# Bearing the Burden of Booms

2026 The Digital Press @ The University of North Dakota

Library of Congress Control Number: 2026933479
The Digital Press at the University of North Dakota, Grand Forks, North Dakota

ISBN-13: 978-1-966360-89-6 (print)
ISBN-13: 978-1-966360-13-1 (Adobe PDF)

Cover Design: Vitoria Faccin-Herman
Interior Design: William Caraher

# Bearing the Burden of Booms

## Energy, Extraction, Communities, and Landscapes on the Plains

Sebastian Felix Braun

The Digital Press at the
University of North Dakota

Grand Forks, ND

For my children

Ursina Gillian Braun
and
Julian Serafin Braun

and for all the people
who bear the burden

I thank everybody who has worked with me.
You are too many to name.
Your generosity has kept me going.
This is how I am trying to give back.

## Table of Contents

On a hot summer weekend in 2007, we went camping in the Little Missouri Badlands between Killdeer and Mandaree, North Dakota. We took a long hike down to where usually the waters of Lake Sakakawea, dammed behind Garrison Dam, would have flooded the valley. In the middle of a terrible drought that summer the waters had receded and left behind a thick, slick layer of mud, which seemed the only water source, and a welcome relief from the heat for our dog. Where the lake had vanished, the mud was penetrated by young, eagerly growing cottonwoods, unaware that they would soon be flooded again. For the duration of the drought, a return to a previous landscape seemed remotely possible, like a brief illusion of freedom and an open future, shimmering in the hot, wide-open spaces. At night, when I took our dog for a last pee behind the tent, onto the plains above the badlands, we saw an illuminated drilling rig a few miles away, and another much farther from us. Under the star-studded night sky, they appeared like alien spaceships. It had been a long day, and the night air was comfortable. It was easy to imagine romantic notions of peaceful coexistence, of coyotes hunting a few rabbits, of running away from civilization. Blissfully unaware of the future the rigs presaged, perhaps like the cottonwoods simply enjoying the moment, I wished the lights would not intrude on my allegories, but they seemed harmless enough.

A year later, we took my mother and one of my aunts to visit Killdeer Mountain battlefield. On the way to the site, northwest of Killdeer, we passed some drilling operations. The rigs, the trucks, the enormous wastewater retaining tank, and other industrial aspects of the site were impressive. I vaguely knew that there had been an oil boom here in the early 1980s, and newspapers had carried some news about a renewed interest, but one had to be an attentive reader to see those stories. The operation, as massive as it was, still did not seem to affect too much land, and on the way back to Killdeer, we stopped and watched some pronghorns enjoying the range. Before we had left home, I had made hotel reservations in Watford City. The manager had told me that as we would arrive on a Sunday, she probably would not be around, but she would just leave the key in the door and leave the room open. Watford City was still largely an agricultural service town. I remembered the display on oil history in the museum from a visit a few years earlier, but it seemed unreal that anything more than a few wells would ever be drilled here. Western North Dakota was where one went away from crowds – open spaces, small towns, the periphery of everything. On the way through Fort Berthold Indian Reservation the next day, we saw one or two more rigs, about the same number as cars we encountered in thirty miles. My mother won two hundred dollars at the Four Bears Casino, and immediately wanted to return the money because, she said, there was so much poverty in the community.

In 2009, we moved to Akron, Ohio. In eastern Ohio, stories about the Marcellus Shale started to become relevant. By 2010, people were talking about hydraulic fracturing, and rumors started to circulate about fracking for natural gas in the Cuyahoga Valley National Park. Eastern Ohio started to become interesting to gas extraction companies, and stories of wealth and of environmental dangers gained popularity. There was a growing awareness of what was going on in Pennsylvania and in West Virginia, although the actual impacts could not be felt in Akron. It was, however, a lot easier to imagine resource extraction in the Cuyahoga valley, between the industrial zones of Akron and Cleveland, than to imagine it along the Little Missouri. While both rivers flow through National Parks, the Cuyahoga had infamously burned several times and was one of the inspirations for the Clean Water Act. The Little Missouri probably carried fertilizer and cattle urine, but otherwise seemed the poster child of clean, unfettered nature. Such perceptions can be deceiving, of course, but they create expectations that in turn influence actions and reactions to the environment.

By the time we moved back to North Dakota in 2011, the Marcellus shale gas boom was in full swing, and so was the Bakken shale oil boom. Along with other oil and gas booms across the United States, these booms, the public was told, were enabled by something called "hydraulic fracturing" or fracking. North Dakota was experiencing the largest economic boom since the days of the fur trade and the initial land rush in the late nineteenth century. At the same time, news about potential ecological consequences of fracking practices started to make the rounds – videos of burning well-water, exploding washing machines, and increasing earthquakes. Much of this news came from Pennsylvania and Wyoming, but if those areas saw these impacts, could they not also affect North Dakota? How would this boom affect the communities beyond the economic wealth it was supposedly creating? What were the social, cultural, ecological, political, and health impacts of the Bakken? And given that there are undoubtedly impacts on individuals, communities, society at large, the environment, and the economy, are those impacts worth it?

Now, in 2025, the second Trump administration is set to take office, having run on the same slogan that already marked the McCain-Palin campaign in 2008. "Drill, baby, drill!" Our answers to energy questions are still the same. We propose more extraction to fuel more needs. Too often, we do not stop to take stock of how this extraction works, what impacts it has on communities and landscapes, and what its consequences will be on our future lives. In this text, I do that by taking another look at an energy boom in context. I am not proposing an answer. I suggest we might ask more questions.

# Introduction

When academics write, we are often told to think of research questions. What has fascinated me about the Bakken oil boom is that it is a case study for the most important question we, as humanity, are facing: how do we deal with our environment, and what consequences does that have for us? It sounds like a simple question with a simple answer, but our common experience of living in the early twenty-first century proves that it is far from a simple question, and that simple answers to this question fall short.

Sometimes, when my daughter could not sleep, I took her along for the last night walk with my dog. We tried to see the stars through the suburban lights. We talked about school. She told me that she wished she was born five hundred years ago so she would not face what she still sees as an extremely bleak future. And I tried to reassure her that in middle school, she cannot and does not have to solve the problems of this world. It was not her responsibility yet. My son, her twin, does not show his anxieties as much, although he also experiences them. I see these same anxieties also in my undergraduate and graduate students. The issues they face seem insurmountable. I always tell them that nobody can fix the larger issues by themselves, but we can all start with simple things: ourselves, how we treat others around us, how we treat our environment, and how we live. How we live is a choice, a choice with many consequences.

I am an anthropologist, and anthropology answers the question of how we should live.[1] It does so by focusing on culture. Culture is how we assign meaning to the world; it allows us to orient ourselves in our environments and tells us what things mean and how we should relate to them. Because culture thus defines our realities, it is very difficult to diverge from it. Anthropology takes a look at how our own societies and other societies construct their cultures, how they live in their realities, and what consequences this has. From this understanding come alternatives—an understanding of how we live, how we could live, and thus a choice of how we should live. It is important to acknowledge

1 Ingold 2018.

that culture is a social construction; many individuals create cultural values through their actions and interpretations, reinforcing assumptions or questioning them. For any given individual to question or take action against established cultural values, interpretations, norms, or assumptions is a radical action. It can lead to being ostracized, belittled, or ignored. In extreme cases, it can lead to being declared insane or a danger to society. The normalizing tendencies of any culture make it hard to think outside of established cultural values.

Culture as a social construction is an abstract concept, but it is rooted both in and also defining for our lived reality. What we do both contributes to and is directed by cultural norms. In order to analyze natural resource extraction—for example, resource booms, or as a narrower example, the Bakken oil boom—we can start with what we know as facts. We know that we, as humans in the twenty-first century, extract, produce, pollute, and consume too many resources. We don't need to know exactly how many resources are too much to come to this conclusion. The basic understanding is simple. In order to fulfill the demands of our economic system—capitalism—we need continued economic growth. In order to fuel that continuous economic growth, we need more resources, thus creating an indefinite demand for resources. However, we live in a finite world. At some point, indefinite demand faced with finite availability means that resources will be, and already are, running out.

Once we have come to this understanding, we have three basic choices. We can reduce resource extraction to a minimum, thus prolonging our time until exhaustion of those resources. We can try to switch resources to those that might be able to be replenished. Or we can ignore the problem and hope that resource exhaustion will happen after a specific time, for example, after we are no longer alive. These are the choices we are facing, complicated by the fact that the use of some resources also contributes to worsening conditions of existence for ourselves and those around us through an ecological crisis that has led to the extinction of thousands of species and the potential extinction of our own species. Every choice carries its own consequence for how we live or how we need to make changes. All of them have advantages and disadvantages.

While we understand this dilemma in the abstract, what a natural resource extraction boom does is demonstrate it in the concrete. The ecological pitfalls, the economic advantages, the collateral damages, the human costs, the political justifications, the global demands, all manifest themselves "in real life" as the saying goes. When the processes involved in what we sometimes describe as "politics," or "economics," or "globalization" are anonymous, understood and guided by "the government," "capital," "academics," or a rather murky "elite," this anonymous nature makes processes seem like laws, and specialists often explain them in the language of laws. The people affected by hunger, or by resource booms, are often told that this is simply a process, unfortunate perhaps, but unchangeable, following the laws of "economics" or "the market." As individuals, we feel powerless, overwhelmed, fatigued, and underprepared to tackle such processes. As it is for my daughter and many of my students, we come to see ourselves in a "hopeless situation for all, except for those retaining an unshakable faith in technical fixes or a monomaniacal desire to profit from others' misery."[2]

I have become convinced that our job as historians, anthropologists, economists, or resource managers is to explode the abstractions, look behind the veil, and discover the systems that we feel are destroying us. Only then can we do something about them. I am writing this book not to push a specific political viewpoint. I am writing it so that you, the reader, can weigh whether what we are doing is worth it. I am writing it so you, the reader, can do something about my daughter, who is scared of her future. I am writing it so we, together, can decide whether communities—local, regional, national, and global—are better off when they experience a resource boom. And I am writing it so we can come to a conclusion on whether we should, then, put that burden on any community, or whether we should perhaps change something about our lives so we no longer have to face the same three choices.

It might seem counterintuitive to figure out how we should live through the example of an extraordinary event like an oil boom. However, we learn most about what cultural values and norms guide our lives in these exceptional moments. They reveal assumptions and values that are otherwise often hidden or taken for granted. Because we learn cultural values as we grow up, we thus find them normal and culture is often taken as "common sense" or natural. Culture is something that runs in the background. Just like most first-language English speakers cannot at the ready explain the rules of when to use an adverb or an adjective even though most know when somebody used one at the

2 Smith and Young 2025:5.

wrong time, so too do we notice cultural rules mostly when they are broken. We notice cultural values in exceptional moments, when the common sense is questioned. An oil boom is one such exceptional situation, and so because in this situation people need to answer extraordinary questions, their cultural assumptions are clearly revealed by their arguments for how to deal with the situation.

On another level, booms and busts, as exceptional and disruptive every single one is to communities, are not historically exceptional in regions that have been subject to resource extraction for a long time. The Northern Plains is one such region, having lived through a series of resource booms over the past five hundred years. To understand such a region, then, we can try to analyze how these booms work, as they all share similarities. In themselves, they are highly disruptive to local communities. Together, they form a history of disruption that can become accepted as normal.

Communities do not like to be disrupted. Every disruption causes pain, an overthrow of old lifestyles, the necessity for adaptation, and many times violence. Such serial disruption is therefore usually not driven by local decisions, but through the imposition of new forms of extraction from the outside. That is, this local disruption serves regional, national, or global interests.

There is much to say about the interaction of specific economic and political systems and the pollution or destruction of the environment. There is much to say about what some social scientists are calling settler colonialism, about Indigenous ways of knowing the environment and about so-called Western ways of dominating it.[3] I will mention some of these issues. However, here, I prefer to look at these issues not from a categorical distinction between historical societies, but from a perspective of local understanding and non-local interference.

In *Does the Earth Care?* Mick Smith and Jason Young write that in the light of the contemporary ecological crisis, "assumptions of theological providence and its successor, progress, are both untenable." They argue that "to describe a situation where the entire world is threatened by an economic system inducing mass extinction and climate change as either 'providential' or a matter of 'progress' now seems entirely implausible."[4] I think that whether or not the earth cares—meaning,

3 See, for example, Liboiron (2021).

4 Smith and Young 2022:4-5.

whether or not we believe that there is a plan, religious or secular, for history—what truly matters in terms of the crisis we are facing is whether we care. I have argued elsewhere that caring means to accept responsibility, to accept relatedness.[5] This relatedness is or springs from rootedness and locality.

What is at stake is whether we look at the earth and its creations as a relative, to whom we carry obligations, or as a stranger, whom we can exploit. People who live in communities that are based on relatedness tend to more easily be able to extend those community obligations to non-human entities. People who look at communities as assemblages of commodities—workers, assets, or resources—tend to have a much easier time to exploit both human and non-human entities in these places.

I have divided this story into seven interconnected parts. They are not actual different realities; they are inherently intertwined and exist only to provide a clearer structure to the narrative.

The first chapter is more theoretical and discusses some of the contexts in which the following story is set. It is not necessary to read in order to understand the rest of the narrative, but it is necessary for me to write. There are multiple avenues and pathways from which to approach something as complex as resource extraction. This text cannot explore all of them. In order to do reality justice, however, I also have to delve into a few. I understand that these are not covered exhaustively, but that is not the purpose.

The second chapter sets the context of extraction, booms, and frontiers on the Plains, placing the story in its historical, cultural, and political setting. This chapter provides a basic framework within which events unfold and meanings are created. The reader will see that this framework itself is not and cannot be one-dimensional. The chapter introduces some historical events shaping resource extraction and touches on some analytical perspectives that are helpful to think with.

The third chapter attempts to provide an impression of the impact of resource extraction on communities. In order to understand how communities changed and how people in communities react to extraction frontiers, I introduce three perspectives: hydraulic fracturing as a process of extraction, national security as a framework for policy, and rural poverty as a complex background. I also explore three

5 For example, Braun (2017).

serious consequences. Education, public health, and emergency services serve as examples of how communities and their governments can be overwhelmed.

In the fourth chapter, I show how resulting partial paralysis of local government, together with the systemic frameworks already discussed, impact the landscape. Communities exist within a landscape, and our identity is in a large part formed by our historical, cultural, economic, and social relations to that landscape. When it disappears as such, communities and individuals are deeply affected. How and whether a landscape is changed also depends on how people live on or within it, and whether and how they are allowed and expected to live.

The fifth chapter analyzes power structures and how the institutions of power on the northern Plains—including state and federal governments, extraction industry, and tribal governments—influence resource extraction and impacts on communities and landscapes. This chapter in many ways picks up ideas from the first three but focuses on how power relations led to, alleviated, and exacerbated the impacts of resource extraction on communities and landscapes. It is important to acknowledge that communities and individuals have agency; just as important, however, is an analysis of how their decision making is influenced by outside agents with their own agendas and interests.

In the sixth chapter, I take a look at resource extraction from the perspective of water. We need clean water to survive. Hydraulic fracturing uses water in immense quantities. Water is trucked back and forth, is polluted, is re-injected deep into the earth to keep it out of our lives forever, and sometimes even catches on fire. Yet, without clean water, there will be no communities. Water is at the heart of both the extraction process and its potential impacts. Even when the resource booms are over, it is water that will continue to ask fundamental questions of extraction. These questions are also related to pipelines and their potential dangers. On the Plains, the Keystone XL and Dakota Access Pipeline projects have garnered as much if not more attention from the press than the extraction itself—and thus also from the world outside the communities and landscapes at the heart of this story.

Finally, I will try to connect the pieces with a short attempt at the economics at play: if the social, physical, and cultural landscapes are in danger of disappearing, or are allowed to disappear, the overarching question has to be, is it worth it? It is that question that underlies any so-called rational decision making. It can only be answered based on a holistic understanding of what is at risk and what can be gained. I hope that by the end of this text, the risks and opportunities will have become clear.

A final note on this text: In order to hold the interest of our projected readers, we are often told to simplify, to reduce the scope, to follow the "human interest." This story is not so much the story of individuals, but of relations. The perspective on events like extraction booms from individuals or families lend themselves to movies or novels, but mostly depend on composite characters that come to embody myriad lived experiences.[6] Instead, I want to focus on two antiheroes for this story: communities and environments. As a cultural anthropologist and (ethno-)historian by training, people come into and walk out of my stories all the time. However, I am not interested in disciplinary territory in this text. I am working from an anthropological perspective, but, having worked for over twenty years primarily in American Indian Studies and now happily housed in a department of political science, I also hold that understanding American Indian or rural realities in the United States—or anywhere else, for that matter—requires a multidisciplinary approach that includes ecology, law, health, economics, histories, politics, and other matters that are both included in "culture" and at the same time often purged from both indigenous and rural studies. This book is not a standard environmental history or ethnography. Instead, it aspires to show the consequences of our actions. Some readers might find the introduction of moral values and interpretation into an academic text to be unsettling. However, I strongly hold that, if it ever existed, the time for environmental history or anthropology as purely presenting facts is over.[7]

6 David Schneider (1980):124, in a somewhat lengthy and perhaps curmudgeonly response to the critique that he omitted the specific data of his interviews for American Kinship, wrote that, "using nice little quotes and convincing little illustrations was, I thought then and think equally strongly now, a form of cheating: it pretends to documentation when it is not that at all."

7 See, for example, Braun (2025).

# Chapter 1
# Extraction and Social Sciences

"Drill, baby, drill"
Michael Steele, RNC 2008

At the heart of this text stands the concept of *extractivismo*. Extractivism is a term, like development, that is often applied in so-called non-Western contexts, and less in Western ones, perhaps because it brings with it connotations of resource imperialism, corruption, greed, and the wanton destruction of communities for the sake of multinational companies. It is tied, in that sense, to a critique of capitalism that stems from Marx and Engels' analysis in the *Communist Manifesto*, namely that capitalism leads to the control of the countryside by the towns, the control of non-industrial nations by industrial ones, and the control of natural resources by capital. The Spanish term, *extractivismo*, then follows other critiques of capitalism from Latin America, such as liberation theology and world systems theory and its successors. These analyses can be applied to Western as much as non-Western contexts—in fact, the division between these seems more a deflection than a categorization of real differences the further one explores the dependencies created by uncontrolled capitalism everywhere.

The most famous chronicler of the processes giving birth to industrialized capitalism is Karl Marx. Marx analyzed the dimensions of capitalism and industrialization, two of the most pressing issues in his day. One of his main critiques was that industrialization led to alienation from the soil and capitalism led to a concentration of landownership and the ownership of capital in the hands of a very few, who then could exert power over the landscape. This power can become so concentrated, and ownership can be so distant from the actual landscape, that the land becomes an abstraction. No real relationship remains apart from an economic relationship. The land, the people on the land, and the environment become a commodity. By the end of the twentieth century, economics textbooks routinely asserted that the land, and its resources, was a free gift of nature, thus denying any responsibilities back to the land for its use.

A resource is, of course, not only defined who owns or controls it. At its heart, though, the term in its application to phenomena in our environment already implies its use. Resources as commodities exist to be used. Because commodities carry only economic values, commodified resources exist to be extracted. Resources are things alienated and economic. If the world is seen as a collection of commodified resources, this creates a fundamentally different approach from one where oneself is an equal part of the world. Thinking of the world as resources to be used leads to seeing the world as consisting of opportunities for extraction. Resources need to be extracted so they can be used. If they are not used, they are being wasted. This equation lies at the heart of *extractivismo*.

Resource booms represent beginnings or new beginnings of *extractivismo* being applied to communities, people, and a landscape. They are moments of great clarity and opportunity and simultaneously of great confusion and loss. For the local communities, they most often happen fast, unexpectedly, and break the existing order. As such, they represent a crisis. Crises are times of indeterminacy. What is happening cannot be interpreted according to established meanings, and events unfold so fast that new ways of attaching meanings have not yet had time to be developed. This creates a situation where local communities are often overwhelmed and are searching for meaning for these events. What makes resource booms different from other such crises of meaning is that the forces that drive the booms are not in crisis mode. For them, the outcome and the meaning of events is not indeterminate. It is, to the contrary, very clear, and they impose their *extractvismo* logic onto the landscape. This imposition is often irreversible because it is not only a philosophical imposition, but a physical change.

Marx was not alone in his insights into the relationship between capitalism and the environment. In North America, for example, some of the founders of the United States had already voiced concerns over alienation from land and the resulting concentration of power. In thinking about the future of the country, a democracy, Thomas Jefferson saw an equal distribution of landownership as essential to the empowerment of citizens. His ideas and idealization of small farmers have been influencing the rhetoric of American farming and democracy ever since, although in practice the emergence of capitalism and industrialization quickly put an end to their application. Homesteading, for example, was always already in competition with railroad land grants and industrial agricultural markets. However, there were still spaces of family farms in the United States at the beginning of the twenty-first century. One was an emerging movement of small-scale farming that had two distinct proponent groups: recent immigrants, often from Latin America, and smaller organic farms and Community Supported Agriculture (CSA) collectives. The other space where family farms still existed, however, was the northern Plains. The soil here was still predominantly owned by those who farmed it. As a result, those who farmed it thought they had control over it.

Because of the history of the concept and its application, capitalism and industrialization are often equated with a supposedly "Western" or European worldview. While it is of course true that both had their origins in Europe (and found their climax in European settler colonies), the argument that therefore Europeans are inherently seeing nature as alienated is a false shortcut. It ignores the history of these concepts and the process of their development in a very specific context.[1] Far from providing this history here, suffice it to say that the first application of capitalist, industrial practices attempted to subjugate European peasant societies. This was never met with an unqualified success. Still today, European peasants, where their economic base has not been replaced by industrial farming, carry responsibilities for their soil, responsibilities that are often mediated by the supernatural. I remember from my own childhood that when we had prolonged droughts, people from the villages carried the relics of the church through the fields and made pilgrimages to sacred places to regain the grace of the supernatural forces.

## Extraction and the Anthropocene

Resource extraction occurs within political as well as natural landscapes, and regulatory regimes[2] as well as economic pressures[3] play their roles in shaping the extent and form of booms. These processes are globally similar. Much of what happens in the Bakken is very similar to many other booms around the world. Workforce recruitment and lodging, as well as the social consequences of a massive influx of outsiders might differ from case to case, for example. However, Haliburton or Target Logistics built the same lodging solutions in North

1 For a critical account of capitalism and the environment, see for example Foster (2000) and Foster and Clark (2020).

2 Sanders, Sandvik, and Storli 2019.

3 Gilberthope and Hilson 2014.

Dakota as everywhere else in the world, and the social impacts on poor, rural, small communities of an influx of single, bored, young males from the outside with an abundance of cash are roughly similar. In this sense, the story of the Bakken fits more or less into the larger story of oil.[4] Accounts of conflicts between indigenous peoples and mining activities in Oceania,[5] of the mining industry and environmental activism in Peru,[6] or of pipelines in Chad,[7] for example, all bear relevance in some ways to this text.

In many ways, the effects of extraction can be approached from the perspective of neocolonialism.[8] Especially in Africa and Latin America, this neocolonial or neoliberal reality is often caught in the phrase "petrostate,"[9] denoting a state that is so dependent on oil that it is in fact governed by the oil industry. North Dakota during the boom could be seen as a petrostate: a state that put its hopes of development and relevance on petroleum oil. A very similar situation could be seen with the Three Affiliated Tribes in western North Dakota, whose tribal government saw oil as the way out of endemic poverty and underdevelopment. "Sovereignty by the Barrel" was the Tribe's motto at the beginning of the boom. In this situation, contemporary and historical events surrounding oil booms in underdeveloped economies[10] have a relevance for the structural understanding of the Bakken. For the tribe, this understanding fits with the long struggle of Native peoples to assert sovereignty and to support that sovereignty through natural resource extraction.[11]

The Bakken, like any other boom, needs to be seen in the context of similar booms, both historical and contemporary.[12] The oil boom was not only embedded in a national and international context of resource extraction, but also in a history of extraction in the area.[13]

4 See, for example, Marrin (2012), Nikiforuk (2012), and Jones (2016).
5 Rumsey and Welner 2004.
6 Li 2015.
7 Leonard 2016.
8 This is an argument that is developed, for example, by Gomez-Barris (2017).
9 Stronen 2017; Hodges 2004.
10 Ghazvinian 2007; Hicks 2015.
11 See, for example, Jorgensen (1984), Ambler (1990), and Allison (2015).
12 Chamberlain 2000; Nikiforuk 2010; McGraw 2012; Wilber 2012; Theriot 2014; Stief, Figgins, and Babcock 2021.
13 Tauxe 1993.

This history established state and industry regulations and reactions as well as public and private attitudes. Yet, there are also narratives of what happened in communities in the Bakken region. Most of these are personal stories. Soon after the boom began, there were blogs by people who worked as truck drivers, as prostitutes, and, of course, as oil workers. Some of the other publications were written by journalists,[14] some by community members.[15] Researchers associated with the University of North Dakota also published several volumes on contemporary and historical aspects of the Bakken region.[16] While many of these narratives emphasize a very specifically local approach, the development of commodity resource extraction in specific places can be thought of as a script happening everywhere, a resource play, as people say, in a global landscape of "non-places".[17]

Resource extraction in a global economy inherently connects local communities to the global market. The processes involved thus opens the communities to the world (and sometimes quite literally opens the land), erasing their specificity and, by imposing a global, economic landscape, turning them into non-places. The local response to these extraction booms thus often centers on trying to re-establish control over landscapes and communities. Such attempts can take many forms, from collaboration with the industries and governments involved to steer as much economic potential as possible into the communities, to radical resistance. The form that these individual responses take is hinged on previous experiences with industrialization, globalization, resource extraction, boom situations, industries, and governments.[18] As such, these previous experiences as well as lessons people have taken from them become visible in the actions local communities take.

To look at extraction not from a narrowly defined perspective focused on natural resources only reveals how the term describes a process. This is important because it is not only natural resources that can be extracted. Instead, the commodification can encompass much more. People, wealth, animals, water, soil, ideas, practices: all of those and more can be commodified, extracted, forced or coaxed to leave, so they can be used. Usually, extraction implies a difference of power

14 Briody 2017; Rao 2018.
15 Peters 2014; Edwards 2015.
16 Caraher and Conway 2016; Caraher and Weber 2017; Conway 2020.
17 Augé 1995.
18 See, for example, Voyles (2015) for an account of such effects at the example of uranium mining in the Navajo Nation.

and an imposition of dominance. This story, then, is not only a narrative about the Plains, or the West, but about peripheral regions in a global system that is trying (successfully so far) to impose a human dominance over the land. The result of this has come to be called the "Anthropocene."[19]

Geologists and social scientists have defined the Anthropocene as the geological age in which ecosystems on earth are defined by human actions. In many ways, dominance over nature is an ongoing process of expanding human dominance over ecosystems, though: a process of extraction. Humans have changed their environments for a long time; since their existence, really, as to be human means to have culture, and to have culture means to disassociate oneself from natural processes by virtue of creating cultural environments. Alfred Russell Wallace pointed this out in 1864, when he concluded, in an argument that otherwise descended into the environmental determinism typical of the times, that "from the time, therefore, when the social and sympathetic feelings came into active operation, and the intellectual and moral faculties became fairly developed, man would cease to be influenced by 'natural selection' in his physical form and structure."[20] Because humans have culture, they can impose themselves onto nature.

Instead of seeing the imposition of human dominance as a sudden event located at some time in the nineteenth or twentieth century, I propose the process is understood in terms of waves of expansion and retraction. It is true that by the early twenty-first century, the Anthropocene was global. No place on earth was outside the reach of human imposition on ecosystems, and the intensity of these impositions had grown so large that geological impacts became clear. However, if we take anthropological insights seriously, we have to admit that ecological impacts alone are a not a new phenomenon. Humans and their impacts on the natural environment have been a global phenomenon for thousands of years by now. We have built our own cultural environments, at first small and contained, then larger and connected, and finally global and seemingly without space.

The fact that humans can impose themselves onto nature, of course, does not mean they have to do so, or determine how and to what intensity they do so. The decision on whether to create an impact on an

19 For a history of the term and its antecedents, see Steffen, Grinevald, Crutzen, and McNeill (2011).

20 Wallace 1864:clxiii.

ecosystem and on how large the impact should be is entirely cultural and thus voluntary. The development and availability of technology does not force humans to use it. There are many cultural values that might prohibit, limit, or negate the imposition of dominance over nature. Many indigenous peoples, for example, have shown a resistance to the imposition of dominance. Instead, they have seen themselves as one part of an expansive, connected natural and cultural environment. As I have mentioned, I would include many peasant societies in Europe in the category "indigenous;" indigenous taken to mean a people that is rooted in a place and connected to a landscape. Being connected to a landscape means that one at least recognizes responsibility for it. Such a connection is based on kinship relations, which are always rooted in reciprocity.[21]

While reciprocity had long been noted as an essential factor in relationships, the anthropologist Marshall Sahlins formulated a model for reciprocal relationships in the 1960s.[22] In this model, forms of reciprocity occupy a range of options, from freely giving to the closest relatives to taking and stealing from strangers. Without a relation to somebody, there are no obligations to them. I am therefore free to take what I want (if I have the power to do so, of course). Disconnected, I have no responsibilities and no obligations. The opposite of being connected—of being related, of having rights and responsibilities to the other—is to be alienated. Alienation is also an inherent component of industrialization. It is no coincidence that the system imposing the Anthropocene, that is, imposing dominance over the now alienated environment, is industrialized extraction.

## Responsibility and science

We are sometimes surprised that people do not act according to scientific facts, for example in the current climate crisis, where we understand that what we are doing is harming ourselves but continue doing it anyway. One of the reasons is that we are not only alienated from our environments, but from scientific concepts themselves. They have become so abstract that we feel no responsibilities. In order to take responsibility, it is imperative to understand systems of meaning and action and to be connected to those who are being impacted by our own systemic behavior. Alienation leads to a focus on the individual,

21 Braun 2017.
22 Sahlins 1965.

away from community, and away from responsibility. The individual is simultaneously everything and nothing: we cut our relations to others to empower ourselves, and at the same time we feel powerless because we are no longer part of a community. The more abstract our lives are, the less responsibility we can and do take. What individuals can and should do to alleviate the present crisis is often undefined. Solutions would run counter to the alienated individualist consumer society necessitated by a capitalist system. Consequences are often not spelled out because researchers are told they would be speculative. And neither a focus on humanity as a whole nor a focus on exemplary human interest stories allow us to understand the system and react to it.

Gregory Bateson once observed that, "People can be influenced, of course, by economic theories or economic fallacies—or by hunger—but they cannot possibly be influenced by 'economics.'"[23] We need, of course, a framework from which to analyze reality, but we should not mistake this map for the territory it describes. Conclusions are always based on theoretical assumptions, namely the values we hold true and apply to our decision making. Any understanding has to be based on an analytical structure to assess perceptions—a theory.[24] But a meaningful conversation cannot revolve around theories alone, and nobody makes decisions based solely on theoretical constructs. The danger of believing that people die from economics rather than hunger is twofold. First, we ignore the real historical and cultural issues that actually affect people and instead put up a shield of theoretical constructs. That allows a shift from a description of reality—historical and cultural facts—to a debate about largely political models. Without a clear understanding of facts, we can ignore the underlying causes for hunger in favor of treating select symptoms. Second, it allows us to ignore the systemic nature of human realities. Addressing hunger as economics, for example, ignores other factors: soil chemistry, cultural values, poverty, environmental concerns, nutrition, well-being, ties to land, migration, history, politics, and so on. In the metaphorical landscape of hunger, as in any landscape, if we rely on maps as an accurate reflection of the territory, we see only what has been mapped. If we stick to a predetermined framework and neglect to look further, we do not approach landscapes. We only approach specific sites, marked and defined in advance.

23 Bateson 1958:281.
24 See bell hooks' discussion of "theory as liberatory practice" (1994:59-75).

If hunger, or the destruction of a landscape during a resource boom, is simply described as "economics," the power to do something about it rests with economists. The processes involved are anonymous, understood and guided by "the government," "capital," "academics," or a rather murky "elite." This anonymous nature makes processes seem like laws, and specialists often explain them in the language of laws. Nobody mentions that these supposed laws are theoretical constructs based on cultural values that can be investigated, changed, and rejected. In order to understand what people do, therefore, it is imperative to gain an understanding of the discourse that is presented to and imposed on communities. Humans act according to cultural values.

In describing realities, we should also refrain from re-ordering realities through new theoretical language. We know what hunger is. We know what extinction is. We know what pollution is. Instead of re-defining these realities in new jargons, we need to focus on what causes hunger, extinction, and pollution. As Vine Deloria, Jr., wrote, "*[S]elf-determination*, *sovereignty*, *hegemony*, *empowerment*, and *colonialism* are nice big words that philosophers and intellectuals use, but what do they really mean? I often feel they assist us creating a set of artificial problems, wholly abstract in nature, that we can discuss endlessly without having to actually do something."[25] If we want to solve a crisis, we need to take responsibility. In order to make clear that we all have a responsibility, we need to be clear about how things are done—how systems work—and what kinds of consequences they have, for real people, landscapes, ecologies, and lives.

## Visions of the apocalypse

When thinking about resource extraction, fights over land use, and the local-global dichotomy in the North American West today—and western North Dakota is in the West—a good place to start is the "sagebrush revolution" in the early 1980s. At this time, western governors tried to gain more control over lands in their states from the federal government. This included gaining control over resources and their extraction, but also, for some, to gain control over the lands for their protection from resource extraction. The Sagebrush Revolution overlapped with a resource boom spawned, in part, by a reaction to the energy crisis of the 1970s. Coal and oil extraction were seen as crucial national responses to that crisis. The consequences of energy

25 Deloria 1998:25.

dependencies, global markets, local energy development, environmental destruction, and an influx of workers into local communities came to define relationships to the land and its resources. Whether people saw these developments as threats or opportunities, they tried to protect "their" lands from outside influences, knowing at the same time that the federal government had the power to limit economic opportunities or deregulate environmental protections. In such moments of perceived threats to local communities, people often emphasize their connection to the land, and they tell stories centered on the land and its changes.

It is through stories that communities solidify their identities and their relationship with the land, and it is worthwhile to begin this narrative with a story about the meaning of the land for people in the areas we are about to visit. This story, like all stories, is not factually true. Its purpose is to prepare an emotional foundation, and to do so, again like all such stories, it creates a historical narrative of the land, a landscape that was changing:

> We saw the West change before our eyes, but the images, the memories, linger still. Glen Canyon. The Virgin River. Kayaking down the Rio Grande and the Dolores and the Yampa—and seeing no one else. Sunflower fields, country towns, the smell of summer rain, Meadowlarks and mourning doves. Cedar smoke on a winter night. The Super Chief, like a silver snake, on the Arizona desert. The misty arc of an August rainbow. This is our West. And it is dying. A new Manifest Destiny has overtaken America. The economic imperative has forever changed the spiritual refuge that was the West. Some of us have made a truce with change. Others have refused. They—we—are the new Indians. And they—we—will not be herded to the new reservations.[26]

The authors here use what they perceive as outside threats to position themselves as the old-timers, the insiders: to root themselves in the land. It might be ironic that the reason for their presence on the land was the original Manifest Destiny, that they now understand the plight of American Indians being driven from their lands, that they

26 Lamm and McCarthy 1982:4.

identify as Native people. Those feelings are certainly not unique.[27] Defending a landscape against its real or imagined destruction is usually tied to a sense of nostalgia, a remembrance of the landscape as it used to be. Within that, however, is also a remembrance of how communities interacted with that landscape. By anchoring identity and communities in a specific landscape, people territorialize their communities; they make themselves and their communities a part of a specific territory or landscape. Territorialization leads to indigenization. What this narrative allows communities to do is to unite against outside forces over which they have little control, and through that to try and regain control and sovereignty.

The narrative also establishes something else, though. It defines the West as a landscape that has seen similar change before. People have been deterritorialized before. Manifest Destiny has swept the land before. And even if the authors here define those previous waves as somewhat benevolent—while Indians had to leave, they were replaced by people who kept the spiritual relationship to the land alive—the recurrence of such displacements cannot be denied. The authors go on to describe "a recurrent nightmare [that] haunts the West":

> Energy combines, unleashed by the government, invade the West. Seeking profit, unconcerned with local fears, they ignore social, political, and economic considerations in the process of building. Huge profits accrue to them and flow out. Little is left to the people and their communities. Boomtowns mushroom across the West's rural face, disfiguring the land. Cedar breaks crumble to strip miners, water fills with toxic waste, mountain valleys fall to tractor roads, and evening sunsets blaze through polluted air. Ways of life change forever. Values, attitudes, customs—the core of western life—shatter. New cities, plagued by crime and violence and nonexistent social and economic services, cannot deal with the change. In time, the energy rush dies. The boomers disappear. Left behind is a wasteland, its skeletal boomtowns and cratered-out landscape a graphic reminder of days

27 Braun 2016a:102-103.

> past. Western people, pawns in an ugly and endless war, regroup and rebuild. And their cyclical history begins again.[28]

This nightmarish vision of places and people continuously subjected to waves of destruction stands in contrast to the interpretation of booms as opportunities of growth, of revitalization, and of survival for poor communities. Whether one sees booms as destructive or beneficial depends on one's theoretical perspective. The story summarizes the very real fears of many local people, overwhelmed by seemingly uncontrollable, or uncontrolled, outside forces. Resource booms exist within historical and ethnographic contexts that are bigger than local events. They create and impose landscapes: landscapes of opportunity, landscapes of extraction, landscapes of disappearance, and landscapes of the apocalypse.

Those visions of a nostalgic past and an apocalyptic future painted above were largely political reactions of resistance and protection. If academic perspectives today see energy development and extraction as at least partially problematic, it is because over the past forty years, social sciences, humanities, and ecology have caught up with fossil fuels, extraction practices, boom consequences, environmental impacts, and the complex relations between local and indigenous peoples and resource extraction companies, policies, and practices. Because of the systemic complexities of extraction landscapes and because of the reluctance of academic disciplines to engage such complexities in a truly interdisciplinary fashion, it took academia a long time to do so.

## Extraction and social sciences

Ricardo Godoy wrote in 1985 that, "Despite his antiquity, the miner, like Geertz's peasant, was recently discovered by anthropologists. This discovery, not fortuitously, came when the energy and environmental crisis made us all aware of the finite supply of nonrenewable natural resources and the limits of industrial growth. If interest in mining came late, systematic studies of mining have yet to arrive."[29] This was true for the interests of cultural anthropologists at the time. Sociologists and economists, however, had indeed led studies on resource booms. Most of these studies did not include Native communities; they were mostly

28 Lamm and McCarthy 1982:5-6.

29 Godoy 1985:199.

technical reports that were often less interested in people and more in what was defined as natural resources. The integration of the different fields—the realization that Native, non-Native, and non-human communities shared and influenced ecosystems and resources and were impacted by exploration and extraction—might have been present in theory. In practice, though, each discipline stuck to its own traditional territories.

Anthropology's attention to natural resource booms is today often triggered through the impacts on indigenous peoples. In those instances, just as in other analyses of the impacts of neoliberal economics on indigenous peoples, there is sometimes the assumption of a dichotomy between indigeneity and modernity.[30] I tend to steer away from such a categorical dichotomy. Although the disproportionate impact in indigenous communities is clear,[31] environmental justice as well as social and cultural impacts affect people in both indigenous and non-indigenous communities.[32] Extraction can impact communities far away from its original focus. Hydraulic fracturing, for example, needs a lot of sand, which can trigger secondary extraction locations.[33] Of interest to the analysis of resource booms are also accounts of activism against hydraulic fracturing,[34] as well as narratives of public relations campaigns by corporations in the name of social corporate responsibility.[35] Both were present in the Bakken from the beginning, involving both Native and non-Native people.

One might assume that cultural anthropologists would have been interested in oil extraction in those exotic places where they worked. However, when anthropologists wrote of oil in the 1940s, 50s, and 60s, they did not mean petroleum, but usually palm oil (in West Africa) or olive oil (in the Middle East). A search through the discipline's journals reveals quickly that texts mentioning oil extraction do so only as a side comment. Archaeologists and historians of course dealt with resource extraction in the historical and prehistorical record. Just like them, cultural anthropologists were interested in oral histories that deal with extraction, or Native perception and involvement in historical extractive practices. For example, Claude Levi-Strauss recounts

30 Gedicks 2001; Bodley 2008.
31 Whitmore 2012.
32 Behrends, Reyna, and Schlee 2011; Shiva 2015; Todrys 2021.
33 Pearson 2017.
34 Wylie 2018; Ladd 2018.
35 Rajak 2011; Dolan and Rajak 2016.

the finding of gold in Cuiaba by Cuxipo Indians, and Julie Cruikshank has Angela Sidney and Kitty Smith tell the stories of Skookum Jim finding gold in Alaska.[36] Natural resources and contemporary mining communities, however, became the domain of economics, sociology, geology, or cultural geography. When encountered in the field, anthropologists circumnavigated these islands of modernity and the modern state. At the same time economists and sociologists who dealt with modernity often seem not to have been equipped to get off such islands and see how the processes they described and analyzed affected Native peoples. In other words, because indigenous peoples were not supposed to be modern, their ongoing experiences with modern extractive industries were largely ignored.

As an example, a 1952 study of "Southern Ute Rehabilitation Planning" has a self-described focus on "the capacity of these people for self-determination," a theme that fit well within the policies of the times. While the authors delve into perceived factionalism and internal cultural differences that lead to patterns of political organization, they ignore the specifics of the underlying economics, but include this tantalizing tidbit:

> The Moache and Capote at Ignacio, heeding the advice of their leader, Buckskin Charley, adopted farming and livestock raising, and supplemented these pursuits with income derived from wage-work and oil and timber resources. The Wimenuche, on the other hand, led by Ignacio, resisted interference and, in 1895, they withdrew to the west into the more isolated region near Ute Mountain.[37]

There is no further word about when the Southern Ute might have started to exploit oil and timber resources, why, in what form, or any other mention of wage-work or natural resources. Similarly, a whole issue of the journal Human Organization on "Human Problems of U.S. Enterprise in Latin America" dismisses any mention of indigenous communities as follows:

> Oil, iron ore, bauxite, and so on, are generally discovered far away from existing cities. Sometimes they are discovered in almost completely uninhabited areas.

36 Lévi-Strauss 1992:205; Cruikshank 1992:64, 186-188.
37 Euler and Naylor 1952:28.

> Even if there is an existing community nearby, it is generally so small that it does not begin to provide either the work force necessary nor the community facilities required by workers and their families.[38]

Such distinctions, a carving up of disciplinary territory, extend well into the height of globalization and the age of oil. It was mostly sociologists who became heavily involved in energy boom-town studies during the 1970s and early 1980s, and the impact on indigenous peoples is almost never addressed in them. When it is, the focus lies on formal organizational efforts, not cultural impacts on communities.[39]

That cultural anthropologists finally began to seriously engage the extraction of mineral resources and the social, cultural, and political consequences of these activities for indigenous communities in the 1970s was not coincidental, and neither was the geographical focus of these early studies. The timing reflects increased awareness of environmental pollution and critiques of a consumer society dependent on finite fossil resources as well as critiques of anthropology from growing social and environmental activist movements. The geographical focus on marginal regions reflected, for the most part, the idea of Native peoples being impacted by modernity, not those who participate in shaping the world. Thirty years later, in the face of global mining industries regularly working in, appropriating, transforming, and negotiating over indigenous landscapes, anthropologists revised methods and theories to encompass the fact that indigenous peoples are modern. "An earlier focus on mining labor and the threat posed by transnational mining capital to the sovereignty of newly independent nation-states has given way to a much broader frame for enquiry that addresses the exceptional complexity of the relationships that coalesce around mining projects."[40] This shift in perspective was also partially caused because the extraction industry by then was employing quite a few social scientists.

While academic anthropology and social sciences in general took until the early twenty-first century to catch up with the mining industry, applied anthropologists and other ethnographers had begun to lay the foundation for contemporary perspectives on the extractive industry in the 1970s. In Alaska, for example, the Bureau of Land

38 Whyte and Holmberg 1956:22.
39 See, for example, Robbins (1980).
40 Ballard and Banks 2003:287.

Management started its Outer Continental Shelf Socioeconomic Program in 1977, "a multi-year research effort which attempts to predict and evaluate the effects of Alaska OCS Petroleum Development upon the physical, social, and economic environments within the state."[41] This program has produced numerous studies over more than thirty years, ranging from socioeconomic to cultural studies to transportation impact reports. The foundations for contemporary thinking about extractive industries and indigenous peoples and the environment, however, had a different focus, although they originated from the same 1968 Prudhoe Bay discovery.

## The Arctic as an extraction revolution

When oil was discovered in Prudhoe Bay, and thus in the waters off the north shore of the United States and Canada, both countries discovered that they had neglected to ever legally acquire the land from the indigenous peoples. Neither Alaska nor the Canadian north were covered by treaties. Oil and mineral discoveries thus quickly led to discussions over land claims and sovereignty. In Alaska, those were settled with the Alaska Native Claims Settlement Act in 1971. In Canada, that process is ongoing, with the creation of Nunavut as a first step.

It was not social science that found the relationship between Native peoples and extraction; the question was raised by legal and political inquiries. The question of dependencies has been a defining issue ever since. If non-Native people are dependent on extraction, but Native people own the rights to the resources, then what happens to the traditional narratives of economic, political, and social power? The issue of Native sovereignty and resource extraction was summarized succinctly by John Borbridge, Jr., at a 1969 conference on "The Impact of Oil on the Future of Alaska":[42]

> For the most part you have easily gotten used to the Alaska Native, because he has needed your help and your assistance ... The relationship between one who gives and one who receives when it has been institutionalized is very easy to accept, to adjust to, and to forget. ... But what happens as the Alaska Native assumes his rightful place as an equal partner in the

41 OCS 1978:II.

42 In Chance (1990):257-258.

> economic, political and other power structures of this state? What happens when instead of coming in asking for help, he comes in by right and asserts his right to share equally in the opportunities and benefits of economic and social development?

This was the question that would be discussed in the neighboring Yukon Territory, where Canada wanted to build an oil and gas transportation corridor from the arctic sea to southern Alberta and beyond. In 1974, Justice Thomas Berger was appointed to lead an inquiry into the planned Mackenzie Valley Oil and Gas Pipeline; his inquiry "has set the scene for all subsequent investigations."[43] He insisted that this would not simply be a feasibility study. Instead, Berger investigated whether the pipeline actually should be built or not. To do so, he asked the people living in the local communities what they thought should happen.[44] In his report, Berger emphasized that what is a frontier to some is a homeland to others. In other words, while outside interests, alienated from the land, saw the local resources as commodities with less value than the profits from the oil and gas transported through a pipeline, for the local people, they were invaluable because they were not commodified. Berger wrote that,

> The choice we make will decide whether the North is to be primarily a frontier for industry or a homeland for its people. We shall have the choice only once. ... The issues we face are profound ones, going beyond the ideological conflicts that have occupied the world for so long, conflicts over who should run the industrial machine, and who should reap the benefits. Now we are being asked: How much energy does it take to run the industrial machine? Where must the energy come from? Where is the machine going? And what happens to the people who live in the path of the machine? [45]

While some of the Native people giving testimony, especially Inuvialuit in the Mackenzie delta, held interest in large-scale development,[46]

43 Young 1995:185.
44 Smith 1977:193-245.
45 Berger 1988:33.
46 Nuttall 2010:70.

those along the route of the pipeline, who did not stand to profit from extraction, feared for their land. Frank T'Seleie told Berger that "there will be no pipeline"; "It is your concern about your future, as well as our concern about ours, that will stop the pipeline," he said. Mel Watkins pointed to the extraction of resources and capital without benefits for local people. "When the resource is non-renewable, as it is for mining and oil and gas, the major legacy of failing to keep the surpluses in the region to seed other activities is the ... ghost town." By the time the resources were gone, he asked, "who knows what cumulative damage will have been done to [the native people's] land and its ability to support them?"[47]

Beyond changing the Canadian relationship with its North, the Berger Inquiry changed the ways in which industry and states relate to indigenous and local peoples. The questions coming out of the Berger Inquiry are still relevant.[48] They are still being asked even though they have largely been answered, and have often become largely rhetorical, a show of good will for public relations. The Berger report serves as an important historical document, as it demonstrates the changes in perspectives on resource extraction between roughly 1965 and 1975. The long-term impact of the Inquiry, however, is that it set expectations for interactions that would eventually lead to the standard of free, prior, and informed consent. There might not be a direct link from the Berger Inquiry to the Brundtland Report or the UN Declaration on the Rights of Indigenous Peoples. But Berger set an important example for the acknowledgment of interactions between economic, cultural, political, and ecological systems.[49] The report prepared the academic and public landscape to engage local communities.

47 T'Seleie 1977:13; Watkins 1977: 90.

48 Dokis 2015; Sacco 2020.

49 Wynne 2015:xi.

# Chapter 2
## Extraction, Frontiers, and Native Peoples

It is difficult to describe the previous landscape, or even to take pictures of it. The immensity of the open skies and the wide horizons is almost impossible to convey to somebody who does not have the physical experience of sensing that landscape. Cell phone reception was spotty at best, if it existed at all. Some people commented that they did not "care for such newfangled things here." Communities were face-to-face, united in the knowledge that anybody who lived here went to the same church where they prayed for the same things—good weather for the harvest, good prices from the co-op, and good health amid hard work. At ceremonies, community get-togethers, powwows, and giveaways people reaffirmed networks by strengthening kinship relations and uniting in mourning and celebration.

Driving into New Town in 2011, I felt like a time traveler. The twenty-first century was all around, of course; trucks of all sizes and shapes, carrying water, sand, pipes, and all kinds of construction materials for roads and houses—although the infrastructure in New Town dated primarily from fifty years before, I saw people on cellphones, cars, advertisements beside the road. The general atmosphere, though, was energetic, chaotic, unbound, uncertain. This was, I thought, the closest I would ever come to experience what it was like to come into a gold rush town in the nineteenth century.

The road to New Town and the roads around it had carried all the signs. Thousands of trucks were driving on roads where a few years before, one occasionally might pass a pick-up, a harvester, or other farm machinery. Where before, on the fifty-mile drive between Watford City and New Town, there might be three vehicles going the other way, there were now traffic jams—standing traffic for miles, seemingly in the middle of nowhere, just because it had become impossible to make left-hand turns, and all the traffic had to stop and wait. And there were accidents. Some happened because local people were not accustomed to driving in these conditions. Some happened because non-local drivers had no patience. And some happened because people were drunk, tired, or on drugs. For a while, the sixty miles of North Dakota Route 23 between U.S. Route 83 and New Town was the most dangerous road in the United States, or at least that was what was rumored. Driving that road, however, the notion was absolutely believable. Traffic was constant. Heavy trucks, carrying water and sand to oil wells, carrying water and oil from oil wells, and carrying equipment to set up drilling sites; brand-new, white corporate pick-ups; all kinds of road construction machinery; passenger cars; farm machinery; grain trucks; and all kinds of other vehicles were hustling down the two-lane road, tearing it up, trying to pass, trying to turn across traffic, and trying to break. It routinely took forty minutes to drive fifteen miles through rural land.

Much of this traffic converged on New Town, because New Town defined the approach to the Four Bears bridge—which is the only bridge over the Missouri River that had been dammed to form Lake Sakakawea between Williston and Garrison—the only crossing point within a hundred and sixty miles. New Town, and the tribal administrative complex and casino across the bridge, also was the only larger town in that stretch, and the headquarters for the Mandan, Hidatsa, and Arikara Nation, the Three Affiliated Tribes of the Fort Berthold Indian Reservation. Tribal government, Bureau of Indian Affairs (BIA) offices, the clinic, the college, tribal police, and other infrastructure was located here. Even in normal times, New Town was a relatively busy town. Now, however, an endless caravan of trucks moved through town, stopped at the lone stoplight in the middle, and clogged the main road to such an extent that residents who wanted to cross the street or join the traffic to get out of town had to wait for literally an hour or more to do so. The town retracted away from the main road as much as possible, as the road had become a thoroughfare for strangers, stranded there and in turn stranding the residents.

In the middle of all this traffic, the state was desperately trying to improve the road, and the pace of the work was perhaps best visible in the construction trucks that were lying on their sides, crashed, without anybody really trying to get them back up. Along the road were visible new scars in the landscape—storage tanks, sand mines, and drilling pads had joined the previous disturbances, which were mostly missile silos for the intercontinental nuclear missiles that made North Dakota the fourth-largest nuclear power. Once, I was caught up behind a missile transport from Minot to somewhere near New Town, behind the convoy of armed Humvees and an armed helicopter surrounding the semi they escorted, stopping all traffic on the road. The impact of all this activity on the communities was near-to unfathomable. Western

North Dakota and eastern Montana used to be one of the most isolated and least populated areas in the United States. Now, these were some of the communities where work was available, where money could be earned. Thousands of people had moved here, heeding the opportunity to get a well-paying job. In a nation scarred by economic recession, people flooded to the area, enticed by newspaper and television reports that readily used allegories of the nineteenth century.

Yet, over all the chaos that ensued, the rising prices for groceries and lodging, the mounting traffic deaths, the overwhelmed law enforcement, the evictions and overcrowded housing, hovered a constant layer of anticipation, of opportunity, of bustling energy. The people who fell into poverty, lost their houses, or left town if they could because the challenges had become too many were only visible behind this mist of energy if one looked carefully and listened to the residents. At that time, very few people from the outside had the time to do this, and many people from the community were too overwhelmed to be able to do so. In an environment of relative lawlessness, and enthusiasm for the companies that created the jobs people so desperately needed, the situation was also reminiscent of the range wars, or of the water and land conflicts that erupted in land and gold rush environments. Within the mist of opportunity was a warning to be cautious, an uncertainty to who could be trusted, and an imperative to protect one's interests.

Before the Bakken boom, western North Dakota and eastern Montana were extremely peripheral to the national consciousness. Outside the people who lived in and between the communities, not many took an interest in the region. When the boom began, some journalists and researchers developed great community connections and began to understand the places they wrote about. Some, however, scratched the surface on their way to a different place, with a new story demanding attention. Community members were not very surprised, especially not those in Native communities, who had lived with that kind of coverage for decades. It was easy, as Richard Edwards notes, "to dismiss the region with a sneer and a boarding pass in hand."[1] This was just as much true for academics. The sudden influx of interest was not a coincidence. The Bakken oil boom, just as the Marcellus Shale gas boom, developed into much more than a natural resource boom. All of a sudden, money was to be made not just from oil, trucking, groceries, drugs, prostitution, lodging, water, sand, and other commodities, but

1 Edwards 2015:175.

also from planning, studying, organizing, and reporting on the boom. It sometimes seemed like one of the first threats to the communities were all the academics and pseudo-academics who claimed to be experts on community development, crime, booms, and western North Dakota, most of whom had not set a foot in the region voluntarily before 2010. Many went to the communities to help the people, imposing themselves and their solutions on communities they did not know. Some outright claimed that the Bakken was "theirs" and discouraged or sabotaged other researchers. Academia, too, if run as a business, can be an extractive industry.

## Frontiers

The American West is a landscape of booms, defined by "waves of growth." If one wants to identify distinct waves, there might be four: steam engines and power looms; railroads, steamships, and electricity; automobiles, airplanes, and petrochemicals; and microchips and post-industrial economies. Of these, some historians and economists argue, the first wave "barely affected" the West.[2] That might be true if we think of such waves in those strict terms, and if we think of industrial booms as only occurring since the industrial revolution. However, if we enlarge the meaning, the West, and here specifically the Plains, have seen succession after succession of booms sweeping across the landscape and the people. It is also important to note "that the cultural changes occurring on this continent were not simply a matter of the activities of the Europeans and their influence on the native groups. The influences were mutual."[3] American Indian nations and individuals have shaped and continue to shape these frontiers, and with them the policies on resource extraction. This has been especially true again over the last few decades.

The story of these booms and busts is the story of the "frontier." Frontiers are not unique to North America, but the frontier is a recurring concept and trope in the history of the American West. Many people think of the frontier in the United States as simply an event that deterritorialized Native nations and replaced them with American settlers. This, the removal of Native peoples, is one aspect of North American frontiers. It is, however, a symptom, not the cause of these events. Instead, frontiers in North America and elsewhere can

2 Nash 1999:xiii-xiv.
3 Holder 1970:7.

be seen as a consequence of, and simultaneously an enabling process for industrial capitalism. The historian Frederick Jackson Turner, who famously coined the "frontier thesis" alluded to this, when he wrote in 1901 that, "The transcontinental railroad, the bonanza farm, the steam plow, harvester, and thresher, the 'league-long furrow,' and the vast cattle ranches, all suggested spacious combination and systematization of industry."[4] Another historian, Walter Prescott Webb, directly tied the frontiers on the Great Plains to technological innovations—overland travel, the six-shooter, large-scale cattle ranching, barbed wire, windmills, irrigation, and dry farming.[5] New frontiers indeed often rely on new ways to access and exploit resources, and the desire to exploit these resources drives innovation: nowhere can this better be seen today than in the current hydraulic fracturing booms of the oil and gas industry.

That frontiers are not unique to North America and that they are more than territorial expansions is shown by the first European frontier originating in the Americas. This was literally a European frontier; plants from the Americas enriched and fundamentally changed European agriculture not only in the Americas, but especially in Europe.[6] The early European frontiers in North America itself—the fur and the deer hide trade, early agricultural land rushes in the Ohio valley, and early gold rushes, such as the one in Cherokee territory—were enabled by and quickly led to industrialization. There are, of course, non-industrial social changes tied to frontiers. European frontiers, however, perhaps because they were initiated by industrializing or industrialized societies, seem to be tied to industrial booms. They happen because people come onto or expand into a landscape with the purpose of industrially extracting a resource.

If frontiers are tied to booms—or, indeed, are booms—they are also the serial expansion of industrialization, capitalism, and alienation imposed onto the land, expanding the human impact (the human "footprint"). Human dominance over the ecosystem is not achieved all at once, everywhere. While its consequences are global, in its local manifestations it is a process that comes and goes in waves, affecting different landscapes at different times more or less severely. With these waves of booms, frontiers, industrialization, control, and the imposition

4 Turner 1953:147.

5 Webb 1931:510-512.

6 Hallowell 1967:328.

of the Anthropocene come and go large numbers of people. The popular idea of a single frontier advancing across North America is a misunderstanding. The story of the frontier as a one-time event, the battle between a superior civilization and a pre-existing wilderness, the displacement of that supposed wilderness, and the settling of the landscape by what the now dominant society deems to be common sense norms, is thus a cultural myth. It is a necessary legitimization of an ongoing industrial process. Frontiers do not simply advance. They ebb away and return in a different form. Thus, the idea that the "closing" of the frontier in 1890, or its reopening in the 1980s, were momentous occasions is largely also based on this misunderstanding.[7] Frontiers are not the expression of population density. Frontiers are tied to the exploitation of resources in booms, which might lead to temporarily dense populations. In landscapes that are revisited by booms time and time again, such as the Great Plains, frontiers close and open and have done so over centuries.[8] The fact that population density grows and declines is not so much a function of the frontier closing and opening as it is of the permanence of the frontier in this landscape.

## Frontiers and Native peoples

Obviously, indigenous peoples, too, used and use resources. Peasant societies all over the world, hunters and gatherers—all humans depend on resources. Native peoples, too, expanded territories in response to resource needs. The Beaver Wars of the Iroquois come to mind, or the Lakota expansion into the Powder River valley (although both of these events were direct or indirect responses to European industrial booms). Indigenous peoples and peasant societies also can and do destroy existing landscapes.[9] Landowners in the Bakken were not conservationists. Running cattle on the plains has many negative ecological consequences.[10] Participating in the global industrial ranching and farming complex carries much responsibility to the imposition of the Anthropocene. All of this is true. The difference, then, lies not between Native and non-Native resource extraction, but between commodified, industrial approaches to extraction and non-industrial, non-commodified approaches. The difference is between an approach

7 Turner 1953:1; Popper and Popper 2006; Braun 2013b.

8 Braun 2016b.

9 Krech 2000; Harking and Lewis 2007.

10 See, for example, Donahue (1999).

that sees nature as a relation and one that sees nature as a commodity. Land and resources in non-capitalist societies have value. That value includes their uses, but that use value is dependent on how it is used and by whom. The value of the earth, then, was and is tied in to social relations, which in turn determine specific rights over resource use, habitation, and spiritual and ceremonial factors. However, commodification excludes all factors in determining value other than exchange value. Social ties—kinship relations—are no longer relevant, and with them, obligations have disappeared. While recognitions of moral obligations to the earth might not lead to actions, they do lead to different views of the world because they assign values differently.

In a non-commodified society, there is, for example, value in the preservation of a landscape—the preservation not of resources or of parcels, but of an area, an ecosystem, as a whole. As a commodity, landscapes have value if they can be sold or bought as parcels, but it is very hard to put an exchange value on a landscape itself other than, for example, as a resource for tourism. In and of itself, however, landscapes have no value in a market society. Similar calculations apply to water, for example. For many people, water has value because it can be used to grow plants or manufacture things, which then can be sold on the market. A river flowing, however, has no exchange value as a flowing river (again, unless it can be commodified as a tourist attraction). Exchange values are not inherent in the land. They have to be imposed. In order to exchange value, landscapes have to be turned into parcels and commons have to be turned into private property. It is the process inherent in frontiers, which parcel the earth into commodified resources to be extracted. Just as narratives of the frontier serve to legitimize the industrialization of the landscape, they also legitimize the parallel process of the deterritorialization of those people for whom this landscape holds more than economic meaning. This is the process inherent in Highlands enclosures, American Indian allotments, and railroad land grants.

The idea of the closing of the frontier conjures up an image of history that draws a hard line between a state that used to be and the progress we have made since that hypothetical time. The closing of the frontier thus fits in perfectly with the idea of Manifest Destiny. While many frontiers had devastating consequences for indigenous peoples, from depopulation to deterritorialization, it is equally true, however, that indigenous peoples everywhere have participated in frontiers, as groups and as individuals. This was the case for the fur trade, and it is still the case for the frontiers of energy and resource extraction. And it has been true as well that the continuous industrial frontiers have worked in similar ways to deterritorialize the newly indigenized peoples, who with the generations living on land they settled also came to see the landscape as more than resources waiting to be extracted. This deterritorialization of the settlers—the farmers and ranchers who benefited from the original Manifest Destiny, the first waves of frontiers and now work the land—often stays hidden. The narrative instead focuses on Native peoples, who have supposedly long since disappeared but can therefore be rediscovered as metaphors.

Hallowell wrote that, "Now that the frontier has passed, our children discover the Indian in the comic books, as well as in the library."[11] It is unfortunately true that many people still assume that indigenous peoples have vanished with the frontier. However, as Hallowell knew well, in reality, American Indians have been involved in all frontiers in North America, and continue to be involved in them. Contrary to the expectations,[12] however, Native peoples have not disappeared, in part because they have neither simply been "victims of progress," nor have frontiers (that is, resource exploitation) simply been "a plague upon the peoples."[13] Reality, as always, is much more complex. Instead, "from the beginning of energy development on Indian lands, Indian people have been actively engaged: as owners and lessees of resources, workers in the industries, consumers of electricity and gasoline, and developers of tribal energy companies, as well as environmentalists who sometimes challenge these enterprises."[14] This does not mean that Native peoples are "eager to exchange their basically satisfying cultures for the dubious benefits of the commercial world."[15] Native peoples have always been modern. No society lives in past times. The fact that industrial societies resort to a rhetoric that makes others out to be backwards, medieval, or living in the stone age is only a reflection of an effort to secure supremacy.[16]

All peoples have been in contact with others and have continuously learned from others and taught them in return. Ceremonies, technologies, techniques, values, ideas: all of these are encountered, studied

11 Hallowell 1967:345.
12 On expectations of Native people, see Deloria (2004).
13 Bodley 2008; Johansen 2016.
14 Smith and Frehner 2010:5.
15 Bodley 2008:37.
16 Lyons 2010; Lévi-Strauss 1969.

to see whether they are useful, and, if they can improve lives, adopted into one's own cultural reality. In this way, peoples are contemporary and modern. They may choose to select different expressions of their contemporaneity, but difference in culture does not mean difference in time. Such a view of modern indigeneity stands in marked contrast to the notion that indigenous peoples are living in societies marked by "a relative lack of change in the major cultural patterns."[17] That view will lead to familiar notions of Native peoples, expectations of "primitivism, technological incompetence, physical distance, and cultural difference."[18] The story of indigenous involvement in resource booms is much more complex than a simple narrative of victimhood, and it deserves more attention than that narrative would allow. Contemporary and historical resource exploitation in North America makes that very clear.

## The beginnings

Natural resources played a large role in the exploration and colonization of the northern Plains. The story of Native and non-Native communities in what is today western North Dakota and eastern Montana can be told as a story of these resources and the series of booms and busts designed to discover, own, and extract them. Already Lewis and Clark noted every coal vein they saw in North Dakota in their journals. Their journey up the Missouri River was in response to a resource boom that had brought wealth to the Missouri River tribes; the fur trade linked the Mandan and Hidatsa to the centers of Europe, and made what was to become North Dakota the key to the control of the continent.

When Lewis and Clark reached the Mandan and Hidatsa in 1804, they arrived at villages where European traders were well established.[19] The tribes had been trading at York Factory on Hudson Bay since 1715.[20] When the French explorer La Vérendrye visited them in 1738, they were well informed about the Spanish presence to their south, and the presence in their villages of conch shell from the Gulf of Mexico, dentalium shell from the Northwest Coast, as well as other

17 Bodley 2008:33.
18 Deloria 2008:4.
19 Larocque 1985:136-139.
20 Ray 1998:55-57.

trade items confirm large, long-standing trade networks.[21] Their settlements were agricultural centers, with fields stretching between villages along the Missouri River.[22] The fur trade had made these centers one of the American nodes of a global trade network, the equivalent to European nodes. It is difficult to say whether the trade began in Paris and ended in the Mandan and Hidatsa villages or vice versa. Yet, the fur trade boom had also already shown dangerous sides to globalization processes. Global connections had brought destruction and would bring more. Epidemics had struck, among them the devastating smallpox epidemic of 1780-81. More would follow, with another, in 1837-38 wreaking absolute havoc in the villages. At the same time, the tribes experienced a decline in intertribal trade as the American and Canadian traders established direct trading posts in other societies' settlements.[23] This meant that the lucrative position as a distributor of European trade goods to other tribes no longer existed. Together, these trajectories meant that the village nations had to regroup, and they did so quite successfully by unifying in a single town, Like-a-Fishhook, and then establishing new communities along the Missouri River on the Fort Berthold reservation.

The next resource boom led to new challenges. The object now was land. The historian Elwyn B. Robinson argued that North Dakota was settled—by Europeans and Americans—in two booms. The first was the Great Dakota Boom, from 1878 to 1886; the second land boom lasted from 1898 to World War I. Robinson thought that the "pioneers had done well" in the first boom, as they had "turned an empty wilderness into a civilized society."[24] Of course, both claims, about the empty wilderness and about the civilized society should be taken with caution. There had been no empty wilderness on the northern Plains, and whether the impending settler society was more "civilized" than the Native societies it replaced and destroyed is a matter of ethnocentric debate. At least, however, the terms show the predominant assessment of a progressing frontier, and the values assigned to it. From the dominant perspective, progress was being achieved, and the processes were both demonstrating and inscribing Manifest Destiny. To be fair, Robinson, despite the praise for the achievements of these settlers, also saw the other side of booms. "The pioneers had done too well," he added.

21 Wood 1967:153-155.
22 Will and Hyde 1964.
23 Wood and Thiessen 1985:5-8.
24 Robinson 1966:133-155, 235-254.

"In the enthusiasm of the Great Dakota Boom, they had inevitably made what can be called 'the Too-Much Mistake.' Retrenchment and abandonment soon followed."[25] Under the economic, political, social, and cultural value systems in place, unfortunately, nobody learned from this experience of wanting too much. The pressures to increase population and production were common-sensical and could not be questioned—I will return to this in the Epilogue. More continued to be seen as better in any circumstance. As a consequence, after the initial settlement booms, there were others: the bonanza farms brought in the industrialization of agriculture, which was met by the collapse of wheat prices after World War I and by the droughts and dust storms of the 1930s, for example.

The land boom obviously impacted Native peoples in very different ways from its effects for non-Native people. For Native people, this was not a boom. To the contrary, they were the people from whom this resource was to be extracted.

## The tribes

The first of today's Three Affiliated Tribes to arrive in the region were the Mandan, who arrived from the east, possibly across the prairies. They arrived at the Missouri by the White River, in South Dakota, and then made their way upriver, eventually settling in the region around the Heart River.[26] Here, they were encountered by the Hidatsa, who also came from the east. It is unclear (and unimportant) when this happened exactly, but the Heart River Phase of villages in the area is archaeologically ascribed to begin around AD 1450.[27] According to Will and Hyde, Hidatsa tradition says that they learned agriculture from the Mandan when they reached the Missouri. However, this seems to be a statement driven by "zeacentrism",[28] the equation of agriculture with corn. It is plausible that the Hidatsa learned about corn from the Mandan; by this time, however, the Midwest had been agricultural for thousands of years, focusing on other crops.[29] That some, if not all Hidatsa groups were or had been agricultural before becoming "the Hidatsa" on the Missouri is supported by Wood's study of oral

25 Robinson 1966:155.
26 Will and Hyde 1964:35-36.
27 See Wood (1980).
28 For an explanation of zeacentrism, see Fritz (2019).
29 For an overview, see for example Shay (2022).

traditions.[30] People sometimes imagine such movements as happening in "frontier" situations—Native peoples moving into wilderness. Far from it, the Missouri valley had been settled for millennia by this time. In the nineteenth century, the Arikara also reached the area, after slowly moving upriver over the past centuries.

The three nations were focused on agriculture and established large village sites surrounded by fields along the Missouri and some of its tributaries. By the eighteenth century, this distinguished them from other groups who were taking advantage of horses to focus on more nomadic hunting and gathering lifestyles. Neither the village tribes nor the hunter-gatherers were exclusive in their subsistence pursuits, and a lively dynamic of trade and warfare developed between them. The peoples living in earthlodges, however, were far more susceptible to devastating epidemics. Eventually, in 1845, the Mandan and Hidatsa began to live together in Like-a-Fishhook village, where they were joined by the Arikara a few years later.

In the first treaty of Fort Laramie, signed in 1851, the Mandan, Hidatsa, and Arikara are treated as one group, claiming a territory encompassing all the lands west of the Missouri from the Heart River to the Yellowstone, and reaching the northern Black Hills. However, the Lakota expansion into the Powder River valley in practice also affected the southwestern portion of these lands. In 1870 and 1880, the United States massively reduced the territory by executive orders. Finally, the current boundaries of the Fort Berthold Indian Reservation—through another massive reduction—were established in the Agreement of 1886, which went into effect upon ratification in 1891.

The agreement included a provision that the lands were to be allotted. Allotment enforced the dominant society's view that the only right way to own land was as private holdings. It therefore broke up communally owned lands and distributed the land base to tribal members. Allotment is a poster child of what Fredric Jameson identifies as "translat[ing] the money form and logic of commodity production for a market back on to space itself." It was indeed "the power of commerce and then capitalism proper" that insisted on this process "to seize upon a landscape and flatten it out, reorganize it into a grid of identical parcels, and expose it to the dynamic of a market that now reorganizes space in terms of an identical value."[31] Allotment parcels

30 Wood 1980:124.
31 Jameson 1998:66.

were—some temporarily—protected from market forces because they were placed into trust; the federal government holds the title to the properties in trust for their Native owners. The process was, however, no less brutal. Tribal members on Fort Berthold primarily chose allotments along and near to the Missouri River, which was where water, timber, and fertile soils allowed for productive communities.

Allotment was a drawn-out process. In 1907, those tribal members who had not yet taken allotments, and those whose allotments were less than 80 acres could take additional allotments. In 1910, another round of allotments took place, and a further cession opened the northeast third of the reservation to settlement. Despite these losses, the people of Fort Berthold were economically self-sufficient again by 1915.[32] The process was completed in 1910, and so-called "surplus" lands—lands that were left over once every eligible member of the tribes had been allotted—were then opened for settlement. As in other cases where reservations were opened for settlement, the state and communities assumed that the 1910 act had diminished the reservation—that the area opened for settlement did not belong to the reservation, anymore. However, in 1972, the Eight Circuit of the Federal Court of Appeals ruled that the act had not changed the exterior boundaries of the reservation. The advance of the frontier—of the process of extracting and deterritorializing resources—was checked in this case. Although the land had been sold, the Three Affiliated Tribes retained important rights. Some of these rights held true for resources below the land.

During early allotment, mineral rights were not separated from surface rights. However, in 1912, Congress reserved mineral rights under allotted lands on Fort Berthold to the tribe, so that all the mineral rights in the 474,422 acres of the allotted area remain tribally owned, either by members of the tribe or the Tribe itself. The tribe also kept ownership of mineral rights on 110,623 acres of the area opened for homesteading in 1910, about a third of that land. In 1914, Congress reserved the mineral rights under reservation lands opened for homesteading for the tribe; it would do the same on Fort Belknap, Fort Peck, and the Crow reservation.[33] However, these mineral rights were only reserved if the lands had been classified accordingly. On Fort Berthold, the initial survey in the 1910s had only found a potential for coal, and it only discovered about half of the actual reserves. "As was

32 Parker 2011:76-81.

33 Williams and Bluemle 1978:2-3; Ambler 1990:44; Fritz 2005:658.

true on other reservations, DOI [Department of the Interior] attorneys later determined that the early mineral classifications were final, and the tribes had no claim on minerals under allotments or homesteads that were not recognized during that classification."[34] Thus, the Tribe itself would eventually come to own only a minority of oil and gas rights because in 1910, the oil reserves had not yet been discovered.

## Oil

The processes that allowed resource booms to occur, the building of the natural resources that are the foundation for industrial capitalism and the Anthropocene, began a very long time ago; in the case of oil and gas booms, long before the current landscapes or their flora and fauna existed. For the northern Plains, it all started with the creation of what is called the "Williston Basin," a geological region so named in 1924, after the city of Williston in western North Dakota. The Williston Basin extends through western North Dakota and eastern Montana, includes some portions of northwestern South Dakota and a tiny bit of northeastern Wyoming, and large portions of southeastern Manitoba and southern Saskatchewan, as well as, for some authors, some parts of Alberta.[35] For much of the Paleozoic era, between 514 million and 252 million years ago, this region was submerged by shallow seas, as was the case again during the Cretaceous period, between 145 and eighty million years ago. Although exposed to above-surface erosion from time to time, the area experienced deposits of sedimentary layers that are thickest in its middle region where they extend to about sixteen thousand feet deep under the Killdeer Mountains.[36] Especially the Paleozoic sedimentation layers, over millions of years, turned into carbonates. The Williston Basin thus contains several geological formations that contain oil, gas, potash, and coal. The most famous of these formations today is the Bakken or Sanish formation, but there are many others, for example the Three Forks, Lodgepole, or Madison formations.[37] Thus, the Bakken boom is somewhat of a misnomer, as not all oil produced in the region actually originates in the Bakken formation.

34 Ambler 1990:46.
35 Barnes 1952; Laird 1956.
36 Sandberg 1962; Peterson 1988.
37 For an overview, see for example LeFever et al. (1991).

Millions of years after the sedimentation of these layers, at the beginning of the Anthropocene, the search for oil extended onto the northern Plains. Oil was first looked for in the areas of anticlines and domes, geological formations whose layers arch up and thus can serve as "petroleum traps"; oil and gas collect at their highest points once less porous rocks prevent them from going higher. The Williston Basin includes several anticlines and domes, the most famous probably the Cedar Creek anticline in southeastern Montana and the Nesson anticline in west-central North Dakota. These two anticlines, important too for coal resources, were defined between 1910 and 1917, and the Cedar Creek anticline started to produce gas from shallow wells in 1912.[38] In 1936, oil was discovered on the Cedar Creek anticline.[39] However, while neighboring areas in Montana saw quickly dissipating oil booms in 1901 and 1904 and started commercial production in the 1920s,[40] commercial oil production in the Williston Basin began only in the 1950s. The first commercially viable discovery in the Williston Basin was made in January 1951 in Manitoba. This well was quickly followed by the famous Clarence Iverson No.1 well in North Dakota in April of the same year and a well in Dawson County, Montana, in mid-July.[41] These discoveries set off a first boom, with increased lease and drilling activities. However, lease activities had already seen a high before 1950, in anticipation of oil discoveries in the region.

These leases also affected Indian reservations in the area, and as is always the case, federal regulations affect Native nations in different ways than they affect non-Native mineral rights and land holders because the federal government holds lands and rights in trust for the owners. Fort Peck in Montana leased 84,411 acres of tribal lands by 1952. In December 1949, tribal members received $287,217.13 for 21,257 acres at a lease auction. In November 1951, Fort Berthold leased 17,290 acres for $588,000. These leases, to remain intact, required the establishment of a twelve thousand feet deep well or a producing well within a year. Other leases took place on Standing Rock and Cheyenne River reservation further south.[42] The latter two reservations, however, although geologically located within the Williston Basin, never saw sustained successful commercial production.

38 Gries 1952; Davis and Hunt 1956.
39 Anderson et al. 1982:3.
40 Darrow 1955.
41 Frantz 1952:45; Laird 1952:16; Goodin 1952:57.
42 Goodin 1952:53-54.

It is important to note two factors in the late 1940s and early 1950s. One is that the Bureau of Indian Affairs still exerted a huge influence on leases, having been accustomed to not having to ask for any input from the tribe for decades. The other is that under the threat of Termination policies, tribes often felt the need to build as many assets as they could. The federal government at the time was planning to end all of its treaty obligations, and tribes were faced with a real possibility of having to take care of their members by themselves. Tribes were thus trying to maximize income and had very real incentives to agree to as many leases as they could.

It is also of importance that by 1950 many other tribes had been involved in oil exploration, production, and leasing. The most famous experience with oil came from the Osage reservation in Oklahoma, where the first oil and gas lease was approved by the Tribe in 1896. However, the Navajo Nation also approved leases from 1921 on.[43] Other reservations were engaged with the industry, such as the Wind River Shoshone and Arapahoe tribes in Wyoming, who were fighting with the federal government over oil leases and for per-capita allocations of revenues from 1908 through 1947. Marjane Ambler wrote that these early experiences show that our assumptions about early Native leaders are often misguided: "Rather than reluctantly accepting mineral development, they sometimes sought it. At the same time, their control was limited by their lack of information, the interference of the federal government, their economic desperation, the terms of leases, and the lack of enforcement of federal regulations and lease terms." The 1934 Indian Reorganization Act (IRA) and the 1938 Omnibus Tribal Leasing Act, which governed tribal mineral, oil, and gas leases until 1982, rectified some of these concerns. This was especially true for consent to leases. Although the terms of the leases were long, and the royalties were extremely low, tribes now had to consent to oil and gas leases before they could be approved.[44] At least, that was what the law now said. How this played out in practice might have been another question.

A short boom occurred in some of the communities in northwestern North Dakota, on and off the Fort Berthold reservation, when intercontinental nuclear missiles were posted in the area in the 1950s. Many communities saw temporary camps for the workers established.

43 Chamberlain 2000; Ambler 1990:49-50.

44 Ambler 1990:48-53.

This was another boom that affected mostly the subsurface, apart from the establishment of the Minot Air Force Base. Occasionally, a missile or a warhead is still transported from the base, in a convoy escorted by helicopters, armored personnel carriers, and police cars. Air Force patrols as well as silo maintenance crews used to make up some of the sparse traffic on the gravel roads before the oil boom, but apart from the fenced-off missile sites—and the missiles in the ground—not much remains visible from the missile boom.

## Water

The bigger boom was caused by the building of the Garrison Dam, a part of the Pick-Sloan Plan to build dams along the tributaries and the mainstream of the Missouri river. This boom did not bring many people to Fort Berthold, but it had a tremendous impact on the communities. Again, like the booms that brought allotment to Fort Berthold, this boom extracted lands, this time for energy production and transportation. And while non-Native people were also negatively affected this time, the brunt of the damage was done to the tribes. The positive effects of the boom were for others.

The Pick-Sloan Plan was a compromise between separate plans by the Army Corps of Engineers and the Bureau of Reclamation to prevent Missouri River floods, produce electricity, divert water for irrigation projects, and provide recreation spaces. It was approved by Congress in 1944 with the Corps as the lead agency, and thus it came at a time when American Indian policy shifted to the Termination era.[45] Termination foresaw the end of treaty obligations through the termination of Native sovereignty and the Americanization of tribal members who would be stripped of their rights as American Indians. Thus, reservations would no longer be needed. They could, therefore, be used in the national interest, for example for the Pick-Sloan Plan dams and the lakes it would create.

In a contemporary book on the plan by the Indian Service, Frances Cushman and Gordon MacGregor spent the last chapter on the impacts on reservations. While they acknowledge that Fort Berthold "will be affected more seriously by the Missouri Basin Development Plan than any other area of Indian land," they assure that the government will pay for losses. Thus, the "whole land ownership problem which has been created by the allotment and inheritance systems,

45 Lawson 1994:3-26; Braun 2008:23.

can be wiped out and replaced by a more useful system." More than that, however, the "sale of land at this time will provide cash for some people who may wish to leave the reservation or go into businesses other than ranching." In accordance with Termination rhetoric, they assert that these developments are "a great opportunity to become self-supporting and independent of the limitation of so-called wardship." In a preview of Termination policies, they write that "[s]tate and county governments might give the governmental services of education, health, welfare, farm extension, work and law and order," and that the "Indian Council might take over the local administration of the reservation."[46] In the logic of industrial booms, local people gain economic opportunities by the development of their resources, and they will use those opportunities to become productive industrial workers and citizens so that they would not need these local resources anymore, which makes it okay to extract them in the first place. On Fort Berthold and elsewhere, thus, the productive communities along the Missouri River (who were already self-supporting), would be flooded so that the people could leave the reservation to participate in the American dream.

How much these expectations were unjustified is not only demonstrated by the ensuing historical reality, but might also be shown by a contemporary publication by the state of North Dakota on the future positive impacts of the Garrison Dam. While the state gives detailed plans for irrigation districts, electrification, and other development plans, in its whole one hundred and twenty six pages, it manages to not mention Fort Berthold once.[47] In fact, so eager was the state of North Dakota to get the dam started that in 1946, Governor Andahl made an effort to change a provision that "none of the money can be used for work on the structure until the Indians have been re-located." Instead, North Dakota wanted it to read "that the Indians cannot be flooded out until and unless provision is made for them elsewhere."[48] Indeed, the Corps began construction in 1946, before the land issues were settled. Fort Berthold lost over 152,000 acres; the reservation became split into different sections by the lake; about eighty percent of the tribal membership had to relocate out of the Missouri River valley; and the reservation lost ninty-four percent of its agricultural lands.[49]

46 Cushman and MacGregor 1948:162-163.
47 State Water Commission and State Engineer 1946.
48 Bismarck Tribune 1946.
49 Lawson 1994:59.

The reservation gained no irrigation. Its economy collapsed. Ironically, despite the assurance from the Cushman and MacGregor that the dam would be a chance "to become self-supporting," the Tribe went from self-sustaining to economically dependent. As one author writes succinctly, "The Fort Berthold economy transitioned from one largely based on agriculture and ranching to one based largely on unemployment."[50] The damming of the Missouri to form Lake Sakakawea and the relocation out of the Missouri River valley became a continuing historical trauma of great proportions.

## Lake Sakakawea

In this succession of booms, each one impacts the others that follow. The Garrison Dam, for example, still impacts the oil and gas booms. In 1951, after the Clarence Iverson No.1 well discovery, both houses of the North Dakota legislature passed identical resolutions to Congress "to so amend federal statutes as to permit landowners to retain the oil and gas rights to their land when it is taken for such projects as Garrison dam."[51] The mineral rights on non-Indian lands surrounding Fort Berthold had in many cases been sold in the hard 1930s so that farmers could pay their taxes. At the time, it seemed like selling mineral rights would not have large consequences, and selling them to save the surface rights and being able to keep farming was a good strategy. Non-Indian farmers were not necessarily enthused by the proposed dams; this industrialization of their landscape would take their lands, and it represented a loss of local control.[52] In response to pressure building from the state, the Corps discontinued its practice to take mineral rights with surface rights in October 1951, and allowed affected landowners to keep their mineral rights. By that time, however, most parcels on the reservation had already been appraised. As a consequence, the Corps acquired the mineral rights of taken lands on the reservation, but did not acquire the mineral rights of lands being flooded off the reservation.

On the Fort Berthold Reservation, as the Army Corps of Engineers took the lands that were going to be flooded and landowners were moved out of the Missouri River valley. The mineral rights of their allotments (which they now no longer owned) were transferred to the

50 Parker 2011:316.
51 Bismarck Tribune 1951.
52 Tauxe 1993:107.

federal government as well. However, in 1984, they were then restored to the Tribe. They were not restored to the individual tribal members who had owned them before. It is therefore the Tribe that owns oil and gas rights under Lake Sakakawea. This move became important when the Bakken boom started. With new horizontal drilling technologies, it now was possible to get at the oil under the lake without having to install expensive equipment in the lake. The former allotment owners pressed for the tribe to return their mineral rights to them. They saw the mineral transfer to the tribe in a way as being robbed twice: first, the federal government had evicted them from their lands, now the tribe was going to use their mineral rights.

The debate over who owns the mineral rights under the lake was far from over, however, even between the State and the Tribe. In September 2016, the North Dakota Petroleum Council (NDPC) sent out a notice to mineral rights owners under the lake that the state might be in the process of claiming all of these mineral rights. "In sum, it is the State's position that the Missouri River and Lake Sakakawea are one and the same," the NDPC wrote, "and since the State owned title to the Missouri River at the time of statehood, the State acquired title to all minerals underlying the Lake due to the 'expansion' of the river caused by Garrison Dam."[53] In 2020, the solicitor of the Department of the Interior indeed issued a memorandum to the effect that "the State of North Dakota is the legal owner of submerged lands beneath the Missouri River where it flows through the Reservation." That opinion rested on the assumption that "[w]hile the Missouri River is obviously included within the *geographic* boundaries of the Reservation, the record is silent regarding whether the Reservation was intended to *include* the riverbed."[54] It is, of course, at the very least questionable whether the State ever gained title to the Missouri River within the reservation at statehood. The State based this assumption on the so-called equal footing doctrine, arguing that a state received title to navigable rivers and lakes unless Congress decreed otherwise. This would have given the State title to the historical riverbed, and thus the State argues that the lake was but an extension of the river.

Tribes are unfortunately all too familiar with this kind of legalistic argumentation. The Three Affiliated Tribes filed suit against the decision; in 2021, the Biden administration issued an Executive Order on

53 NDPC 2016:3.

54 Department of the Interior 2020; italics in original.

its first day in office, specifically mentioning the memorandum as one decision by the first Trump administration that would be reviewed. In general, it should be mentioned that according to United States law (25 U.S.C. § 194), the burden of proof in trials over property between American and Native parties rests with the American party.[55] At least theoretically, then, it should be the state of North Dakota who has to prove that the riverbed within the reservation is its property. In 2022, the Biden administration's solicitor for the Department of the Interior issued another memorandum, concluding now that "the minerals underlying the submerged lands in question here are held in trust for the Nation."[56] The State promptly challenged the decision. At stake are about $100 million in unpaid royalties.

The lake is more than a cause for lawsuits over mineral rights and royalties, though. Perhaps most importantly, it remains an ever-present reminder of historical trauma. In 2012, the flooding of the Missouri was a common referral point for reservation residents worried about the negative effects of the oil boom. Their fears were that just like Lake Sakakawea, the Bakken boom would sweep away social and cultural landscapes, networks, and practices. In conjunction with the flooding of the Lake, another image that was often brought up in conversation at that time was that of a tsunami. This was undoubtedly a reference to the tsunami that had hit Japan in 2011; the fact that the event translated as a metaphor to the northern Plains, however, shows that the experience of the Garrison Dam is still very powerful. Like a tsunami, the lake flooded lives, memories, and communities. Unlike a tsunami, it did not recede. Whether or not the boom would impact landscapes and communities permanently or temporarily, it was clear to even those who saw the boom as a positive development that the dangers were similar.

## Sacrifice areas

After the initial oil boom in the 1950s, and following the water and electricity boom of the Garrison Dam, the next big boom on the

55 The Trade and Intercourse Act of 1834, article 22: "That in all trials about the right of property in which an Indian may be a party on one side, and a white person on the other, the burden of proof shall rest upon the white person, whenever the Indian shall make out a presumption of title in himself from the fact of previous possession or ownership."

56 Department of the Interior 2022:2.

northern Plains came with the energy boom of the 1970s and early 1980s. The initial phases of this boom were mostly focused on coal. These years demonstrated the inverse connection between global energy supplies and northern Plains energy booms: although the planning activities foreshadowed energy shortages in the future, the extraction boom itself was triggered by and lasted only as long as the energy crises themselves. The booms were supported and planned by the federal government, which threw its weight behind energy companies. A public alarmed by the urgently felt need for more energy was supportive of the boom, and the energy companies began to put into motion a massive expansion of extraction and processing capacity. "If American citizens were blissfully ignorant of the restricted availability of domestic fossil fuels," one author wrote, "the energy companies were not. Throughout the late 1960s and early 1970s, they were busy developing plans for extracting and processing ever greater amounts of coal, oil, natural gas, uranium, tar sands, and oil shale."[57] While American citizens might have been blissfully unaware of these preparations, however, once the plans began to be put into action, people on the plains and elsewhere—both Native and non-Native, and often in collaboration—responded quickly. Energy extraction in the 1970s and the response by the local, national, and international public, in concurrence with the raising awareness of economic, ecological, social, and cultural consequences of extraction, in many ways laid the foundation for contemporary technologies and practices but also political reactions to energy extraction. This is the context for the apocalyptic visions of deterritorialization in the first chapter.

On the northern Plains, government-industry initiatives to increase electricity production continued the vision laid out by the Pick-Sloan plan, but now focused away from water and on coal. The major driver of these efforts was the Northern Central Power Study, an effort that began in May 1970 in Omaha, where at "a meeting of top executives of major power supply utilities Assistant Secretary [of the Interior] Smith outlined a plan to combine hydropeaking with major thermal plants utilizing the enormous coal resources in Montana, Wyoming, Colorado and North Dakota."[58] It was a foregone conclusion that "the further development of the vast coalfields of the North Central region

57 Little 1978:63.
58 NCPS 1971b:1-2.

of the United States is almost a certainty."[59] The question was not whether to turn this coal into electricity, but what the most efficient way to do so might be. The answer was the building of mine-mouth power plants and transmission of electricity to the "load centers," that is to the industrial and population centers. In other words, open pit mines would extract the coal and feed it to local power plants. The consumers of the electricity generated would not be impacted by either mines or plants. They would simply be able to consume, without experiencing or carrying the burdens of production. Those would be shouldered by the local people in the rural, sparsely populated areas that would not benefit from the electricity. In fact, a Ford Foundation report pointed out these consequences of the projects in passing: the temporary influx of workers during construction and its social impacts, and the fact that energy extraction projects often channel that energy to other regions.

> [T]he development and operation of mines and power plants in the western United States more nearly resembles, in its economic and demographic aspects, the development in underdeveloped areas than it does the development of industry in major metropolitan areas. The magnitude of the projects in money and energy is huge, and their development potential enormous. The area developed, however, is not necessarily at the site of investment.[60]

In other words, it was clear that these projects were a continuation of extraction not only of minerals and energy. They were also a continuation of an extractive economy as a whole, further extracting social, environmental, and economic capital from rural areas and transferring them to the urban population centers. The Ford Foundation simply pointed out the reality that could be experienced in other regions of extractive economies, from mining in Appalachia and the Upper Peninsula to cotton in the South, from timber in the upper Great Lakes to industrial agriculture in rural areas everywhere. It was that report which introduced the term "national sacrifice area"[61] into the global vocabulary of development.

59 NCPS 1971a:5.
60 Ford Foundation 1974:104.
61 Ford Foundation 1974:85.

As discussed, the idea that extractive economies create social and environmental inequalities and alienation goes back to Marx and Engels' analysis that capitalism has globally subjected the country to the rule of the towns. Osha Gray Davidson, in writing about the farm crisis, very succinctly summarized these dynamics when he wrote that the "disintegration of rural life—the breakup of families, small-town organizations, and whole communities—fits the pattern established by colonial powers throughout the Third World."[62] The Ford Foundation report, far from taking any ideological sides, studied the proposed development of energy resources, the scientific data on rehabilitation efforts, and the legal frameworks in place. It came to the conclusion that any consideration of nonrenewable resources as the driver of economic development must first invest in an effort "to identify and assess the environmental, social, and economic objectives, the resource development potentials, and the ecological, social, and economic conditions of that development" to hopefully "provide a basis for an acceptable balance between the needs for environmental protection and those for technological development."[63] The report found that these basic assessments were being given "no consideration" in the planning. The boom, in other words, was not in any way guided by a framework that could have taken into account the impacts on local environments and peoples. The concern was focused solely on energy extraction for what was seen as the greater good.

Caught up in the development of coal resources in the Powder River Basin in the 1960s and 1970s were the Northern Cheyenne and the Crow reservations. Eventually, the Northern Cheyenne decided to pull back from mining contracts on their reservation when they had an opportunity to do so in 1973. They were able to finalize that decision in 1980.[64] The Crow ostensibly went a different path, one of capitalizing on their mineral resources. This path led to a prominent role in coal development until today. However, the decisions were not that different in other ways. Both tribes decided to protect their lands. In the 1970s, the Crow decided to only lease mineral rights for coal extraction on lands off their reservation, so that the reservation lands would not be directly impacted by coal mining.[65]

62 Davidson 1990:159.
63 Ford Foundation 1974:105 .
64 Allison 2015; Ashabranner 1982:100-116.
65 Allison 2015:98-124.

During this time, tribal activist also worked with the non-Indian resistance to energy extraction; such coalitions are ongoing today, perhaps most prominently seen in the "Cowboys and Indians" alliance against the Keystone XL pipeline. Ranchers were and are just as intent to keep coal mining and other disturbances from resource extraction off their land, and many of them have deep connections to the landscape.[66] Ironically, it is often Native nations who hold more leverage against energy projects, though, because they are sovereign nations who hold treaty rights. In 1980, for example, the Northern Cheyenne managed to gain leverage over the nearby power plants at Colstrip, Montana, by invoking their right to clean air under EPA rules.

## Native control

The fundamental question emerging in this context was, and has been ever since, "Can tribes control energy development?"[67] Of course, tribes had been trying to do exactly that for decades. In the 1970s, though, in the larger context of Self-Determination policies, courts that were beginning to enforce treaty rights, and a public that was more intent on listening to marginalized peoples, tribes were in a position where their voices could be heard and where they could organize to project real power. One way to strengthen their position was to share information and build a common interest group. In 1974, tribes on the northern Plains founded the Native American Natural Resources Development Federation (NANRDF), and in 1975, a national organization was founded: the Council of Energy Resource Tribes (CERT).[68]

However one stands to CERT as an organization, it seems clear that the organization helped gain funding for tribal planning purposes and provided a large impetus for tribes to engage in planning. Thus, while in 1978, the answer to the question of tribal control over energy development was "an unqualified 'Maybe'."[69] twelve years later, Marjane Ambler came to a much more optimistic conclusion:

> No longer the nation's energy colonies, several tribes have become energy developers, and others have gained significant control, making their own decisions with the help of consultants and attorneys, many of

66 Grossman 2017.

67 Owens 1978:49.

68 Allison 2015:127-184; Ambler 1990; LaDuke 1984; Ambler 1984a.

69 Owens 1978:61.

> them Indian. Smaller tribes still must struggle to retain even minimal staffs and hired expertise. Although intertribal jealousy still exists, when tribes need advice they now often look to one another, either informally or through tribal organizations such as CERT. ... The energy tribes have moved from a time when they were totally dependent upon the federal government to a time when a few pay most of the cost of providing services and economic development on the reservations.[70]

Here was the beginning to the answers that John Borbridge had asked in 1969 in Alaska. Thirty five years later, the economic potential of tribal energy development was obvious, although the costs to the environment, both locally and globally, had also become much more visible.

Whether tribes have the opportunity to take advantage of energy resources is of course dependent on their location. If they do have resources, however, the potential is not only tied to economic development. As Borbridge had predicted, hand in hand with economic independence comes political sovereignty, a connection that was never lost on American Indian nations. Control over energy development also meant political control. The then head of the Northern Cheyenne Oil and Gas Office, Joe Little Coyote, explained that very succinctly: "Every American Indian tribe is caught in the dependency trap," he said.[71] "We must help ourselves. That doesn't mean we will close our eyes and ears to the outside world. We know we're a part of America and we know our economy is tied up with the national economy. But from now on we intend to see that Cheyenne affairs and the Cheyenne economy will be directed and controlled by members of the Cheyenne tribe. We must determine our own destiny." Energy development was one route tribes could chose to try and gain power over their own destinies. As the Northern Cheyenne demonstrate, however, the refusal of energy development is another route.

The different paths, sometimes simply based on different situations, different ideas, or different individuals in leadership positions, are still evident. The Navajo Transitional Energy Company, for example, became the third largest coal producer in the United States after it

70 Ambler 1990:261.

71 Ashabranner 1982:119-120.

bought three coal mines in Montana and Wyoming in 2019.[72] One of those coal mines is located on Crow Nation mineral rights. The Crow have long depended on coal extraction for jobs. In 2016, plans to export mostly Crow coal through ports on the West Coast saw setbacks when the Lummi Nation stopped the building of coal shipping terminals. Weighing economic development against ecological protection is still a very difficult decision. The fact that tribes take different positions on the dilemma is not proof that some are more in touch with traditional culture than others. It demonstrates that they, like everybody else, are partaking in the very complex decision making of the twenty-first century and that they are looking out for their specific interests as sovereign nations.

At the same time that American Indians came to be in a position in which energy resources had the potential to increase political sovereignty, energy-rich western states also perceived those opportunities. They feared, however, that the federal government, in search of a solution for the national energy crisis, would sacrifice them for the national good. The governor of New Mexico said, "the West will not become an energy colony for the rest of the nation," and the Western Governors' Regional Energy Policy Office pushed for federal laws that would allow energy development on federal lands only with strict environmental regulations.[73] In times of the Arab oil embargo, President Carter had proposed a switch from imported oil to U.S. coal, coupled with a call for reducing energy consumption.[74] However, the public did not want to make sacrifices in their daily lives, and the western states feared a federal enforcement of coal production on lands within their territories. While the Sagebrush Rebellion in its infancy was thus a reaction against a fear of forced development, this would change to a fear of too much environmental regulation a decade later.[75] In the late 1970s, the West saw itself at the beginning of yet another boom cycle; this time, however, it was one they feared would not be controlled by them, but might end up in stripping states of their sovereignty. Thus, the people who had profited from the earlier booms—land, agriculture, minerals, water—now feared to be in the position of those they had previously exploited, and thus called themselves the New Indians.

72 For a history of Navajo coal development, see Curley (2023).
73 Cawley 1993:79.
74 Jacobs 2016:219-232.
75 See Pendley (1995).

## Lessons learned

In North Dakota, coal development during the 1970s led to the building of a coal gasification, or synfuels plant near Beulah and Hazen, about four miles south of Lake Sakakawea and close to the Fort Berthold reservation. In his proposed solutions to the energy crisis, President Carter had put an emphasis on synthetic fuels, although he thereby angered the growing number of environmentalists.[76] Perhaps in a seemingly exemplary demonstration of Sagebrush Rebellion fears, the synfuels plant was pushed through against objections by the Mercer County Landowners Association. What became apparent in the negotiations around the permitting process was an issue that would repeat itself in most industry-driven booms. Rural communities in western North Dakota, just like in much of the West overall, were run by volunteers. County commissions and boards were not prepared to stand up to international corporations operating in the national interest that had professional staff dedicated to research every single aspect of their operations. "As a commission, we try to make an intelligent decision based on what is presented in our own research, and sometimes a gut feeling. But with their resources, they can do whatever can be done," said the chair of the county's planning and zoning commission.[77]This issue would repeat itself over and over again in the Bakken oil boom. Local people knew the land intimately, but not in the formal way required by the hegemonic discourse of the law and administration. Added to that was the reluctance of local people to follow their county commissioners in gathering such information and apply it. "There was little support among the local population for the comprehensive plan or for the legal formalisms of planning procedure," wrote Tauxe about the discussions surrounding the synfuels plant. "Systematic development planning was seen by many locals as one aspect of a general intrusion by outsiders, and its enforcement evoked the strong insiders-versus-outsiders conflict characteristic of the boom years."[78] Thirty to forty years later, the situation had not changed. Local governments did not have access to data that would have allowed them to make decisions on the Bakken oil boom, and communities were not in support of legal planning efforts.

76 Jacobs 2016:236.
77 Tauxe 1993:140.
78 Tauxe 1993:141.

Just like in other powerplant and energy extraction locations close to or on reservations, Native people started to work in the synfuels plant and gained or further applied skills. It would be a mistake to assume that Native people were not involved in these plants, or in energy policy and practice in general. In 1980, the Three Affiliated Tribes at Fort Berthold founded ONRED, the Office of National Resources and Energy Development, which was established with the goal of regulating exploration and extraction on the reservation—a role that the Bureau of Indian Affairs claimed for itself. The tribe was able to assert itself in this role in part because of severe understaffing at the local BIA office. Overwhelmed with permits and applications, the Bureau needed the tribe, and the tribe was not satisfied with simply assisting the BIA.[79] The boom years of the late 1970s and early 1980s led to more consequences than tribal assertions of sovereignty, however. Many towns in North Dakota were not equipped to deal with the influx of workers and families. New schools, housing developments, and infrastructure projects were initiated. When the boom ended, these towns often had no other choice but to declare bankruptcy. Those lessons were well learned, and would influence the reaction of town and county leaders to the Bakken boom twenty-five years later.

79 Ambler 1984b:195-197.

# Chapter 3
# The Boom

In January 2012, I was visiting New Town with a colleague from the University of North Dakota. We were staying with one of his former students and visited a tribal oil development conference that brought together mostly different oil service companies, as well as representatives from the tribal, state, and federal governments. On the first day of our stay, we visited with staff at the new Elbowoods Memorial Health Clinic, which had just partially opened in October 2011. The clinic was based on a so-called 638 contract between the Tribe and the Indian Health Service. 638 contracts are opportunities for tribes to take on and manage federal responsibilities themselves. Based on the Indian Self-Determination and Educational Assistance Act of 1975, Public Law 93-638 (hence the name), the federal government will transfer responsibilities for programs to tribes, but retain its funding requirements at an equal level. The Three Affiliated Tribes then were able to inject their own money—in this case from the oil development on the reservation—and build a brand-new clinic and health center. This was one of the earliest and most important contributions of the boom to the welfare of tribal members. A second contribution was at that time still in the planning stages. Over the next few years, a new housing development would be built across the road from the clinic. In 2012, however, the housing crisis weighed heavily on the community, to the point that doctors at the clinic had no housing. The Tribe, just like other communities in the region, was trying to catch up. One of the staff at the clinic said that if a boom has fifty percent positive outcomes and fifty percent negative ones, that would be a great overall situation. At that time, he said, for those people with royalties from mineral rights it was probably thirty percent positive and seventy percent negative. For those without mineral royalties, the situation was almost all negative.

That evening, I had a conversation with our host. He said that as long as people analyze the boom only in terms of money, they miss a major point. What many people were missing, he said, was the spiritual component of taking things from the land. When one takes something from the land, one should give back. This is true for sweetgrass, sage, and other things; it should also apply to minerals and oil. People attributed some of the bad things that were happening in the communities, such as the increase in deaths, crime, drugs, inflation of prices for groceries and housing, and other issues, to this lack of giving back. One of the other big issues he saw was that people stopped visiting each other. "Visiting" is a major social activity in rural communities, on and off the reservation. Visiting means keeping up social connections, keeping kinship and community bonds working, and talking through things—often without saying anything. Now, our host said, some people were getting rich and others not, and people got disconnected. "We need another summit," he said, in reference to the oil summit we were there to attend. "A different summit; a summit of the spiritual leaders to interpret what is happening." However, he concluded, spiritual leaders would only be heard if the political leaders and the community were humble and thought long-term. In the atmosphere as it was at the time, this was not the case, either on or off the reservation.

In his words was the nucleus of resistance, and as the boom developed, that resistance to unabashed visions of growth, greed, and extraction would grow. It might be tempting, perhaps, to see this resistance as one of "traditional" against "progressive" forces, or of those left out from royalties against those with royalties. These arguments were present, of course, but overall, that was not the case. Rather, this resistance pitted those who fought for their communities against those who were perceived to broker outside interests. Narratives of local resistance to outside capital are as much a part of booms as are other events that constitute resource plays. The Bakken is as much an illustration of attempts by local people to wrestle capital away from outsiders and gain control over it themselves as is any other situation where communities have to make decisions over their own futures without having control over the full discourse.

## Rural communities

Nobody has been able to survive on the northern Plains outside a community. People need each other. Ranchers can, of course, live "in the country" rather than "in town" and living in the country can mean that they live twenty miles away from a town and fifty miles away from a grocery store. People from Parshall or New Town went to Minot for anything other than basic needs, a seventy-five mile one-way trip, and about an hour and fifteen minutes without traffic. Yet, the towns constituted communities, and everybody knew who belonged to that community and who was a stranger. "Visiting" defined the networks, and because visiting is a public affair, the networks were defined for all to see, thus reinforcing themselves.

With the large influx of people during the beginning boom, that clear understanding of the world was no longer there. All of a sudden, strangers lived in the community. Mancamps sprung up everywhere—some in houses, some specially constructed, some in trailer parks, and some in campers. People were also no longer equal, as some had mineral rights and others did not. While the new wealth was often hidden in an attempt to preserve community, it became the subject of speculation. Trips to Minot or Williston became two-day affairs, especially since driving after dark was like Russian roulette. Trips to neighboring communities became dangerous. Kinship relations began to be strained. Who was still a relative and who was a stranger, and which strangers were potential future community members and which ones were not good candidates for that became increasingly difficult to assess. Overwhelmed, people lost control over their communities and the communities lost control over people. There were many more people there now, but the communities were disappearing.

It is no secret that rural communities are the peripheries in the United States, as they are in most industrialized countries. Heavily dependent on regional, national, and global centers for loans, technology, education, markets, and services, smaller communities experience a constant flow of raw products and population to larger, often more urban, centers. Rural reservation communities are not structurally different from other rural communities, except that they are usually the peripheries of these peripheries, in turn dependent on the border towns around them. Rural and reservation poverty has been studied, debated, discussed, and addressed for decades. Much of the discussion on rural poverty has focused on Appalachia and the rural South, perhaps because of the underlying racial discrimination, perhaps because of historical precedence and in the wake of groundbreaking work on poverty in these areas. The Midwest and the Plains, however, have been seen as the heartland of America, where communities are assumed to be homogenous and healthy, living both the American Dream and its past pastoral traditions. Poverty and the destruction of the environment as concepts are antithetical to this perspective. When there were problems, such as the Dust Bowl or the Great Depression, they were explained as aberrations of nature or historical exceptions as a result of outside influences.

On the Plains, as well as in the South, American farmers extracted so much from the land that their practices could only be sustained by appropriating "abundant, cheap fossil-fuel energy to import enormous amounts of synthetically manufactured nitrogen onto their fields."[1] This exploitation of the land, however, seemed common-sensical or natural and followed "a cluster of traditional American attitudes." Farmers were improving the land, not depleting it; they were keeping alive American values, not being oppressed by them; and whatever caused rural communities to suffer could not be manmade.[2] The narratives circulating about the rural heartland emphasized independence and prevented people from understanding how farming practices could lay at the root of dependency and poverty. So ingrained were these ideas that when, in the 1980s, farmers began to buckle under the stressors of industrialized agriculture and global markets they were now dependent on, they could not understand that the failure of their farms was systemic. Instead, they blamed themselves, thinking they failed "several generations of relatives (both backwards and forwards into those unborn generations who will now not be able to farm)" and saw themselves "as the one weak link in a strong chain that spans more than a century."[3] The farmer suicide crisis during the farm crisis in the 1980s seems to continue today, for much the same reasons.[4] In her ethnographic studies on the Canadian plains, Müller found the following:

> Most farmers I talked to seemed to be caught in the traps of market ideology and family tradition. The myths they created around their self-sustaining autonomous ancestors who seemed to be able to withstand alone all the hardships of settling the prairies, put a tremendous pressure on them to prove themselves successful in an environment that appears much more civilized and benign than the one their forefathers had to face. As the dominant worldview of the prairies is so firmly committed to the value of

1 Cunfer 2005:219
2 Worster 1977:231, 238
3 Davidson 1990:95
4 Weingarten 2018.

> hard work and the belief in progress, it became almost impossible for them to rethink their situation and envisage alternatives.[5]

Worldview is powerful and creates and limits the world for us. Such hegemonic ideologies can strongly limit how we react to new challenges: instead of critically investigating root causes, we abide by the discourse already available to us. This is especially the case when such ideologies are imposed on us from the outside—rural America as a concept has always been created as much if not more by urban dwellers as by rural people themselves, just as Native America as a concept is mostly created and controlled by people outside Native communities. Poverty, for many reasons, perhaps including to differentiate themselves from stereotypes of Native communities, is not a value that rural communities can accept as a descriptor of themselves and is not a value expected of them by outsiders. According to most narratives dominant in American worldviews, the American capitalist system is not supposed to create rural poverty: to the contrary, the system is supposed to originate in these communities, derive its values from them, and benefit them.

Yet, by now "ownership and management of agricultural enterprises have more in common with the characteristics typically associated with extractive industries—loss of local control, outside ownership, and large-scale intensive exploitation of the land." And while "a movement is underway in extractive communities and regions to gain greater control," it is still true that the industries "continue to exercise considerable control over the communities where they are located."[6] It is here, at the nexus of agriculture, extraction, alienation, and the expansion of central control over local resources and residents' lives, that it should be recognized that the values governing this system are not American, but industrial. What differentiates the Soviet expansion over Siberia from the American expansion of control over the West is not the systemic application of control or the violence used to exert it, but, on one hand, the pretense of a free market system and the privatization of the power exerted and, on the other, the discourse of individual responsibility and the denial of systemic power.[7] The

5 Müller 2008:401.

6 England and Brown 2003:327.

7 Braun 2013b:218-219.

acknowledgment of systemic responsibility for oppression goes against all hegemonic American narratives, which depend on a projection of individual "freedom" associated with rural pastoralism.

Even in places like North Dakota, however, where local control had remained more intact up to this historical point than in other agricultural regions, the realities of alienation began to reveal themselves during the boom. For example, local control was challenged by split estate rulings. All of a sudden, somebody who lived half a continent away, or on another continent, somebody who might have never seen the landscape, never lived it, never experienced it, could decide what was going to happen with this land because they owned the mineral rights. Farmers and ranchers were confronted with the notion that whether or not they owned their lands was largely immaterial, as long as somebody else owned what was under their land. Local land ownership turned in some ways from a symbol of local control to a symbol of helpless frustration as more and more drilling wells were established. This created truly existential dilemmas for many farmers and ranchers. They had subscribed to the dominant discourse and the politics of individual responsibilities for so long that when they were confronted with the realities of systemic oppression they could neither simply change political views and parties (if that mattered) nor deny that their politics had, in part, created or supported the system that now harmed them. As a result, they—and their communities—often became politically paralyzed, as they were caught in a double bind.

For decades, these communities had seemingly faced a single existential problem, which was outmigration. They had shrunk and shrunk, and some had stopped to exist. The boom at first looked like a great solution to this problem. Very quickly, however, it created new issues as communities became overwhelmed. Without trying to anthropomorphize a historical event consisting of many separate events, it might help to imagine "the boom" as a living organism, being born, growing up, changing shapes, and then disappearing into middle age, although roaring back from back from time to time with intensity and anger, until finally dying away. In order to understand the boom and how it has impacted communities and landscapes, it is also helpful to investigate very briefly some of its parts. It is not necessary to discuss each one to its full extent here, but to provide enough of a background to facilitate an understanding of how these issues then affected communities, landscapes, and people.

## Fracturing

The Bakken boom—like the Marcellus, Eagle Fork, Permian Basin, and other oil and gas booms developing after 2005—was dependent on so-called "new" technology that would allow the extraction of fossil fuels that could not economically be reached by traditional methods. It is sometimes assumed, therefore, that hydraulic fracturing, the method most often used in these booms, was a new technology. In fact, it had been an experimental method from the 1930s on. Since that time, the industry had developed a number of different fracturing methods, all aimed at fracturing shale and rock that contain fossil fuels, thus setting the fuels free, and then pumping them up to the surface. In one of the more extreme methods, since at least 1959, discussions had been ongoing on using nuclear energy for oil shale fracturing.

In 1967 and 1969, nuclear devices were used in the United States to test whether this method could stimulate gas extraction.[8] Tests for using explosions from nuclear devices to extract oil from oil shale were proposed at the same time, but not conducted.[9] As a 1970 assessment pointed out, "Hydraulic fracturing cannot compete with nuclear energy as a means of rubbling rock; however, where in situ thermal recovery processes are planned that are to be conducted through a fracture system, hydraulic fracturing offers advantages over the mass rubbling process."[10] In other words, nuclear devices were really good at reducing a lot of rock to rubble, but they did not leave much to extract. The Soviet Union, too, started conducting tests to stimulate oil production with nuclear explosions in 1968, but did not end the experiments until 1987.[11] Contrary to much rhetoric about hydraulic fracturing as a new technology, then, it was not in itself what allowed the gas and oil booms of the first decade of the twenty-first century. Instead, the factors were two other developments: higher oil prices made the expensive extraction economically advantageous and refined hydraulic fracturing processes were combined with advanced precision horizontal drilling.

The first horizontally drilled oil well that reached the Bakken formation was completed in 1987.[12] By 1989, about eighty percent

8 Howard and Fast 1970:188-192.
9 Russell 1980:113-114.
10 Howard and Fast 1970:188.
11 Rogers 2015:66.
12 Deans, Scherrer, and Pulley 1991:95.

of horizontal Bakken wells were fractured wells, but it emerged that the production decline rate was exceptionally steep. While companies began to experiment with re-fracturing—stimulating the well again and again—the conclusion at that time was that, "If and when horizontal Bakken wells can be effectively stimulated, their success will be assured. Until then, their full potential will only occasionally be realized."[13] As the fracturing process was improved, and as oil prices rose in the first decade of the twentieth century, the technology available now became economical to deploy despite steep production declines, however, and the Bakken boom was born. The second part of the equation—the global oil market driving the prices up—is important to keep in mind. Despite the advances in technology, it was the interplay with oil prices that created the boom. And so, like all booms, when prices would eventually fall, there would be a bust. The promoters of booms often focus on the technological advances alone precisely because they want people to ignore the boom-bust nature of such events. By selling the oil and gas booms of the early twenty first century as driven by new, ground-breaking technology only, they could sell them as sustainable. Here, it was claimed, was the proof that new technology would continue to provide cheap energy and jobs well into the future.

## Depression economics and politics

Two further driving factors for the gas and oil booms were just as well hidden in plain view as their dependency on global energy prices: national security and an economic crisis. In 2008, just as the hydraulic fracturing booms in the United States began to shift into high gear, the economic system broke down. In essence, the average individual had become the periphery to the wealthy few who constituted the political and economic center, and the system began to recognize that debts could no longer be repaid: the credit system collapsed and because the American economy is a consumer economy fueled by debt, the economy broke down. In order to save the economy, the government would use public funds to bail out the most important creditors who were thus enabled to continue to lend. Before that happened, however, unemployment, homelessness, and economic recession had spread over most of the country. Because of this nationwide—and then global—recession, natural resource booms gained national and international

13 Deans, Scherrer, and Pulley 1991:99.

attention as economic hotspots; they represented the salvation of the economy; and the dominant discourse about and to communities was that not only did they have a chance to improve their economic situation, but in doing so they would save their country.

The Great Depression of the 1930s might be most memorialized in its impacts on rural areas, especially where it coincided with the Dust Bowl on the southern Great Plains. Just like it, however, the 2008 depression also began in the cities on the east and west coasts. Both events impacted rural as well as urban areas because in most places agriculture is tied to and dependent on financing and land ownership by corporate industry. In many states, "loss of local control, outside ownership, and large—scale intensive exploitation of the land"[14] define an agricultural industry largely alienated from the land and thus susceptible to economic changes like any other industry in a super-capitalist economy. This loss of local control—the extractive nature of industrial agriculture—had already led to farm crises marked by depopulation and deterritorialization. By the beginning of the twenty-first century, rural communities on the Plains and elsewhere had experienced at least thirty years of economic, social, and cultural crisis.

North Dakota was not an exception, but benefited from some different underlying factors. It had recovered from its population low in the 1930s, and had a population of around 650,000. That number had held more or less steady since the 1940s, although there had been a marked shift from rural to urban areas. The state had a long history of outmigration and an agricultural economy based on family-owned farms. This was often seen by North Dakotans—and portrayed by outsiders—as a negative: the state just could not hold its young people because there was nothing going on. In a time of crisis, however, it was a positive factor. The history of industrial agriculture has one of its main beginnings in eastern North Dakota. At the beginning of the twentieth century, "bonanza farms" in the Red River Valley showcased how agriculture could be industrialized. Despite this, however, local control and ownership over farmlands had largely remained intact in North Dakota. When the recession hit in 2008, the State of North Dakota could also fall back on a legacy from its socialist past: while in other states, privately owned banks could no longer provide credits to farmers, North Dakota has a state-owned bank, the Bank of North Dakota, the main purpose of which is agricultural loans. A lean

14 England and Brown 2003:327.

agricultural economy not directly run by multinational companies, a state bank that continued to provide credit, and the beginnings of the oil boom thus created a protective bubble for the state. North Dakota was not prosperous by any means; however, in the face of a crisis, it was at least stable. This economic stability was also matched by political, cultural, and social stability that in part resulted from relative isolation—evidence of outmigration without much immigration.

In other states, people were waking up to the realization that the prosperity they had been taking for granted was based on a system that favored inequality and that labor had become largely contingent over the years leading up to the recession. While in the 1970s, the top one percent of the population had taken between eight and nine percent of income in the United States, in 2007, they took 23.5 percent.[15] At the same time, the national security crisis after September 11, 2001 and the U.S. wars in Afghanistan and Iraq had doubled the defense budget in ten years to $680 billion in 2010. In particular, highly skilled young, urban people—who had so far escaped the economic devastation of globalization, unlike their peers in the rust belt and other manufacturing regions—felt especially betrayed by the system. Political unrest began to grow with the Occupy movement and others.[16] This political situation was an important contributing factor to the decision by the federal government to stabilize the banks and some large industries. Any economic sector that showed promise of growth and employment was a welcome sight.

## National security

During the buildup toward the financial collapse—and not entirely unrelated to it—energy had become a mainstay of national security concerns. A long history of patriotism and nationalism in wartime coupled with as long a tradition of an extractive and exploitative economic system was still fueling what Eisenhower had called the "military-industrial complex", which had indeed expanded and was now in charge of the "scientific-technological elite" through its influence on the federal budget. Increasing inequality, the lingering effects of globalization and the shift of manufacturing jobs outside the United States, as well as the beginning of the realization that industrialization is indeed destroying the world through climate change raised fears and insecurities

15 Maharidge and Williamson 2011:212-213.
16 Hedges and Sacco 2012.

and created tensions between those who simply wanted to continue their lifestyle as was and those who advocated for real change. The wars in Afghanistan and Iraq raised questions about the actual global dominance of the United States.

The economic collapse of 2008 brought all these tensions into the foreground. Yet, political demands were simultaneously defused in the national consciousness because of two factors: on one hand, any sign of socialism is anathema in the late twentieth- and early twenty-first century United States, and, on the other, the ongoing wars continued to fuel an aggressive patriotism. Technological solutions to the ecological crisis, the economic crisis, the crisis in national security, and the renewed energy crisis could, it was hoped, bring salvation without confronting the systemic inequalities at the root of these problems. While the ecological crisis, the most existential crisis, was denied credibility and dismissed, the oil and gas booms, like a *deus ex machina*, were here to save the day for the economy, for energy needs, and for national security. The political concerns were condensed into easily understandable slogans—"Drill, Baby, drill" during the 2012 election cycle—and eventually re-channeled into the traditionalist/Nativist/anti-globalization movement that brought Donald Trump the presidency in 2016 and again in 2024, when the slogan was prominently reactivated.

This connection between national security, energy development, and the salvation of the economy becomes perfectly clear in political rhetoric. As one example, here is then governor of Montana, Democrat Brian Schweitzer, addressing a symposium on the oil boom in 2011:

> You know, as long as we depend on oil from these petro-dictators, we'll send a generation and another generation, and still more generations to defend an oil supply for these petro-dictators who don't share our values and we will be enhawked [sic] to them forever. It's time to break our addiction to foreign oil and this is the generation that oughta get it right. Now, right now, the Montana National Guard, and I suspect the North Dakota National Guard, you've got men and women in Iraq and Afghanistan and I, um, I'm absolutely convinced that I'll never send the Montana National Guard to the North Dakota border to protect an oil supply. And furthermore I promise you this, the men and women in the Montana National Guard will never go to the Alberta border to protect

> an oil supply. That oil supply that we have in Alberta is conflict source of energy [sic] and anybody who tells us that we don't want and we won't use those oil sands, well then you oughta just put them in a military uniform and have them go fight for one of those dictators. Because these are our friends straight north of the border and we can count on them and they are part of the solution to break this addiction to foreign oil. And that's why I'm such a proponent of this Keystone XL pipeline. [...] So I went back to Calgary [to Transcanada] and I said okay this is the way it works: I want you to completely understand it, that there will be no pipeline that comes through Montana unless there is an on-ramp for North Dakota and Montana Bakken oil—well, do you understand that? Yes! And it was eleven days later we signed the contracts in Billings.[17]

The quote makes perfectly clear that the boom allowed the hegemony of the narrative of oil-dependent development to not be broken. Americans did not have to reduce oil consumption or adopt different lifestyles. They simply had to switch oil supplies.

This political rhetoric also perfectly illustrates how environmental and social concerns raised against oil extraction activities— or in support of limiting them—became associated with anti-Americanism. In that discourse, poverty, national dependency, and international despotism were all linked to objections against drilling activities. "Every job that we produce in the energy sector produces another five or six jobs around it," Schweitzer continued, "and as long as we continue to buy that oil elsewhere, we're going to be making jobs for somebody else, not somebody in our communities." Bakken oil was the salvation. Rural communities in the Bakken could save themselves and the greater nation. And if they refused, or objected, they would let everybody down. To that effect, their decisions on the matter were immaterial. Decisions had already been made for the greater good.

17 Dickinson State University 2011.

## Rural invisibility

At the same event that Governor Schweitzer gave his remarks, historian Clay Jenkinson spoke up against the invisibility of the local communities and people, pointing out that western North Dakota was a homeland for people. In a comment eerily mirroring Berger's forty years earlier in the Yukon Territory—and many others on resource extraction enterprises in communities around the world since—Jenkinson noted that "North Dakota is a place, not a platform. It's a homeland, not an energy sacrifice zone."[18] Such local voices were becoming more common at the time, but because the communities were largely invisible for the larger, national audience, they could be acknowledged and then dismissed as local concerns, and then ignored against the larger benefits.

For most people, North Dakota was a platform. It was a platform that they did not even know existed unless they were reminded of it, and then they thought of it as fly-over country, populated by some hardy but unsophisticated relics of American history that would probably be better off if they had some money so they could leave. Most people had never experienced the landscape, had no sensory understanding of the land (and really, any land) as home, as connected to oneself and one's community. It was easy to dismiss rural people and communities. Steaks came from the freezer, cows belonged in zoos, and the Plains were boring. Most people did not know about the care and devotion that connect people and the landscape through rodeos and powwows and sundances and church picnics. They could have cared less about what it means to get a star quilt or a first saddle or where to find sage or medicinal plants or how the earth smells when a thunderstorm is approaching. North Dakota was a platform, nothing more. The people and the landscape were invisible. Nobody had to care what happened to them.

In 1992, Terry Adams and Greg Duncan wrote that, "Rural poverty is all but invisible to the average American. The rural poor rarely come into contact with most urban residents, and media stories about poverty focus almost exclusively on the urban 'underclass'."[19] This neglect and ignorance changed somewhat with the 2016 election of Donald Trump, largely seen as propelled by rural poor to become President of the United States. The renewed focus was at most momentary and not

18 Dickinson State University 2011.

19 Adams and Duncan 1992:63.

sustained, however: neither the president nor his political opponents really understand, or care to understand or support rural communities. In that way, the past ten years have been similar to other episodes when rural poverty became the focus of interest, only to disappear again—the War on Poverty comes to mind, but also moments of perceived rural crisis: metamphetamine, religious fervor, education, depopulation, and crime, the latter often associated with natural resource booms. Instead of trying to understand the issues rural communities are reacting to and thus understand the reactions, such efforts are often left as superficial projects of categorization. Rural people are too often simply dismissed as uneducated, ignorant, and incapable of taking care of themselves. At most, efforts might be taken to educate them on how they should live to have better lives. In that sense, rural Americans are indeed treated similarly to Native peoples.

The issues of poverty and hegemonic ideology that push continued dependencies onto rural communities and many tribes are important in the context of natural resource extraction because they explain some of the reactions by communities to resource booms and opportunities. Rural counties, communities, and tribal councils are usually presented with but one choice to improve their economic conditions: increase or attract production to increase their share in the global market. While this strategy does not solve dependencies, it fits nicely into the existing system, which is often presented as the only one that makes sense. In this situation, resource booms seem to present a salvation, a sudden, and therefore urgent opportunity for growth. Those who would try to resist them, then, are resisting the common good, the nation, and its salvation. Once communities were able to react to the stressors placed on them and began to resist some of them, this was the political rhetoric that had been prepared as a useful discourse to counter any of their efforts of limitation and resistance.

## Geographies

North Dakota is traversed east-west by two main roads, Interstate 94 and U.S. 2, which roughly split the area in three equal slices. I-94 runs through Bismarck/Mandan, where it crosses the Missouri River and then continues west to Dickinson, and then to Glendive in Montana. To the north, U.S.-2 runs through Minot to continue west to Williston. These four cities (or, before the boom, business centers) form a slightly westward leaning parallelogram, with the Missouri

River crossing from Williston in the northwestern corner to Mandan, and with the Fort Berthold Indian Reservation about straight in the middle. The Bakken shale, one of the oil-bearing layers in the geological formation fittingly called the Williston Basin, is centered around the northwestern corner. Minot, Bismarck, Dickinson, and Williston became crucial staging and support points for the boom. They all featured commercial airports and components of the university system that could readily be upgraded, and they had good road access. Other towns became secondary centers: Watford City, Killdeer, Tioga, and Stanley formed a smaller trapezoid in the heart of the Bakken exploration efforts. The Bakken shale efforts also roughly cut through the Fort Berthold reservation, with the eastern third not seeing much exploration, and efforts concentrating around New Town and Mandaree.

Before the boom, western North Dakota, just like the other areas "in the Bakken" was cowboy country. Small communities based on ranching were connected to regional centers. It was dark at night, distances were long, and school districts were fighting for survival. Until the 1990s, more of the population of North Dakota lived in the few miles wide strip between I-29 and the Red River on the far eastern side of the state than in the rest of the state. Fargo and Grand Forks had the two larger universities, and many people in those cities had never set foot across I-29 to the west—the State was focused toward Minneapolis. Money, education, and power was centered in the east, and while Bismarck was the capital, it represented an outpost of that establishment. Minot was a similar outpost, largely connected to Minot Air Force Base. If Bismarck represented State power, Minot represented national and global power, and neither one was seen by most people in western North Dakota as a representation of local interests or control. When I began to show up to events and meetings about the boom impacts on communities after 2011, I was usually the only person from eastern North Dakota in the room, and people frequently commented on that. The University of North Dakota and North Dakota State University, and with them Grand Forks and Fargo, were not perceived to pay any attention to the rest of the state, and were often seen as thinking they were better than everyone else. In North Dakota, like in most other rural places, that is not a compliment. With the boom, however, came a perceptible shift in the geographies of resources, power, and investment, and the scramble for access, grants, and academic opportunity that ensued often contributed to a newly empowered west rejecting the seemingly arrogant outside experts' advice.

Much of the government and public service structure in western North Dakota was based on volunteerism. It was the responsibility of those who had the fortune of having been successful to serve on city councils and county commissions. They usually also knew the land and the economic, social, and political landscape. Very similar dynamics govern reservation politics. In these places, those who are known, who are established, who have large families rooted in the area, are elected into office and run for office. It is much more important to have a large social and political network and to have proved oneself in the local economic and cultural systems than to have a title or a formal education. Histories are family- and land-based, and so are knowledge and status. Outsiders are often seen as experts, but insiders who try to claim expert status often become outsiders and are no longer trusted. This enables communities to defend local control: those who give advice do not have access to local power, and as long as the centers of knowledge are located far enough away, they cannot project power over local communities. However, once the advice needed falls outside the accumulated knowledge of the local community, it also can no longer be evaluated. In normal times, that is not the case, and the system works. In times of disruption, however, all of this changes. And in the Bakken, everything was about to change.

## Boom!

The first accounts of the oil boom in the Bakken came as seemingly ridiculous stories. The Walmart parking lot in Williston was so full of RVs that locals could not park there anymore. McDonalds paid $20 an hour. Municipal employees were leaving jobs, especially those with truck driving licenses: some waste collection truck drivers were hired off their routes, leaving their trucks right in the middle of the street. They could now make a six-figure salary. There were traffic jams on the streets of Williston and Dickinson—and then there were traffic jams in the middle of nowhere. In Grand Forks, people circulated these stories, not sure what to believe, although some of them were seemingly backed up by circulating correspondence by sheriffs in the region and by eye-witness accounts. But none of it made sense. It could not be, and to realistic, grounded people—as one has to be to survive in North Dakota—that which cannot be, is not. Some old-timers remembered the short oil boom in the late seventies, but even with that comparison in mind, the stories seemed out of proportion. Still in 2011, Clay Jenkinson pointed out quite rightly that "most North Dakotans don't live in the oil sector [sic], the media in North Dakota is a relatively weak one because of our population base, most of the people of North Dakota are literally not aware of what's happening in the oil fields—they haven't seen them, they're aware that *something* is going on out there, but they are not aware of the magnitude and the impact of this thing."[20] To gauge the magnitude, and the responses from people in communities in the region, a few quantifiers are needed.

In 2015, the then mayor of Dickinson explained to a workshop I participated in that because the oil boom expanded roughly north to south, from Williston outward, Dickinson had initially gained a bit of time to prepare. The motto the town adopted, he said, was "don't let this turn into Williston." Williston, the commercial center of the Williston Basin boom, had gone from a population of around sixteen thousand before 2008 to twenty-two thousand in 2010, with estimates of a coming population explosion to reach 190,000 by 2015.[21] Even though those projections were not based in reality, they show not only the optimism for growth and the rhetoric of growth by state experts, but also outline the perceived planning needs at the time. The city doubled in population within about five years, and the city administration was simply overwhelmed. Before the boom, Dickinson had not built a single apartment building since the 1970s; by 2010, almost all building permits were for apartment buildings. 2009 saw 118 new building permits. 2012, the highest year, saw 783. During those early years of the boom, the city was absolutely overwhelmed by building permit applications, to the point that the city of Grand Forks helped out by lending its workforce to go over building plans between 2009 and 2013. Apartment buildings were needed because, as the mayor explained, the people who moved into the area after 2007 either had no credit or were not sure they wanted to stay, so buying a house was out of the question. The city also recalled the lessons learned from the last boom, when a whole neighborhood of single-family houses had been built, on the quick and cheap, only to have that investment drive up debt for the city. The houses remained unsold because nobody wanted them.

In 2015, the population stood at 28,000. Demand for apartments was so high that a two bedroom apartment went for about $2000 a month between 2010 and 2014: this was quadruple the rent from

20 Dickinson State University 2011.
21 Gabriel 2012:9.

before. Exorbitant rent was not the only consequence of the population influx, however. Between 2010 and 2012, for example, water consumption in the city grew fourty-six percent. In 2015, Dickinson still had an issue with water storage, and the issue was not only drinking water; the mayor estimated that fighting a potential fire for three hours would probably be a problem because the city water would run out. The city needed $250 million for infrastructure build-up. It had received $110 million over three sessions of the state legislature, but was projected to be $104 million in debt by fall 2015. It had begun to develop a comprehensive city plan in 2011 to address the capacities it could mobilize. The plan was adopted in 2013, but by 2015, the city was ranking development projects in triage efforts to curb spending on infrastructure. At the same time, airport boardings had gone from fewer than nine thousand in 2009 to close to sixty thousand in 2014.

In its planning, the city had become dependent and reliant on engineering firms, and simply had to trust that these firms had access to the latest information and numbers, that their projections were correct, and that they knew what they were doing. The city's general fund had been $8 million in 2009, but had reached $17 million in 2014, most of it spent on public safety. It was running a $3.5 million deficit on its general fund in 2015. About a dozen professional firefighters had been hired, as there was now a need for professional first responders. Volunteers were still needed, but could not respond fast enough, anymore, and the toll had become too high on them. In 2009, the city saw 218 calls for fire service. In 2014, there were 559. The city was paying $6 million in annual debt service, and needed about $20 million per biennium well into the future. Dickinson was no exception, and, as the mayor mentioned, was actually in a lucky position. It had a city government in place, it was already a regional population, business, and service center, it had Dickinson State University, and while it quickly became a staging center, it did not lie in the Bakken area itself. Its sales tax revenues went from $4.3 million in 2009 to $12.7 million in 2014; other towns in the Bakken that had no grocery stores, car dealerships, truck maintenance facilities, and other services were not so lucky. "It is not clear that we can do much about it," Jenkinson said about the oil boom in 2011, "except brace ourselves, to profit from it where we can, and to coordinate where we find ways to do that."[22] Communities and counties tried to do exactly that. One of the problems apparent

22 Dickinson State University 2011.

in Jenkinson's phrase, however, was that communities were not sure where or what they could coordinate, how they could profit from outside investments that went mostly to outsiders, or where they had the power to control, to limit, or to direct the forces that were fracturing their very essence.

## People

It is tempting to compare the hydraulic fracturing underground to the fracturing of communities, and as poetic metaphors go, that comparison carries a lot of truth. The simple truth to the fractured communities during the early years of the oil boom, however, was that they were overwhelmed. The personal experience of the boom—and for most people, there was no other experience than a very immediate, personal one—was not only all-encompassing, but every fractured experience in itself was life changing. Perhaps people could have made sense of, assigned meaning to, and reacted to each one of these changes if these had been isolated. The totality of them, however, resulted in changes that were paralyzing. Many communities, not sure how long the boom would last, at first took lessons from the previous boom. They had made investments that led to communities going bankrupt. Not willing to give up their lives or take another plunge, they decided to bunker down and let it blow over. When the problems became unbearable and the state and other actors convinced them that this boom was here to stay, they began to address the issues one by one. The most pressing was the change in population.

An example can be provided by McKenzie County, the largest county in North Dakota with an area of over 2,800 square miles. Extending from the Missouri River south of Williston to the Montana border in the west and about halfway the distance to I-94 in the south, it also encompasses the northwestern corner of the Fort Berthold reservation in its east. The county saw a population of less than six thousand in 2000; by 2018, its population was estimated at over 13,500 people. Watford City, the county seat, had 1,700 inhabitants in 2010. Eight years later, the estimate was for a population of slightly over seven thousand. The town had been absolutely transformed. When I first visited in 2005, it was a typical business center of the rural northern Plains, having lost almost half its population since 1920. There was a small exhibit on oil exploration in the county museum, a country club on the outskirts of town, and two hotels serving mostly tourists visiting the north unit of the Theodore Roosevelt National Park about fifteen miles south of town. In 2013, the heart of town had been replaced by a large new building including a banquet hall, a movie theater, and a large restaurant. New roads had been built to divert truck traffic around the town. Mancamps and new housing developments had sprouted on the outskirts of town, including single family housing developments that sold for $200,000 and up. In the words of one editorial writer, "a 2-mile-square small town" had transformed "into a sprawling community that seems to have no outer limits."[23]

Dealing only with a population increase would have created problems, but could have been managed. Watford City was a mirror of Williston on a smaller scale, and Stanley and others in turn mirrored Watford City. The towns hoped, and were supported in this hope by outside experts and by the state, that this was not a boom, but a sustainable development. Finally, the population pressure became so large that communities began to do what they had done in the last boom: expanding housing and infrastructure. Williston, by 2013, was bordered on its northern side by complete neighborhoods consisting of new long-stay apartment hotels and developments. According to the signs advertising "great deals" the long-stay apartments rented for $699.99 weekly. A two-bedroom apartment went for about $2,500 a month. Companies rented whole buildings, and sometimes building managers would rent out apartments on the side if they knew the workers who were living in them had a week off and would not be there.

The city itself had only paid off the last of the debts it had incurred from the investments it had taken during the last boom a few years before. Having learned from that experience, the city now asked developers to pay up front for the costs of development, so that they would not just leave the city high and dry if the boom ended. Because the projections communities were handed predicted that this development would be ongoing for decades, and as population growth was seen as a great development for communities—oil extraction was portrayed as dependent on a technological development, and the discourse of progress and growth was deeply ingrained—communities became convinced that this situation was different from the last booms. Maybe there really was not going to be a bust. All across the region, the secondary and tertiary centers of the boom saw single family housing built

23 Geiver 2014a.

in the hopes that the newfound wealth of the oil workers would translate into an influx of permanent residents. Stanley, for example, had a whole new neighborhood. However, most of the houses sat empty. They were too expensive for local people, and if people could afford the prices, they would rather buy a house elsewhere. Most workers rented, rather than bought houses—even those who brought their families with them. The population and housing boom brought other problems, too. For example, Watford City's sewage lagoon had been built for 1,500 people, but by 2014 at least 6,500 were using it. The city was trying to replace it with a $20 million wastewater treatment facility.[24] Simply providing housing, however, was a problem in itself.

## Housing

The first problem with housing was the building process. There was not enough housing for the workers who were going to build additional housing. Often, the people who were building the housing had to live a few hours' commute away. This was a real issue in the first few years of the boom, and it illustrated the overarching problem with housing in the area: many jobs could not be filled, many projects not be undertaken, many issues not addressed because there was not enough housing, and because housing, if it existed, was not affordable. In New Town, the agency town of Fort Berthold, the Tribe had built a new section of housing by 2014, but in that case, the reservation was addressing not only an influx of workers but also a long-standing housing crisis for tribal members that had been aggravated by the boom.

Building new housing was possible, although it took a long time, but it only addressed one issue, and at that only superficially. One of the main consequences of the boom for communities stemmed from the absence of any rent or price control. This meant that rents spiraled out of affordability and it quickly became impossible for anybody not directly profiting from the boom to afford lodging. As companies outbid each other on apartments for their workers, and as workers themselves formed informal housing cooperatives in order to perhaps afford lodging, the local people, especially those on fixed incomes, were left without alternatives other than to leave. Housing was not the only thing to see rising prices. Groceries, gas, and other commodities and services also rose in price. In many ways, this aggravated an already existing housing crisis, especially on the reservation. In 2011 and 2012,

24 Geiver 2014b:36.

two trailer parks in Newtown evicted their residents. Solutions were hard to find, especially in a housing situation that had already experienced much stress before the boom. It was not unusual for two or three families to move into one space simply because they could not afford to live any other way anymore. Sometimes, four or five families lived together. In July 2012, a hook-up for a trailer behind the Motel in New Town went for $550 a month, and the owner was going to raise it to $600. In Watford City, a cement RV pad cost $1,200 a month. The Tribe, just like county and town governments, urgently needed to hire doctors, nurses, law enforcement officers, social workers, and other employees to address issues brought on by the boom, but could not find any housing for them. One new police officer, for example, lived in a little trailer behind the police station for a year—not a great way to attract employees.

While areas around the Fort Berthold reservation saw formal mancamps built, there was a striking reluctance to build infrastructure like that on the reservation. The outskirts of New Town saw the development of more or less informal mancamps, as did other communities on the reservation, such as Parshall. These were large conglomerations of camping trailers on gravel lots. However, camping trailers, tents, and improvised camps often also appeared in fields or around barns, both on and off the reservation. From my first visits to the region, it had been apparent that the usual establishment of formal mancamps—built by global companies like Halliburton, ATCO Structures and Logistics, and Target Logistics (now Target Hospitality)—was skipping around the reservation. Around Williston, however, there were between ten thousand and twelve thousand people living in such mancamps.

Mancamps have been global solutions for increasingly contingent and migrant workforces. Whether it is cell phone manufacturing companies in China, dam construction sites in India, mining enterprises in the arctic, or oil extraction sites in North Dakota, there is a need to provide temporary, efficient, and tightly controlled housing to workers who follow job opportunities, often leaving families behind. The companies building mancamps in the United States often brought direct experience from providing logistics and security services to armed forces installations around the world. The wars in Afghanistan and Iraq, border security operations, and the global "War on Terror" operations provided the same logistics challenges as the natural resource booms in rural areas—in the United States, in Canada, in Mongolia, in Peru, around the world. A contingent workforce had to be moved, housed, and fed efficiently in remote locations without sufficient or sufficiently secure local housing available. These people worked in shifts and had communications needs, and their work locations were themselves contingent, so their housing had to be able to be moved quickly.

Management solutions were readily compatible once they were in effect divorced from the purpose of the work, which made a global upscaling extremely efficient. Carolyn Best from ATCO gave the example of building 250 beds in Fort McMurray, Alberta, within ten days, from initial meetings to completion—modules are ready to go, and simply need to be dropped, connected, and washed.[25] Mancamps, or as they were preferably called by the industry, crew housing, are nothing new, of course. There were always needs for housing solutions at temporary work sites. Already in 1939, there were reports of boomtowns in Oklahoma where it "was not unknown for a condition of scarcity to force men to spend the night walking about or sleeping exhausted on the ground."[26] The drive toward globally efficient, rapidly deployable, and compatible housing solutions dates at least to World War II.

That resource booms create issues with a stream of incoming population has always been known. Most infamous in terms of the effects on Native peoples are probably the gold rushes in Georgia, California, the Black Hills, and Alaska. While the first sociological studies of boom migration and its impacts on (non-Native) communities date further back,[27] during the energy booms in the 1970s and 1980s, the influx of workers into small rural towns became an important topic for sociologists, giving rise to so-called Boomtown Studies. Many of these studies came out of reports for the industry or in collaboration with assessments for projects or improvements for communities. In those efforts, researchers conducted surveys of workforces at energy extraction and conversion sites.[28] One survey found that in Rock Springs, Wyoming, at the time "the most notorious of the present-day boomtowns,"[29] fifty-three percent of workers were nonlocal, or had moved to the community over the past five years. Only a quarter of the

25 Dickinson State University 2011.

26 Forbes 1939:396.

27 Forbes 1939; Whyte and Holmberg 1956:22-24; see Myler (1981-82) and England and Albrecht (1984).

28 Wieland, Leistritz, and Murdock 1977.

29 Myler (1981-82):213.

workers were born in Wyoming. In the Beulah coal mines in North Dakota, on the other hand, only about a fifth of the workforce was nonlocal.[30] Boomtowns have not always been fueled by immigration from far away. They are, however, usually associated with sudden, large population increases that do present challenges of scarity in housing stock, underlying infrastructure, and other supplies.

One of the models for oil boomtowns over the past forty or fifty years has been Fort McMurray in Alberta, and it provides a good idea of a typical energy boomtown. The town had a population of about a thousand inhabitants before 1964. Then, Great Canadian Oil Sands (GCOS) began building its tar sands (or, preferred by the industry, oil sands) operation about thirty kilometers north of town, starting commercial extraction in 1968. By 1978, Fort McMurray boasted a population of twenty-eight thousand . In those ten years, Syncrude, the other early tar sands extraction company, had spent $180 million to build around 2,700 houses. Despite the fact that Fort McMurray is now a new regional center, a 2007 report found that seventy-five percent of the mobile workers in the area were not considering moving there permanently, most because the housing costs were too high.[31] The dynamics represented in these studies applied very similarly to the Bakken.

## Schools, healthcare, and emergency services

In boom situations, housing is only the tip of the iceberg an early indicator of other issues. A larger population meant more students in schools, even though the rising student numbers were not proportionate to the rising population numbers because most workers came without their families. Enough brought their families with them, however, to have a serious impact. The McKenzie County Public School District #1 in Watford City had an enrollment of 538 students in spring 2010. In January 2012, there were 740 students. The district hired eight new teachers and hustled to provide new classrooms. Based on growth projections, Watford City would go from around 1,500 people to around nine thousand within three years, and the schools would need new facilities, including teacher housing, worth around $30 million. Ray-Nesson school district saw an enrollment increase of 56 percent, from

30 Wieland, Leistritz, and Murdock 1977:11, 20.
31 Maugh 1978:758; Nichols 2007:15.

164 to 255 students.[32] Williston public schools had an enrollment of 2650 students in 2011/12, up from 2100 in 2006/07. The projections for 2012/13 were for 3850 students, around three hundred of whom were projected to be homeless students, mostly living in trailers. The school district hired fifty-two new teachers. However, their starting salary was $31,000 a year; the school district owned eight apartments, and asked every teacher to share one with another teacher.[33] By 2014, the city was working on a $50 million new high school project, half of which was not yet funded.[34]

If teachers could not find housing, neither could parents. Forty percent of children in Watford City schools in 2014 were classified as homeless. Many were simply transient, and the transient living situation of many students' families very quickly also became an issue for schools. Because families often moved dependent on their job and housing needs, students would be enrolled and disenrolled in different schools during the middle of the semester. Often, they had no documents on previous schools, and the teachers did not know how their knowledge would fit in with their new school's curriculum. One student in Beach, North Dakota, had been enrolled in thirteen different school districts. Demands for special education and new language learning resources were often new in these mostly rural school districts. New bus routes slashed the life-expectancy of school buses in half. Teachers, if they could be recruited, needed reasonable accommodations they could afford. New facilities needed to be built, but without a good understanding of how many people actually lived in the school districts, and with many of them living in transient accommodations, cost and funding projections were at best educated guesses.

Just like education services, health care services became stretched to the breaking point and beyond. Public health was quickly entering a crisis situation. This was not only a consequence of inadequate facilities and staffing—Watford City, for example, had one doctor. New demand grew exponentially because of the nature of the oil field jobs, the increase in traffic accidents, and an increase in crime. North Dakota had experienced difficulties finding physicians to work in rural communities, anyway. The new demands and the increased cost of living created more physician turnover. Some communities tried

32 Energy Development and Transmission Committee 2012.

33 HUD 2012:11.

34 Geiver 2014b:36.

to hire nurse practitioners to cover the more basic health care needs. However, one of the rises in medical needs were trauma cases, mostly from accidents. Even where doctors were present, trauma treatment centers and timely access to them were lacking in the region. There was also much more demand for care related to STDs and family planning services; western North Dakota had been a region with a rather older population, but the population influx was mostly young. These young oilfield workers often did not carry medical insurance and had no established physician in the area. Their use of emergency rooms meant that local hospitals were losing money at the same time that they became strapped for resources. The hospital in Dickinson saw around 1,200 emergency room visits per month in 2011.

There were other emerging challenges for health care providers, however. In 2012, all providers I spoke with at the Elbowoods Memorial clinic identified the housing issues as a public health problem. There were up to four or five families living in one house, which created issues with privacy, aggression, and depression. They also named prostitution and human trafficking, issues that would come to the public forefront a few years later. Sexual assaults were on the rise, and one provider explained that this was also a consequence of the housing crisis. Often, families now living together did not know each other too well, and without privacy, behavior could no longer be controlled. One provider mentioned that a single county now had 145 registered sex offenders, but those were only the ones who registered. People feared that most who lived in mancamps or trailers or other transient housing situations would not register. The Tribe had formed a human trafficking taskforce; over the next few years, those with families who could afford it would often relocate their children to Bismarck. Others would tell me that they had prohibited their children from leaving their fenced-in yards. People were worried about rumors that sexual predators were roaming the edges of powwows looking for young people.

One doctor said he was also increasingly worried about the environmental consequences of hydraulic fracturing and flaring; neither the water nor the air quality was being monitored very closely. He mentioned that he was seeing more and more cases of respiratory problems, perhaps from the dust thrown up by the thousands of trucks running the gravel roads to the oil wells. Sodium chloride and magnesium chloride was frequently sprayed on gravel roads to suppress dust. This also meant that the substances were put into the air with the dust. The other problem he saw was an increase in Hepatitis B, and he connected that to shared needle use. By then, a new drug had found its way to western North Dakota—heroin. While law enforcement and public services were used to meth and marijuana, heroin would in fact become a big problem and would also bring Mexican drug cartels onto the reservation.

A third immediate priority for communities, although less visible than education and public health, was the overwhelming of emergency services and their inadequate resources to deal with the new developments. One response was to enlarge the regional Dickinson training facility for fire fighters. That facility had been developed since 2005, primarily as a response to the oil and gas industry already gearing up for the boom. The training facility was often the first place where fire departments learned how to use foam and were taught how to put out oil and gas fires. It was also, however, one of the only places where they could learn how to put out a fire in a three- or four-story building. In 2008, most of Williston's fire department was still volunteers, with just a few professionals on the staff. The city had twenty-five volunteer firefighters, and would have liked to get forty; it projected that it needed a professional department once the population hit twenty thousand, but said it wanted to avoid that, if possible. One of the problems with volunteers that was beginning to emerge was that many people now no longer worked in town, but out on the oilfields. This was beginning to prevent volunteers to respond in adequate time, or at all. The ambulance service was housed at the one fire station, but covered 1200 square miles with four ambulances.[35]

While in 2008, communities were still optimistic that things might not have to change all that much, and that a ramping up of existing resources might suffice, it became very clear over the next few years that this was not the case. Between 2007 and 2011, for example, Billings County ambulance services saw a 270 percent increase for service calls; McKenzie County had an increase of 151 percent, New Town experienced eighty-six percent more calls, Westhope ninety percent more. Even smaller towns saw an increased demand. Parshall, for example, a small town about fifteen miles east of New Town, still on the Fort Berthold reservation and along ND 23, dubbed the "suicide road," saw an increase of 41 percent for ambulance calls.[36] Such new demands put

35 Dickinson State University 2011; SRF 2008.

36 Minot State University 2012.

enormous pressures on services mostly run by volunteers, who, all of a sudden, saw themselves overwhelmed with calls—sometimes to such an extent that they had to make a choice between their employment and their volunteer service to the community. Those are hard choices to make in places that are close-knit and dependent on volunteers for providing any services.

By 2012, even small towns no longer knew how many people lived in houses. Emergency services did not know what kinds of chemicals were transported in trains or trucks. Even if they would have known, they did not have the equipment or the training to deal with them. Emergency departments could not keep up with knowing who to contact to ask questions about these issues, because there were so many different, new companies that operated trucking services, oil well services, drilling, and hydraulic fracturing. Most dispatch centers also did not have that data available, or even if they did, they could not readily match the telephone numbers with specific locations.[37] With many new roads and most of the drilling rigs and wells so new that they were not on maps yet, emergency services often literally did not know where to go. The volunteer fire departments were not equipped for the kinds of situations they were facing. This was sometimes a problem at the very basic level—some communities that now had three-story buildings had no ladders reaching to a third floor. Departments also had no suits for chemical incidents, no mobile command centers, and no equipment or training for oil, chemical, or wastewater spills and fires. These issues began to be alleviated with an influx of new equipment from around 2012-on, much of it donated in the name of corporate social responsibility by oil companies active in the communities. Of course, the equipment was also donated because the companies had to have somebody protect their investments and their workers.

## Local governments

With county and city governments overwhelmed by such immediate, simultaneous, and urgent problems, it is no wonder that concerns for the environment were not a priority at first. Local governments felt helpless to address the needs of their communities; how could they deal with regulations that many felt were out of their control, anyway? Many of the older, long-time residents of their communities—and sometimes service providers and officials themselves—were

37 Minot State University 2012; Dickinson State University 2011.

considering to relocate. At a meeting in Mountrail County in 2011, one of the county commissioners said, "We're experiencing frustration, overload and burn-out. The stress level is becoming intolerable." This was true across the region.

Counties and cities became especially concerned with permitting and inspections. Being overwhelmed with immediate response priorities meant that building and environmental inspections were often not carried out in time, and that the communities lost control over the enforcement of their rules. A participant at a public meeting in Mountrail County in 2011 pointed out that, "Everyone is so busy playing catch-up, they don't have time to look forward." One of the largest issues, especially in the context of landscape, was zoning. While some counties, like Golden Valley, were zoned, others, like McKenzie, in the heart of the oil activity, were not. McKenzie did not even have building codes of its own, and adopted those of the state when it decided that it needed a zoning ordinance for the county in 2012. One of the first challenges for the planners was to establish an inventory. Throughout the first few months of meetings, there were concerns over the regulation of private property and grandfathering-in existing land uses. Repeatedly, the county zoning commission was asked if it could put a moratorium on mancamp construction. Also repeatedly, the commission adapted the emerging regulations and zoning maps to the wishes of businesses. However, it declined to allow industrial and commercial uses of agricultural lands, although it then allowed projects like waste management facilities on agricultural lands under conditional use permits.[38]

Regardless of how or whether larger areas were zoned, one problem that could not be regulated by the counties was the specific location of the oil wells. This was especially an issue because oil companies most often also did not consult with landowners on well placement. About seventy percent of mineral rights owners did not own the surface rights. The ranchers and farmers who owned the land but did not own the mineral rights could get very bad surprises on where wells were placed. The placement of pipelines, both for oil and for the wastewater used to fracture the wells, also presented issues. Both wells and pipelines also spilled. At a meeting in Bowman in 2011, one participant pointed out that they saw about one spill per week, but that "The problem is that the State doesn't want to emphasize the bad side."

38 McKenzie County 2012-16.

Although the bad side—spills and other damages—was not widely discussed, by 2011, most people were aware that wastewater spills were by far more damaging than oil pipeline spills. "Oil can be a good fertilizer; the downside is if it has production water in it. That water does the damage," one participant in a public meeting said. One question people began to ponder was whether the wastewater would get into aquifers, the Missouri River, or other waters, and how that would affect drinking water for communities or water for fields and pastures.

It was on the county level that the emerging dilemmas of the oil development efforts manifested themselves the most and the earliest. While the state government was dominated by commercial voices, rural western North Dakota was still mostly ranching country. This meant that county governments had a strong ranching influence, often by families who had been long established as large landowners and still projected as much influence as the families who dominated the commercial environment of towns and cities. Much of the ranchland, however, was split estate—the mineral rights had been split off from the surface rights, and the ranchers now faced not only an economic and range management challenge, but also a threat to their personal and cultural identities and their relationship to the land.

If it was at the local level where these dilemmas were manifested, it was also the personal, community, and county levels that carried the burdens of the boom. Schools, emergency services, healthcare, housing, law enforcement, and local infrastructure were overwhelmed quickly. While the industry, the state, and the federal government promised that the development would eventually pay off economically, they focused on investments to enable and subsidize more development, not on technical assistance or other help for local governments or individuals to manage these challenges. Many people I talked with were not against the development as such, but wanted it to be slowed down so it could be managed better. Communities and counties needed a break, a pause to catch their breath, to regain control, and to recalibrate relations between people and with their social, cultural, economic, political, and also physical environments.

Carrying the burden thus had economic connotations. Communities had to scramble to pay for new infrastructure, from fire engines to schools, from health centers to roads, from water lines to housing. The overwhelming burden, however, was emotional and psychological. Communities became divided into those who successfully jumped onto the boom train and those who became literally or emotionally uprooted and displaced. Displacement can lead to nostalgia, and in many ways rural communities on the northern Plains have been living in this state for decades, longing for what once was. Simultaneously, this nostalgia led either to encouragements to embrace the boom in hopes to reconstitute economically successful communities or toward resistance to the boom because it destroyed relationships.

In many ways, the boom upended social dynamics. It was the people living outside of towns who had been able to weather previous booms the best, at least so it seemed. From the nostalgic perspective of rural America, they still lived authentic, traditional lives. Now, though, with a boom that grabbed the very foundation of this rural life, minerals under their lands, it was the business owners and entrepreneurs who gained more influence. Local governments, although they were squeezed and overwhelmed, also gained power if they bought into the boom. Incentivized from all sides to do just that and told that they could either adapt and grow or resist and disappear—told that, in fact, resistance meant disappearance because it was futile, as the boom was not stoppable—the choice was still not easy. People and communities saw the potential for uprooting and understood the dangers and lurking trauma.

"Planners," writes Oliver-Smith, "tend to perceive the culture of uprooted people as an obstacle to success rather than as a resource."[39] They think communities can be planned, when in reality, they evolve over long periods of time through trial and error. It could be said that planners see culture as an obstacle and therefore uproot it, so it can be replaced by something else, often something more efficient. Schools can be built. Healthcare, law enforcement, and other services can be planned. Housing can be developed. None of this, however, will build communities. Communities are built by telling stories. These stories are often complicated, complex, and inefficient. The disruptions that result from negating or ignoring these stories are carried by local communities that are often torn apart in this process. As they become torn, however, as planners gain the upper hand over the more cautious, the strangers over the rooted, these disruptions also tear apart relations with the environment.

39 Oliver-Smith 2005:55.

# Chapter 4
# The Land

The landscape that was my home when I grew up is defined by a prehistorically documented triangle of sacred mountains, the lines between which form an astronomical calendar. The intersections of these lines define powerful places that over time were appropriated by different religions; the exterior points of reference form the boundaries of the ethnic place we call home. Christianity is tied to these places and to the land, not the other way around. Pilgrimage places are set upon these and other places of power, and in my youth, it was still common for people to pray on and for the land. Other places are marked by religious symbols so that they are remembered as places of story.[1] Our language does not have a standardized writing system—instead, we learn other languages in school to read and write in. This landscape is transected by national boundaries imposed upon it and, so I was taught by my ancestors, utterly irrelevant for our cultural understanding that flows from the land, the language, and a shared history. These nations have, increasingly over the last fifty years or so, tried to enforce national (or perhaps colonial) consciousnesses over the landscape, tried to carve them up, and have encouraged and restricted mobility and kinship within national boundaries. Yet, for those who are native to the landscape, it is whole, and the lines carving it up into land are temporary disturbances.

Upon arriving in the Bakken at the height of the boom, it was hard not to see the landscape simply as the backdrop to the social crisis that was unfolding. The problems of housing, population influx, crime, education, and healthcare were so urgent and immediate that it was difficult to see past them. The scale of these issues was so large and immediate that in the necessary triage of responses, the environment came a distant second. It was simply hard to understand what happened to the landscape, however, because the landscape was too large and not easily accessible.

1 See, among others, Fichtner (1988); Schäfer (1996); d'Aujourd'hui (1998); Hagmann (2006); Fingerhuth (1999); Stohler (1939).

Driving through the area, some of the impacts were, of course, immediately visible. Drill pads, especially while active, were probably the most obvious. These were spaced along roads every so often; they also could be seen sprinkled across the landscape from the vantage point of a butte, and were marked, especially at night, by spotlights and otherwise by open flames burning off the natural gas. Other impacts on the landscape were visible, but not readily seen. The fact that many roads were enlarged, that traffic volumes had increased manifold, that suburbs appeared overnight, that the night sky was no longer visible, that trucks drove where before there had been no roads: all of these impacts could only be seen by those who had been familiar with the landscape before. To somebody not familiar with the landscape as it used to be, these were normal because they were expected from other landscapes that had already experienced these changes. If anything, many people saw them as a sign of progress, indicators that North Dakota was joining the rest of the country.

## Three stories

Three stories led me to pay attention to this process of local people literally becoming uprooted from the old landscape and simultaneously feeling helpless or being overwhelmed by this new landscape now imposed. One of these stories encountered me as the now late Marylin Hudson, who was in charge of the tribal museum, took me out to her father's allotment, where the family had had to move after the flooding of Lake Sakakawea. As I mentioned, many tribal members observed that the oil boom felt like a tsunami, a flood reminiscent of the removal from the river settlements. On this allotment, with a lone old house in the middle of what for most people would have been literally nowhere, the contrast in landscape changes hit me. To move from a community along the river, below the bluffs and nestled in trees and fields, to this flat, treeless, and exposed land where neighbors lived apart must have been an incredible shock. After first trying to establish churches to hold the now dispersed communities together, most people left their allotments within a generation to settle in one of the older communities or in New Town. The flooding of the lake had forced many people out of communities, onto the plains, into isolated allotments, and then into new settlements. The oil boom forced them to live in communities that were now being overrun, yet again changing the landscape to the point of it no longer being familiar. What both events had in common was that they destroyed rootedness in the landscape by destroying the old landscape and replacing it with one that was strange, alien, and therefore barely livable.

The second story came within a conversation with Tom Abe, who taught science at the tribal college. We were talking about possible ways to engage people with the community and with the boom. Many people were so overwhelmed that they retreated, and there was not much information on how to re-engage with this now unfamiliar environment. Taken out of familiar territory, all of a sudden strangers in a now almost unrecognizable land, finding ways to organize potential resistance against these changes or simply to negotiate ways in which impacts could be softened was difficult. As most people in tribal and rural communities are not avid readers of legal texts, I brought up that one way would be to run writing workshops for community members, where they could write plays about their experiences. These could then be performed to share information.[2] Such an approach could combine storytelling with a much-needed campaign for land rights education. Tom listened to me, agreed that this would theoretically be a good idea, and then told me a story. One of his aunts, he said, had been approached by a landman who wanted permission to lay a pipeline under her property. She listened to him and, being a generous person, initially agreed on a lease for $100. When she told some of her family members, they advised her that this was much less than what she should get from the company. So, when the landman returned, she asked for $10,000, a price tag that was way too high. You can try to educate people on their rights, Tom said, but what will you do when people do not know the economic worth of their land because they do not live in a money economy? Being overwhelmed is not simply a consequence of the lack of information. It might also be a consequence of that information being outside the scope of cultural values needed to make sense of it.

The third story that triggered my interest in the landscape and its changes was my participation in a symposium for mayors and county leaders organized by Dickinson State and Minot State Universities in Minot in 2012. During this Energy Impact Solutions Conference, it became obvious to me that these local leaders did not know what was happening on the lands they were responsible for. The landscape was changing so fast that even those in leadership positions simply did

2 See May (2014) for an example of this approach.

not know what it looked like, anymore. They were literally living in an unrecognizable landscape, as it no longer matched their knowledge or any available representation. Town and county leaders did not have the data they would have needed to take decisions. Without access to data, local governments were prevented from reading their landscapes. Instead, they were dependent on the data, and on the interpretation of the data, that the state and the industry shared with them. While the State tried to convince these leaders that it was looking out for their best interest, there was a legacy of mistrust toward the State and other actors, stemming from previous booms. I came to see the situation as a repeat of the events surrounding the establishment of the synfuels plant in Mercer County that I described earlier. It was painful to hear representatives from Beulah and Hazen, the towns industrialized in that process, mention that they were not aware of any records relating to those decision-making processes. When I told them about Tauxe's study describing what happened, they were interested, but the book is an academic study out of print, and so is itself not accessible. The most important solution, I came to understand, was to provide local communities and governments, and ideally everybody, with the data they needed to come to their own assessments and decisions.

## Protecting the land

It is a tempting notion that wise or beautiful landscapes make wise people. In reality, however, they form each other. There are no wise landscapes without wise people. There are no wise people without listening to the land. Far from being undisturbed, the former landscape in the Bakken had been inhabited mostly by people living with the land. Despite the grid and the presence of a market economy, and the fact that some of the practices imposed on the land were heavily disruptive and sometimes destructive, most people on the land listened to it. The relative absence of the state made sure of that. In the western parts of the Great Plains, the grid's imposition onto the landscape began petering out, as there was no purpose to carve up lands where it is pretty obvious that 160 or even 320 acres will not make anybody self-sufficient. It is one of the ironies of forced assimilation that Native lands are some of the most carved-up in this region. While the government forced Native peoples to be competitive private landowners and individual farmers with limited land holdings, non-Natives were allowed to cooperate and to buy and lease more land to create larger holdings.

In this region, the capitalist market system governed economic decisions, but its most salient expression—the consumer society—was present in little enclaves in the regional centers an hour, two hours, or three hours drive away. Frontiers and booms having come and gone, this landscape was not yet, or not anymore, a procedural landscape.[3] It was still being negotiated. In the absence of a procedural landscape, Niobe Thompson observes, "the price of survival [is] ultimately a deeper condition of rootedness."[4] Dwelling in this kind of a landscape was far from romantic notions of harmony and bliss,[5] especially in western North Dakota and eastern Montana. It is simply a fact that in the relative absence of the state and its imposition of procedural order, people are forced to listen to the landscape. As the landscape was carved up, as the procedural landscape imposed itself, this rootedness was being eroded.

It is much harder to run an industrial ranching operation than it is to turn farming into an industrial enterprise. It is not impossible, of course, and feedyards, calving operations, and specialization have turned cattle raising into the meat industry.[6] However, it is still hard to run a ranch as an industrial operation. While planting, spraying, and harvesting can be accomplished with machines, fences still need to be fixed by hand, cattle need to be sought personally, especially in the buttes and ravines that litter western North Dakota, and range conditions need to be seen and experienced personally. Since settlement, ranchers had built a relationship to their lands that was highly personal. That relationship also drew from popular depictions of their lifestyle, their perceived marginalization in national politics, society, and more recently economics, and the resulting resistance to outside dominance. Now, ranchers often discovered that because of split estates, they were not actually in control of their lands. Companies began to trespass on and survey their lands, left gates open, littered, rutted out the roads, and built oil wells on their pastures and pipelines through their ranges. Some ranchers told me that they called the sheriff when oil workers trespassed, but the workers knew that the sheriff would take at least an hour to respond. Families began to feel insecure in their remote homes which they had always left unlocked. The land changed. There were now roaring gas flames that threatened grass fires and sometimes

3 Braun 2013b.
4 Thompson 2008:136-143.
5 Ingold 2005.
6 Braun 2008:137-138.

were located a few hundred yards away from houses that used to revel in their solitude and quiet. The night sky disappeared. Large hotels and mancamps appeared almost overnight. Access roads and well pads dissected the land. Farmers were concerned about spills and illegal dumps on their land that might poison their animals and plants.

County commissions and boards were mostly made up of experienced community members who felt it was their turn to provide leadership, but they had no experience with the forces now imposing themselves onto their landscapes. They were not prepared for the sudden onslaught of new problems and issues. They could not have been. Their carefully calibrated world, where one could make a living if one worked hard and treated the land well, was turned upside down: working hard and treating the land well all of a sudden were seemingly at opposite ends of a spectrum now imposed on them. While commercial interests in towns were hopeful that the rising population and the new business opportunities would benefit their communities, and were often optimistic that the traffic, crime, and social issues could be alleviated over time, ranchers faced issues with their lands that were definite, permanent, and potentially catastrophic. Many ranchers did not like what they saw. This was all the more true if they did not own the mineral rights under their lands and thus carried the negative consequences without reaping benefits. But even those who received royalties mostly did not like what was happening to the land.

This is not to say that ranchers turned into environmentalists overnight. Many struggled, because they had been told and perceived that environmentalism was a romantic, progressive, and restrictive outside interference with individual land rights and commercial opportunity. Yet, now their lives were threatened by this exact economic opportunity set free. The same people they had been trying to get off their backs because they tried to regulate how they used their lands now became their only allies as they tried to regulate how others would be able to use the lands that were still theirs but which they no longer controlled. Many began to mourn, at first privately. "It bothers me that my grandson will never know what this country was like before the oil was here," one Mountrail County resident said, and "We're mourning a lifestyle that will never be the same," another. "I don't like what [the oil boom has] done to our communities and lifestyle. We had a good life, and now it's gone forever, or at least for my lifetime," said another rancher.[7]

7 Edwards 2015:178. On mourning for environmental loss, see Willox and Landman (2017).

The old discourses were hard to forget, of course. Some rural people connected these changes in lifestyle to changes in the environment, while others did not. The economic boost provided by the boom also benefited ranching communities, especially those communities that served as regional commercial centers. Those that were trying to regulate the impacts onto the environment were still seen as threats by people who were standing to profit from the new landscape. In 2011, the mayor of Crosby worried that if the Environmental Protection Agency (EPA) were to get tough on regulation and enforcement of hydraulic fracturing, it would at least temporarily hurt exploration and production. In turn, that would hurt his community's dreams for renewed viability through growth and expansion.

## Landscape

The reluctant engagement with environmental concerns is not unique to North Dakota. It seems to be fairly typical of rural communities in the twenty first century United States. In the Marcellus Shale, for example, rural people similarly became concerned about and active for the environment only after a process of disbelief.[8] To become active for the environment in these situations requires a personal act of political and economic revolution and revelation. Sara Ann Wylie writes that for residents in areas impacted by the shale gas industry, "harm is not 'inherently uncertain.' They *know* it through their *senses* and from their *experiences*, and they *learn* it through their shared *histories*."[9] This is very true for those who have allowed themselves to recognize and acknowledge the harm they experience. The way to this recognition and acknowledgment, however, is often buried so deeply that many people have almost no access to it. It is buried beneath economic dreams of seeing these communities flourish; beneath the complicated and often arrogant language and behavior of scientists who can no longer connect to their audience; beneath layers of political indoctrination of nationalism; beneath the politics governing the public education system; beneath the economic interests of those who should know better but still employ short-term calculations over those of long-term impacts; beneath PR discourses of bucolic ideals that have come to shape the identities of those who have no real connection to the land, anymore; and beneath the awareness that speaking out against all of these values can mean to become ostracized in the very community one wants to

8 Wilber 2012; McGraw 2012.
9 Wylie 2018:280, italics in original.

protect. It is important to recognize that all of these discourses deeply impact communities and prevent them from engaging in anything but the mitigation of technical issues—traffic, crime, housing, infrastructure—while refraining from asking the truly fundamental questions.

This avoidance of foundational questions about the concept of land and especially landscape is not an accident. It is tied to the academic approach to landscapes in many disciplines—landscape geography, landscape archaeology, landscape design, and so on—that have all defined landscape in ways that are somewhat counterintuitive. Cultural landscape studies, for example, defines a landscape as any space in which people and nature interact. A kitchen garden or a barbed wire fence can thus be a landscape.[10] Landscape archaeology is interested in the reconstruction of prehistoric landscapes, piece by piece, but often without acknowledging the larger context. In the United States until recently many archaeologists have been opposed to efforts to understand what a landscape means in cultural terms or what it meant for others, for example indigenous peoples.[11] While it can be argued that a reconstitution of a landscape site by site might result in an idea of what the whole landscape looked like, the meaning of the whole as a whole is lost or ignored. These definitions of "landscape" create a vision of landscapes as puzzles in which pieces can be exchanged, destroyed, or repurposed without hurting the whole.

From an anthropological perspective, this widespread inability to focus on a landscape as a whole cannot come as a surprise. The focus on narrowly defined sites is duplicated in other endeavors. In ecology, for example, the quest for Traditional Ecological Knowledge (TEK) often focuses on specific practices but rejects their foundational context of ceremonial, social, spiritual, economic, and ecological values and perspectives. This often amounts to a silencing of those who have a connection to the total landscape. Their voices will not be heard unless they speak about specific sites, places, and practices. Such a practice, however, would already represent a shift in cultural paradigms and

10 Groth 1997:1

11 As noted, these comments refer most specifically to the United States. European archaeology is in many ways very different. Even in the U.S., there seem to be interests in slow change, although not many archaeology programs actually teach their students how to interpret a landscape. Ethnological interpretation and ethnographic methods are often seen as foreign by archaeology students. See, for example, Fleming (2006); Fowles (2010); Kluiving and Guttmann-Bond (2012); Branton (2009).

actually compromise their understanding.[12] There are not many things more frustrating than to see and hear academics dismiss and denigrate what they see as unfocused, irrelevant, or personal opinions by people who talk about their cultural connections to places, plants, animals, or other entities in their world.

Empiricism, ethnocentrism, and a focus on efficiency have primed perspectives which pretend that knowing many trees is equal to understanding a forest. These approaches are learned, but have become so ingrained that they are now "common sense." The founder of landscape studies, J.B. Jackson, wrote that on the Plains, the grid system was "the *only* practical and speedy method of organizing space." The grid then eliminated, "once and for all" the traditional spaces.[13] As Fredric Jameson argues, this homogenization of the landscape is a consequence of capitalism applied to the landscape that drives peasant farmers and indigenous peoples into extinction.[14] The only way to perceive a grid system imposed on a landscape as practical (and to see practical and speedy as foundational values to apply onto a landscape) is in the name of efficiency. The traditional method of organizing and perceiving the landscape was, of course, practical according to traditional cultures on the land. The newcomers, however, rejected those perceptions. They did not see a landscape. They saw a patchwork of resources. Where land is seen as a commodity, landscapes cannot exist as meaningful cultural spaces.

Where landscapes are valued, this valuation is most often purely aesthetic. The aesthetic notion of a beautiful landscape is tied not to an understanding of the landscape's history or cultural meaning, but to a romantic notion of the seeming absence of human traces on the landscape—or to the commodification of that idea for tourism. Landscapes as coherent, whole systems are, however, recognized in large federally-owned lands. The prime example in terms of protected landscapes is the National Park system, but these are exceptions. Even here, what remains protected as landscape is often simply the most desirable view—that is, what can be profitably extracted. Other public lands are not established for the protection of the environment. National

12 See, for example, Ellis (2005).

13 Jackson 1994:154.

14 Jameson 1998:65-68.

Forests, for example, cover large tracts of land, but are often valued for timber, mineral, and rangeland extraction more so than for anything else.

In places like National Parks, conserving the landscape is an effort to conserve what is often considered a pre-human history of the land, but what is, in North America, more accurately a pre-settler landscape. These ideas, tied to the concept of "wilderness," are illusions that relegate American Indian peoples outside of human history. In the perception of those newcomers who have remained settler-colonialists, presumed wilderness includes Native peoples. No better example of these ideas can be found than the proposal by the painter George Catlin to preserve some of the landscape of the plains. In his desire to save the buffalo from extinction, he included the Native peoples as inhabitants of a national park, "containing man and beast in all the wildness and freshness of their nature's beauty!" This could only be achieved by "a system of non-intercourse", that is, by Americans staying away from the Plains (apart from enjoying all of the "natural" beauty).[15] Nature, and by extension all those people who are supposedly still living in a state of nature, should be left alone to be valued by others. So-called unspoiled nature carries the most aesthetic value. This is a parallel valuation to the notion that in order for indigenous peoples to have value or to be recognized as indigenous, they, too, should be "unspoiled" by civilization and as "natural" as possible.

The aesthetic value of landscapes is, thus, connected to its difference and distance from ourselves—to its exotic and alienated nature. Ideally, aesthetic landscapes should not be inhabited. It is not surprise then, that most local people do not look upon their own landscape from a purely aesthetic perspective. Aesthetic perspectives are, instead, imposed upon their landscapes by outsiders, for whom any meaning the land might carry for the people who live there is of no interest or relevance. Nature, under these conditions, becomes the playing field of ourselves. "The world," as Terry Eagleton puts it, "is no more than a notional constraint against which the ego may flex its muscles and delight in its powers, a convenient springboard by which it can recoil onto itself."[16] This process is also the description of the frontier, as discussed earlier. The imposition of an aesthetic value, it can be argued, imposes ownership over landscapes; this can be seen readily

15 Catlin 1841:260-264.
16 Eagleton 1990:123.

with the history of National Parks in the United States. Native peoples were welcomed as tourist attractions and as representations of majestic nature, but they cannot be allowed to have inhabited these areas, as that would deny the claim of unspoiled nature. The resistance to environmentalism by ranchers, Native and non-Native, similarly often originates exactly in a fear that their practices and existence on the land, their being at home here, would be prohibited for aesthetic reasons.

## Home

The most foundational question in the American relationship to the land seems to be ownership. Land is valued and has value when it is owned and because it is owned, as it is on that condition that it generates wealth. Property—land ownership, or "real estate"—ties into many facets of culture, in part because it creates specific interests. For example, once I own land, I am interested in the State protecting my title. Beyond that, however, specific kinds of ownership depend on, express, and in turn create cultural values. In American culture, property ownership lies at the heart of economic, personal, and social core values.

> Property institutions not only regulate the complexity of human interaction, but also *shape the character of those interactions.* Property is not only about the allocation of scarce resources, the management of complex information, or the coordination of land use among competing users; it is about our *way of life.* If this is true, then property law should reflect and shape our deepest values. Property is not just about information or complexity; it is about promoting "Life, Liberty and the Pursuit of Happiness."[17]

In the United States, ownership is an exclusive right. It regulates access. Relations to land can thus only be built on specific parcels that are either owned or provide "public access." There are alternative

17 Singer (2014:1299); whether the phrase "pursuit of happiness" in the declaration of independence is directly connoting property is controversial, especially among more recent historians. There seems to be no real question, however, that it at the very least implies property ownership as one, if not the most important pursuit leading to happiness.

models to ownership, further undermining the idea of a "Western" ideology of land, ownership, or landscape, with an "Indigenous" ideology as its opposite. In Scandinavian and Germanic countries, for example, the free visitation on foot of private forests and pastures is anchored in law; as long as no damage is done, everybody has the right to be in a landscape. While American law protects private property against the public, these laws limit private property in the interests of society.[18] This makes it possible for anybody to relate to a landscape, as although private property rights exist, they do not absolutely alienate other people from the land.

When we are able to build relationships to the land, we create landscapes. People might live on or off the land, but they dwell in landscapes, and landscapes are not a differentiation between nature and society: they are both, simultaneously. This is, for example, defined as such in the European Landscape Convention.[19] The ways in which landscapes are perceived in Europe are different from the cultural approaches to landscape in the United States, in part because of property rights, which are then connected with very different ideas of discipline, order, and other cultural concepts. The differences between perspectives on land and landscape, and on how they can, should, could, or must be used, protected, visited, perceived, and dwelt in, depend on specific cultural practices and values, shaped and formed through history on, in, with, and sometimes against landscapes.

A few years ago, I was giving a talk in a small regional center in Iowa that had gone to great lengths to revitalize their historic downtown. I was asked what I would recommend the community could do more to stem the flow of people to Des Moines. My answer was that people should have access to the landscape. Communities could negotiate and build a network of paths, especially along creeks, in forested areas, and along property boundaries. In order for people to feel

18 In Germany, the term for this is "Sozialpflichtigkeit," which means the social obligation of private property; see Kube (1997).

19 Council of Europe 2000. The European Landscape Convention has the following to say: "Le terme 'paysage' est défini comme une zone ou un espace, tel que perçu par les habitants du lieu ou les visiteurs, dont l'aspect et le caractère résultent de l'action de facteurs naturels et/ou culturels (c'est-à-dire humains). Cette définition tient compte de l'idée que les paysages évoluent dans le temps, sous l'effet des forces naturelles et de l'action des êtres humains. Elle souligne également l'idée que le paysage forme un tout dont les éléments naturels et culturels sont considérés simultanément."

at home in a place, they need to build a connection to the landscape. In American community building, the "built environment" is usually seen as a representation of and influence on social relations.[20] Community building is thus often relegated to urban planning. Most often, however, this leaves out social relations with land and landscapes and negates the ability to make stories in the landscape. Landscapes need to be experienced over and over again because they change. They need to be listened to. Elders need to be able to show meaningful places to grandchildren and teach them about the landscape—not just in parks, but all around us. This is how we feel at home.

If "built" is removed from the environment, that is, if social relations—the community—are enlarged to its appropriate standing as encompassing all of our environment, the connection between community, landscape, home, and culture can be achieved. "To permit the development of community," says Anthony Oliver-Smith, for example, "the [...] environment must take a form that is both recognizable and appropriable in organization and substance in local cultural terms."[21] If there is no recognition of the culture in the environment, we do not have a community because we are not at home. Two developments can trigger this: a cultural change or the inability of a culture to listen to a new environment, and a sudden change in the environment against people's wills or that leaves people without time to adjust. On the Plains, the first process followed the enforcement of forced cultural assimilation of Native peoples and the imposition of a settler-colonial society. The second process followed the imposition of extractive regimes, for example during the Bakken boom. It was no wonder that communities became disoriented.

When the eminent anthropologist Claude Levi-Strauss first set sight of the coast of Brazil, he commented that the landscape was different from that of Europe because the people in control of the landscape—settler-colonialists, we might say today—had not yet had time to establish a relationship with the land. He describes the landscape as chaotic, a scene of confusion. He describes agriculture in the "New World" in very similar terms to scholars in the twenty first century, as an extractive industry without regards to the reciprocity that existed in Europe. "A rapacious form of agriculture," he wrote, "appropriated what was readily available and then moved on, after wresting some

20 See, for example, Oliver-Smith 2005.
21 Oliver-Smith 2005:52.

profit from the soil."[22] This sequence of events, as well as the cause for it, has been cited by scholars from Karl Marx to modern agricultural specialists. In North America, its most infamous consequence might be the Dust Bowl, but less obviously visible examples of this ongoing process of destroying the soil, the land, and the landscape are daily occurrences.[23] Rather than to differentiate the quality of relations to land by time spent on the land, however, it might be more useful to do so by the reciprocal relations with the land.

Because there are American Indian reservations and trust lands in the Bakken area—Fort Berthold, Fort Peck, and Turtle Mountain and the lands within the Trenton Indian Service Area to start with—the temptation might be strong to differentiate an American from a Native way of looking at landscapes, as in differentiating a "Western" or "European" from an "Indigenous" perspective. As anthropologists have pointed out, "such an approach is limited, if not flawed, and often yields a superficial or one-dimensional view of the complex and unique relations of peoples to places they inhabit."[24] Just as cultural constructions with the land stemming from a history of inhabitation are not simply inherited from generation to generation but have to be learned, so do cultural constructions overall. Learning relationships with the land is a matter of practice and of engagement. People chose to engage with the land or not to engage based on different variables; where our ancestors lived might come into this equation, but it is not a necessary or sufficient variable to determine our relations. Aldo Leopold argued that the mistake in relations to land was "the assumption, clearly borrowed from modern science, that the human relation to land is only economic." Instead, he wrote, the relationship is also, "or should be," aesthetic. What he meant by that was a bit more than imposing our own notions of beauty onto selected landscapes. He suggested that people should learn to "read" the land—to read the story that "soils and rivers, birds and beasts" spell out.[25] Simply reading the land, assembling meaning from the "alphabet of 'natural objects'," as Leopold suggests, however, is not enough to appreciate landscapes, just as

22 Lévi-Strauss 1992:92; but see throughout *Tristes Tropiques*.

23 This argument is the same as brought forth by Cunfer (2005) for modern agriculture on the Plains. Worster (1977) and Foster (2000) provide ample examples of the history of capitalist extractive agriculture. See also Buckland (2004); Knobloch (1996).

24 Thornton 2008:7; see also Braun (2008).

25 Leopold 1991:337.

reading a letter or a book is necessary, but not sufficient to appreciating its meaning. In order to truly understand and appreciate landscapes, we need to learn to listen to them. Some landscape archaeologists acknowledge that landscapes are neither simply aesthetic nor natural. Instead, they are seen as documents or palimpsests of different histories and present views.[26] However, documents are still archived out of context, and are read in the way Leopold suggests. I suggest that we should see landscapes as stories.[27] These stories cannot be broken into pieces and put back together without a loss of substance and meaning. Landscapes are either whole or they are nothing. This view, of course, eludes human control—and that is the point. Listening to somebody gives them agency. Homes have that agency. They draw us in and keep us. They make us take care of them.

## Stewardship

From an American perspective, the Plains possess few aesthetic qualities that would trump economic exploitation. Even today, they are seen as not exotic enough to protect on a large scale. Tall- and shortgrass prairies still exist in pockets, along roadways, and in small preserves. Most of the ecosystem, however, has been destroyed by farming and ranching, in an effort that is comparable to the current destruction of the Amazon and other tropical forests, and with just as much destructive consequences. Today, monocrop rows of soybeans and corn grow where once the tallgrass prairie flowered in its diversity, and beef is raised where once prairie dogs, bison, and elk grazed the shortgrass prairie.[28] Especially on rangelands, perceived as without aesthetic value, existing in the periphery of the nation and of modernity itself, the people and the land were seen as marginal. Without an understanding of the land, its history, and its meanings, and approaching it from a commodity perspective, having all this open land was a waste. To turn this land over to a yet more profitable method of extraction seemed common sense because the land existed, from this perspective, purely as a commodity resource. The pursuit of happiness demanded it.

26 See, for example, Scazzosi (2004):339; Turner (2006); Harvey and Waterton (2015); Johnson (2012); Meier (2012).

27 Braun 2013c:9-14.

28 For a discussion of Prairie ecosystems, see for example Samson and Knopf (1996).

Newcomers to places are often convinced of their own cultural truths to the extent that they are not willing to engage in negotiations with peoples or landscapes. Instead, they try to impose their ideas. This is all the more the case when these newcomers see the landscape they approach as a desert, ready to be inscribed afresh. Among such cultural truths for Americans was the assumption that private property led to civilization. Allotment was the imposition of these concepts onto Native peoples and the landscape. Allotment had immediate consequences for how people were supposed to live on the land and use it. The previously commonly owned landscape was now a patchwork of different land parcels. Communities were bound to specific parcels. These parcels became resources. For those who received fee title to the lands, they became commodified (and often were lost). Social and cultural consequences followed. The land now had to be viewed in its present context. Even lands that had not been allotted had to be seen differently, as they were now "reservations," governed by "tribes."[29] Some cultural values survived, of course. Those who were still able to live on the land had the opportunity to keep their connections to the land alive. But even their relationship to land changed from a relation to the landscape to a relation to specific places: those in the family. When people in communities talk about land today, they mostly talk about their relatives' parcels, not all the land. It is those places that keep the relationship alive, along with a few specific places that are meaningful to the whole community. These have often have become sacred in a sometimes political way. They are often significant for the nation as a whole because they act as a historical or cultural symbol for the nation.

All cultures change. All cultures find certain meanings and values no longer useful and replace them with others. While cultures pretend that their practices, meanings, and values have not changed, that they are "traditional," traditions are the cultural projection of stability.[30] The idea of an actually existing unchanging culture is nonsensical, as Raymond DeMallie made clear; "culture and culture change," he observed, "are, in effect, the same phenomenon."[31] We could just as well say that landscapes and landscape change are the same phenomenon. As landscapes change from public to privately owned parcels, values might

29 See Wagoner 2002:51-93; Lyons 2010:165-167; Ruppel 2008.

30 As Hobsbawm 1983:2 put it: "The object and characteristic of 'traditions', including invented ones, is invariance."

31 DeMallie 1993:533.

continue to be held in regard. In the continuity, reinvention, and reinterpretation of historical culture, ethnic places are constructed as places of resistance, often based on explicit differences in relations to land. The places and relationships to land are sometimes lived, as continuously changing, pragmatic, flexible, cultural practices by what are often called traditional people. They are also sometimes professed and demonstrated as dogmatic programs and demonstrations of ethnic difference and resistance.[32] However, these ideas and values are often no longer influential on lived practice.

None of this means that Native cultures have disappeared or assimilated. The imposition of private ownership simply meant that cultural practices and values changed, too. "One has to be very naive or dishonest," Levi-Strauss observes, "to imagine that men choose their beliefs independently of their situation."[33] Changes in land ownership and consequentially changes in relations to land, although forced and imposed, have become a part of Native cultures. Simultaneously, cultural values might have stayed the same for some people, even though they are no longer lived. First, as Hobsbawm wrote, "objects or practices are liberated for full symbolic and ritual use when no longer fettered by practical use."[34] Traditional connections to the land, especially as symbols of nationhood or indigeneity, can continue to be celebrated even though practical relationships to land might have changed. Second, this is the case because practical ecological behavior, in contrast to ceremonial ecological behavior, is pragmatic. Igor Krupnik, in a discussion of Arctic hunters, makes a distinction between "ecological experience," the beliefs about and knowledge of the environment, and "ecological behavior," the actual practices relating onto land, plants, and animals.[35] This distinction is applicable elsewhere. It explains why people who are connected to the land sometimes engage in practices that are extremely destructive. It would be difficult to tell small-scale American farmers apart from a small-scale Native farmer, or industrial American farmers from industrial Native farmers, or county and state governments from tribal governments—in their practices. Native people and tribes do have different relations to land from their American neighbors or from American governments. However, the general

32 Lyons 2010; Braun 2013a; Kurkiala 1997; on ethnic places see Hoelscher (1998):13-28.

33 Lévi-Strauss 1992:148.

34 Hobsbawm 1983:4.

35 Krupnik 1993:238-239.

expectation that the response by tribes to the Bakken boom and its impact on the landscape would be fundamentally different—conceptually separate[36]—is more informed by romantic or nostalgic politics than by reality.

Stewardship for land and landscapes makes them beautiful, but this is far from only an aesthetic value. The sublime harmony of landscapes is instead "the result of agreements painstakingly evolved during a long collaboration between man and the landscape," as Levi-Strauss wrote.[37] A harmonic landscape tells us about our collaboration with other entities. Without this long collaboration, without the agreements and compromises, there is no harmony. Instead, there is only imposition. A totally disciplined, dominated landscape teaches us about ourselves. Wilderness, were that to exist, would teach us about others. In contrast to harmony, which is, in its own order, always a bit messy, American values of landscape harmony emphasize "an appearance of readable order," that order of course imposed onto the landscape. The American dean of landscape studies, J.B. Jackson, wrote that it was seen to be essential, to assure the survival of "the most efficient, the most enduring, the most beautiful design," to discipline the "anarchic instinct" that led to disorder.[38]

This idea of an imposition of order onto a "wild" landscape might have indeed sprung from the renaissance, and Catherine Howett speaks of a resulting "cultural predisposition of Western societies."[39] However, there are differences between so-called Western societies, as can be seen in the approaches from Levi-Strauss and Jackson. The difference between Europe and America is that in Europe, the pre-Renaissance or pre-modern landscape was already encoded onto the land and could not simply be swept away; another, more modern, ordered, disciplined, efficient vision could not simply be superimposed. Such planned landscapes were thus confined to specific spaces. No such inhibitions existed in North America, where previous tenure and stewardship of people and landscapes was explicitly denied in order to create a supposedly new, unprecedented society. Thus, the landscape could be seized and flattened out, gridlined, and transferred into a commodity. It is in North America that this process could be and was enforced.

36 Lyons 2010:136.
37 Lévi-Strauss 1992:93-94; see also Ingold (2005).
38 Jackson 1994:5-7.
39 Howett 1997.

## Scale

The fears about deterritorialization and the destructive legacies of energy booms expressed in the narratives mentioned earlier come to the forefront here. Notions of kayaking on free-flowing rivers, sunflower fields, the desert marked by a passing train, and country towns evoke a landscape that is experienced through other senses—smelling the summer rain and a cedar fire, listening to the birds. In contrast, now the booms disfigure the land, pollute the air and water, and leave behind a wasteland. However, with the physical landscape, the cultural landscape also is changed and destroyed: values and customs are shattered.

The French anthropologist Marc Augé writes that, "When bulldozers deface the landscape, the young people run off to the city or 'allochthons' move in, it is in the most concrete, the most spatial sense that the landmarks—not just of the territory, but of identity itself—are erased."[40] In the boom regions on the northern Plains, communities who have experienced depopulation over the past century, some people might have accepted a tradeoff in that the economic boom was hoped to stop the young people from leaving. But that balance, what people are willing to give up, reaches its limit when the physical and cultural landscapes get changed beyond recognition. When environment and communities seem to reach breaking points, home is no longer home, and people feel exiled and alienated. One state senator and farmer expressed it like this:

> Certainly, the mineral owners have the right to access their property, that must never be in dispute. But the surface owner has a commitment to be a steward of the land that existed long before oil development, extending long after the oil is gone. We need to have laws and regulations that honor their place on the land.[41]

Overwhelmed, anxious, afraid, confronted with a reality they could not address, communities in the Bakken looked for help. Ingrained in the idea that help needed to come from engineers and economists, they turned to exactly those people who would answer each question with a precise and narrow answer, presenting hypotheses and projections as hard facts, and intent on development and growth. Once

40 Augé 1995:39.
41 Merry 2011.

people in the communities realized that there was, actually, harm being done to them, they were faced with the uncertainty of how to respond. There are few people who have the strength to stand up against the combined discourse of state, industry, and academia and rely on their own experiences, senses, and histories. Even when there are people who are that strong, they might face a long fight to convince others that they are being harmed and that the harm that is being done is not normal, is not expected, and is not a requirement for the community to flourish.

One difficulty for people on the northern Plains to assess changes and damages to their landscapes is the scale of the landscape itself. In order to understand and assess landscape impacts from a quantitative perspective, what is impacted needs to be a measurable unit. This is why landscapes need to be defined before they can be assessed. Where landscapes are really big, this can be a problem. It is not really feasible to collect data points spanning hundreds or thousands of square miles.[42] Ingold says that landscapes have horizons, not boundaries.[43] If the landscape has to be defined, the horizons need to be defined as boundaries. On the Plains, however, horizons just keep re-emerging out of themselves. A qualitative assessment would, of course, solve that problem. However, because environmental assessments are usually measuring the relation between what is disturbed or destroyed and what is not, qualitative responses are usually not enough to change policies.

## Data

When not even town and county leadership have the data to know, understand, and assess their new landscapes, the first step to solving any problem has to be gaining access to such data. This is important for planning purposes. However, it is also important to assess what kind of damage is done to the environment. If local leaders do not have access, then local ranchers, farmers, activists, and the public usually have even less access. Their access to data has to be as current as possible, and as cheap as possible. Citizen involvement in data gathering would not only cut costs but also create relations with the environment. As social scientists, anthropologists are often unsure as to what we can contribute to communities with which we are involved. One thing we

42 Holdaway, Douglass, and Fanning 2012.
43 Ingold 2005:507.

have is networks, research skills, and access to knowledge. I began to research the feasibility of balloon mapping, a low-tech solution for researchers and activists that want to get clear visuals of specific places. Balloon mapping is a low-cost tool, and the Public Laboratory for Open Technology and Science, now Public Lab, was distributing guides, software to knit pictures into maps, and selling balloon kits. It seemed like a perfect tool to get community involvement, interest, and information. The sheer scale of the potential project, as well as the time pressure, however, led me to look for different solutions. After all, the U.S. government has quite a few satellites that take pictures for everything from agriculture to security. I began to wonder if there was a way to get high quality satellite imagery for current and previous years that would demonstrate landscape changes.

Eventually, I found the USGS Earth Resources Observation and Science (EROS) Center in South Dakota, which hosted the National Agricultural Imagery Program (NAIP). When I talked with Tom Abe about the potential to contact them and get imagery to look at landscape changes, he told me he had already done so. In fact, he had contacted the tribal liaison officer, who had told Tom that the officer could not provide Tom with the images he wanted because "somebody could not be happy with that." During the height of the boom, many public employees were cautious in sharing data with the public (which was their function), especially if that data could be used to critique extraction activities. After some more digging, I found the USDA Natural Resources Conservation Service's Geospatial Data Gateway, a government website where the imagery was actually available for download by county. The imagery came in an obscure format, but I found the software that was needed.

With these datasets in hand, I began to stitch them together and to compare changes over the years. The whole process was so labor intensive and needed so much open-source but niche imagery software products that it could not have worked as a means to distribute information effectively, however. States and industry forces have GIS departments with tools and experts to do these sort of things. Counties and towns in North Dakota obviously could not spare the resources or get the data to achieve this. In order to get this information to the public, I went to my colleagues in the Geography Department at the University of North Dakota, Brad Rundquist and Michael Niedzielski, and they and their students created a browser-based GIS map. The map combined several data sets—well locations, divided into active and inactive wells with date of drilling, spill data, and underground fracturing lines—with NAIP imagery over twenty-five years and, for the reservation, the original survey maps from 1910. All of this was searchable as well as measurable in terms of distances and areas, and the data was downloadable. We signed an agreement with the tribal college on Fort Berthold, the Nueta Hidatsa Sahnish College, and I promoted the site to anybody I could. I demonstrated the site to several organizations, including Fort Berthold POWER (Protectors of Water and Earth Rights). Many stakeholders loved to engage with the data and great discussions flowed from the maps, whether on locations of old wells on people's lands, anecdotes of illegal waste water dumps on specific parcels, or landscape changes.

The result was an actually public collection of datasets in one space that provided users an immediate view of the current landscape as well as a comparison of the changes to the landscape over a quarter of a century and more. In theory, all they needed was a browser—and a good connection. In practice, the site combined so much data that many connections in rural North Dakota were overwhelmed. The site worked, but it took a long time to load. However, with some patience, people did have access to the data. The discussions that the site fostered were proof that such access can spark new insights, bring people together to share stories, and create important new information from this sharing. The website was maintained for about four or five years. Then, the links to the data had been changed so much that the site ceased to be functional. But for that time, people had a chance to work from a relatively evened-out information landscape.

These efforts were not an attempt at "counter mapping," although the intent was similar.[44] Making mapping solutions available to local communities can begin to shift power by giving access to information and thereby greater ability to make decisions. Extraction companies make extensive use of GIS data and have almost real-time information on landscape changes. ESRI, the entity behind the ArcGIS software that provides GIS mapping solutions, provides specific services to oil and gas companies.[45] They offer a newsletter and an annual conference. All of the methodology, technology, and knowledge can, of course, be used to minimize the impact of extraction. To be realistic, however, the

44 See, for example, Chapin, Lamb, and Threlkeld (2005); Elwood (2006); Norris (2014):263-264; Wainwright (2019):288-289.

45 Esri 2021.

main marketing for the products is for strategic location of facilities, efficiency of operations, and integrated planning. Even if extraction companies were to use these integrated data primarily to save landscapes, the point is that so long as they have access to these kinds of data solutions while communities do not, there is an absolute imbalance of intelligence and power. The same applies to federal, state, and tribal governments.

## Terrain

Understanding the terrain provides huge advantages. Strategic and tactical deployment of resources, efficient planning, and placement of infrastructure all depend on an understanding of the terrain. If these are terms that are shared between military, civic, and business operations, that is not a coincidence. It flows from the fundamental understanding of an area as a terrain. A terrain is the sandbox of efficiency and the deployment of resources. It is a very different concept from a landscape, as it is not interested in the stories or meanings of the landscape, or only as far as they relate to efficiency. While local communities might have a better knowledge of the landscape, this is of no use in the realm of commodity extraction, ownership, and control. In these areas, power over the land belongs to those who conceptually control the terrain. Changes in the land can be fast, and the landscape is always partially a historic construct. Local communities reacting to changes in the landscape are thus always a step behind state and corporate actors that have already implemented these changes based on an analysis of the terrain. When local resistance is successful are those times and places communities can contest, deny, or obfuscate the imposition of a terrain and instead impose their landscapes as the defining aspect of the area.

The mapping project was geared to provide equal access to data, in hopes that communities could overlay this data with their meanings and make decisions based on both, the overview of the physical landscape and their cultural meanings of this landscape. The result would have ideally been the construction—at least for the communities themselves—of an instrument for decision making in almost real time that could be used from a landscape perspective. This needed an active participation of communities, because, as Joel Wainwright observes, "although maps are often important in struggles for geographical justice, participatory mapping projects solve nothing in themselves."[46] Like any tool and any data, maps need to be used and interpreted to create knowledge, and that knowledge needs to have a voice. Maps are instruments to share information. If a community or individuals does not want to share landscape information, for example because they understand that their voices will not be heard anyway,[47] participatory mapping projects can be impossible. If the information shared is misappropriated, they can also be dangerous to communities. As mentioned, geographical data—maps and imagery—are also instruments of power. Those who control access to the data hold power.

The non-sharing of data, even by public officials whose positions it was to share exactly these data, raises the question of what public access to data, or open data, means in these instances. While the state makes the data available, finding it requires wading through different websites, downloading and accessing shapefiles, and being able to bring datasets together and represent them on a map. These are not skills many people in rural communities have, should they even have the bandwidth to download the data in reasonable times. The NAIP imagery presented even larger issues. A few weeks into the first Trump administration, the Geospatial Data Gateway developed a functional error and was no longer accessible. The website has since been restored, but without access to NAIP imagery. Instead, the imagery can be downloaded from a box fileset, and although the county codes necessary to understand which imagery to access for specific areas are in shapefiles themselves, not all counties are uploaded; even for those states included in the list, the imagery itself is, as is usual for such files, in MrSID format, for which one needs to find, download, and install specific software. To build the files into mosaics requires other software. Many counties today, as well as private companies, make GIS datasets and NAIP imagery available, but not in time-lapse sets that would allow comparative perspectives.

Some people in the field have told me that they do not have any troubles accessing NAIP imagery. This is absolutely true for researchers within institutions and with computer and research skillsets. For the average person, however, dispersing the data, publishing it on sets of files in obscure formats, and problems with download speeds creates as effective an obstacle as putting the data behind a paywall, if not

46 Wainwright 2019:289.
47 Braun 2020:18-19.

more so. While this creates an issue of privilege for researchers, it also creates an opportunity. One of the future tasks for anthropologists, for example, might well be not only to serve as a data conduit from more or less exotic communities to home publics. Instead, anthropologists and others should become two-way conduits, in return collecting and making accessible data of the state and other large actors to the communities.

Of course, as Kregg Hetherington writes in a very different, yet structurally similar context, "there is something almost quaint about the suggestion that what poor people really need is a little more, and a little better, information about their condition."[48] That is undoubtedly true. It became very obvious that providing access to information was not solving any problems. Without this information, however, communities were not even in a position to double-check information they were given by campaigns and agencies that had their own interests at heart. What became apparent was that tools could be built relatively cheaply by people who have the expertise and have access to data. What also became apparent was that in a situation where state and corporate entities outrightly deny or bureaucratically hinder access, that role falls to universities. Collecting data and giving access to that data is not in itself a political action, although it is often portrayed as such. It is what universities are supposed to be doing; when they do not fulfill that responsibility, however, that choice can quickly become political.

## Impacts

Regardless of these issues of access and power, which I will return to in the next chapter, what became apparent from both the NAIP imagery and the overlay browser map was tremendous change on a huge scale. A similar comparison to imagery from other areas of oil and gas booms—Pennsylvania, Texas, Colorado, Louisiana—demonstrated very similar patterns of landscape changes. The defining mark of areas of oil and gas booms are the well pads, dotting the landscape like pockmarks. They are connected by access roads, fragmenting the land like spiderwebs or, on the Plains, finally imposing the grid onto landscape, making it a physical reality. Roads are widened and new roads are built around towns. Industrial zones sprang up around towns like Williston, Dickinson, Killdeer, and Watford City. From aerial

48 Hetherington 2011:5.

photography, it becomes apparent that between 2007 and 2015, Williston grew new industrial neighborhoods that were two times larger than the city itself. The same is true for Watford City and Killdeer. Williston built a new airport farther away from the city. Industrial zones also appeared, however, in places in between—truck repair shops, storage facilities, man camps, and all the other services needed for the extraction industry sprung up around very small places, like Alexander, or simply around crossroads, like Johnson Corner, or other places acquiring strategic value. The impact of these changes is not readily apparent from driving along the roads because the scale of the changes is not comprehensible from a surface level. It is also not really comprehensible from topographic maps because while these show new roads, they do not show the extent or the ecological qualities of the areas these roads provide access to.

Every well pad by itself takes relatively little space compared to a landscape that stretches to the horizon; the other well pads are not visible on a relatively flat landscape apart from the water and oil storage equipment and gas flares. Even when only looking at one pad from the air, the trade-off between total area of a land parcel and the area of the pad might seem reasonable. A study in Colorado found that from a 171 square mile area (443 km$^2$), the direct effects of producing and non-producing well pads was 6.75 sqm (17.5km$^2$).[49] In Webb County, Texas, about 10 sqm (25.8 km$^2$) were well pads in 2008 – until 2014, when an additional 8.5 sqm (22 km$^2$) were added.[50] Webb County has a total area of 3361 sqm (8700 km$^2$), so this might seem like a relatively small number, even when keeping in mind that these wells were built in smaller portions of the county, not distributed evenly over its territory. A well pad in Pennsylvania takes up about 2.47 ac (1 ha) of space. In North Dakota, a single-well pad was on average about 3.35 acres. However, consolidating multiple wells onto the same pad shrank the acreage needed per well to about an acre for an eighteen-well pad.[51] This meant huge pads, but fewer of them, which was more efficient for farmers. Minimizing impact meant minimizing the competition between two extractive industrial enterprises—agriculture and oil extraction. It also allows the industry to make the argument that they

49 Baynard et al. 2017.

50 Pierre et al. 2017.

51 Dalrymple 2016; see also Adhikari and Hansen (2018); Nasen, Noble, and Johnstone (2011); Slonecker and Milheim (2015); Fitzgerald et al. (2020); Baynard (2011).

are trying to be sustainable. One global report touting those credentials mentioned that horizontal drilling "reduced impacts to surface areas"—the exact argument the state and industry used in the Bakken to show environmental responsibility. "Fewer wells mean fewer drilling sites," the report maintains: "The end result: less environmental impact per barrel of oil produced."[52]

In the North Dakota Bakken area, between December 2006 and January 2016 when the Bakken boom occurred, 10,149 wells were established. If we assume the average of 2.47 acres per well, this would amount to about 39 square miles (101 $km^2$) of well pads, a little smaller than mainland San Francisco. This number is deceptive, however, for two reasons. First, it only takes into account the actual area of the well pads, not the access roads and other infrastructure needs (like, for example, the industrial support areas around regional cities, man camps, access roads, pipelines, etc.). Second, it is deceptive to base an assessment on these numbers because there is no contiguous area of well pads. Nobody took thirty-nine square miles of North Dakota and turned it into a gravel pad. Instead, these pads are distributed throughout the region.

On one hand, this seems to lessen the impact. There is less direct impact on any individual parcel of land. In reality, however, it actually increases the impact. While the direct impact is distributed throughout, so are the indirect impacts. All of the Williston Basin has been turned into an industrialized zone; all of the landscape has been changed. The areal measurement of direct impacts leaves out the main issue: the fragmentation of land. Every well pad needs an access road. These roads are needed to build the pad, to bring in drilling rigs, water, sand, and chemicals, and to take out brine and oil. Especially during initial drilling and fracturing, intensive truck traffic marks these roads, and because they are gravel roads, dust becomes a major issue for surrounding areas. From a landscape perspective, the whole landscape is impacted and changed. About five percent of the impact area for wells stems from clearing land; ninety-five percent stems from land fragmentation and resulting animal behavioral changes.[53] If we apply this numerically, the affected land base from well pads alone reaches 780

52 IPIECA and OGP 2002:5-7

53 McDonald et al. 2009:4.

square miles (2020 km$^2$). And yet, because the disturbance is distributed across the region, the actual area is much bigger. In fact, the actual area is not numerical. It is simply the landscape.

The conceptual and real dissection of landscape into land parcels also affects how people perceive a landscape conceptually. This has impacts on decision making processes. Comprehensive assessments of impacts are almost never done, which leads to piecemeal policies and enforcement.[54] The physical fragmentation of the landscape, partially encouraged by this absence of a conceptual acknowledgment of a landscape as a whole, goes beyond that. It is an actual destruction of relationships within a landscape. Animal species, from antelopes to birds, are heavily impacted by fragmentation because their habitats are dissected. From a scientific perspective, assessment thus becomes a matter of measuring fragmentation, not simply measuring the percentage of space converted to industrial extraction.

The fragmentation of landscapes in energy extraction areas—oil, gas, wind—becomes very clear when viewed from above. Every installation needs access, and roads can span out like spiderwebs laid onto previously nondissected areas. In North Dakota, the State was very proud that it tried to prevent this from occurring. After the *Grand Forks Herald* ran a story on a public presentation I gave using aerial photography, where I compared fragmented landscapes in Wyoming, Pennsylvania, Texas, and North Dakota, I received a call from the state government the next morning. The basic message was that I should stop talking about these issues, because in North Dakota, the State was focusing on what they called Energy Corridors. These energy corridors were an attempt at an orderly development along gridlines. Basically, the idea was that well pads would be established along every other east-west (in some cases north-south) section line, or every two miles. Because horizontal wells could reach about a mile, all the oil could be accessed from these wells, with horizontal drills reaching out to the north and south on both sides of these energy corridors. Theoretically, the well pads would be located on already existing roads, which would prevent further fragmentation. In practice, these roads had been used to access farmlands. Seasonal traffic was now replaced by hundreds of truck loads. The roads had to be improved, which made them into hardened barriers, which present a higher risk for wildlife. Along each side of the roads, north and south, a well pad was established about

54 Allred et al. 2015:402.

every three hundred to four hundred meters—sometimes less, sometimes more. Because they were often not directly opposite each other, the effect of a fully developed energy corridor was a four hundred to five hundred meter-wide zipper line crossing the landscape every 3.2 kilometers. Very few of these corridors came close to being fully developed by the time the boom ended, but the patterns on the land are clear enough.

From a qualitative perspective it is irrelevant how much of the landscape is altered. If enough meaningful places are changed, then the landscape (as a whole) is changed. The quantitative approach eases decision making, and therefore both lends itself to and defines resource management. Decision making is eased because only one variable is allowed into the equation. For land as commodity, that variable is economic. For species habitats, that variable is a single species. For resource management, it is that resource. However, because single variables are almost indefinite in complex settings, all of these variables cannot be taken into account. "Because initiating new location and species-specific studies is not practical for every proposed energy project," observes one study, "we recommend complimentary analyses that quantify the impacts of energy development on indicators from a landscape perspective."[55] The demand to quantify data is also a demand to narrow the scope of an investigation. Every quantification is an exclusion of data that do not fit into the specific categorization used to arrive at numbers. The demand for quantifiable data and a reduction of variables, however, are not coincidences. Efficient management of resources is itself a baseline and a stepping stone for capitalism, which is the reduction of qualitative variables to a single, quantitative, and universally effective and efficient number: exchange value.[56] Resources as commodities are of necessity quantities devoid of other qualities, and the introduction of qualitative variables into resource management threatens to complicate the decision-making process to the point of becoming inefficient.

55 Jones, Pejchar, and Kiesecker 2015:298. See also Davidson (1998); Fischer and Lindenmayer (2007).

56 Dussel 1998; Dussel 2006.

## The sacred

As discussed, it is in the qualitative aspects that human and nonhuman concerns come together to form a landscape. Gregory Bateson observed that under the conditions of capitalism and the value of growth, this reduction of a whole mere to economic quantities is not only a necessity, but also the only allowable epistemology. Landscapes have to be disciplined, and the grid is the only efficient organization of the landscape. These premises are the same whether they are applied to the land, animals, plants, or people. "The premises that led to conflict between settlers and American Indians were the same as those that led to the destruction of the tall grass prairie and that today threaten the rain forests of South America and their inhabitants," wrote Bateson.[57] The alternative to a quantitative reduction and abstraction would be an acknowledgment and affirmation of complex and mutually integrated relations. "Such a perception of both self and other" and their relationships, obligations, and connections, is, Bateson observes, "the affirmation of the sacred."

The sacred does not depend on measurable quantities—in fact, it depends exactly on the absence of measurement and quantification. It cannot be measured. If it is, it is no longer sacred. It is, in effect, the opposite of commodification. Recognizing the sacred means to recognize that the system of social relationships that makes a whole from parts is too complex to be taken apart. Culture, flora, fauna, water, and landscape are one, and an injury to one takes away from the whole. This is not an indigenous or a New Age realization. It flows from being native on and with the land—to recognize the power of the land, to listen to it, to identify special places of meaning, and to realize that the system that binds it all both gives life and takes life. This realization does not stand in opposition to "Western culture." It stands in opposition to quantification, efficiency, commodification, and unbridled capitalism. It stands in opposition to carving up the landscape into resources.

The landscape is the visible representation of the system and simultaneously its foundation. When people in the Bakken reacted first to light pollution, to access roads, to well pads, and to industrial zones, they felt that the sacred qualities of their landscape, their home, were under threat. Native people and non-Native people constructed different meanings for this landscape, but it was a meaningful landscape

57 Bateson and Bateson 1987:175-176.

to both. When it began to be fragmented, it was no longer home. People were uprooted. They were deterritorialized. Their landscape was gone.[58]

The sacred is what Levi-Strauss called the sublime harmony of the landscape, the result of collaboration and of relationships. It is no coincidence that an industrial landscape is mostly not seen as sacred. It might carry meaning; after all, it is also a representation of specific cultural values. However, this representation is not a collaboration, is not about relationships. Industrial landscapes have been imposed, and it is this imposition that is visible in the landscape. Such landscapes do not have to be bleak factories, storage areas, malls, or well pads. Most suburbs, for example, are industrial landscapes in that way: rows and rows of same-colored houses along streets that are designed to either look cute from above or laid out in the most efficient ways to fill a subdivision, with lawns carefully kept devoid of any natural intrusions. What rules suburbia is the attempt to keep property values up. It is only after exchange values have relatively dipped anyway that some sort of collaboration with natural forces can be allowed. In western North Dakota, one sure sign that the landscape was changing was the appearance of suburban neighborhood developments.

Extractivism simultaneously denies meaning in the landscape and remakes the landscape in its own image. It defines the land as a commodity and then makes that happen, by imposing and inscribing this perspective onto the land. As less land can be inscribed with sublime harmony, as meanings other than exchange values are banished from the land, literally extracted from it, as the sacred gets disciplined, limited, and retreats into ever smaller areas, at some point, the nature of the landscape changes. No matter whether there are still roadside prairies where certain plant species can hang on. There is no more prairie landscape. It has disappeared. Similarly, the people in North Dakota noticed that their landscape, of which they were proud, which made them a home, with which they had been forced to collaborate, was being taken away. Because landscape is dependent on meaning, it does not even matter if the physical aspect of a landscape is restored

58 "The built environment in which we live is a material instantiation of our social relations. It expresses and shapes our social relations." Oliver-Smith 2005:51.

in some way. As long as I know that over the next hill there are ten drilling rigs, that under this shortgrass there runs a pipeline network, the landscape is damaged.

The Bakken oil boom, and in fact every resource boom, every expanding frontier, extractivism as a concept applied, is a demonstration of capitalism. Capitalism, as a system, needs to expand, depends on growth, and will eventually eat its own. In the twenty-first century, we, as humans, are faced with this consequence, which I will have to get back to at the end of this text: we are on the brink of destroying all relations with nature, all harmony, all collaboration. Some people argue that this development is okay, forgetting that humans are animals, a part of nature ourselves. Landscapes like the Bakken are a demonstration that we are destroying ourselves.

Those people native to and with the landscapes in extraction zones—Native and non-Native—know that their world is being changed and possibly destroyed. The new landscapes are imposed on them, too. This is what motivates the apocalyptic visions with which I started the book. However, what they miss is that this is not "a new Manifest Destiny." It is the same old Manifest Destiny that their ancestors had followed. The West became a spiritual refuge for them as they became native to it. The settlers, their ancestors, had themselves imposed their economic imperatives onto others that were native. Native people have to be convinced of the necessity to change and destroy their landscapes, or these decisions have to be imposed and enforced on them. In order to see how the system of extractivism works on the land, then, how it disappears the landscape, it is necessary to look at power, its relations, its use, and its imposition onto the landscapes.

# Chapter 5
## States, Tribes, Industry, and Power

The Bakken oil boom, like most resource booms in rural, relatively poor, and peripheral politico-economic systems, combined the national security aspects of oil with the real and potential economic power of multinational companies, a desire for relevancy by marginal communities, and the commodified approach to the environment. Hydraulic fracturing energy booms meant opportunity: for the Three Affiliated Tribes, an opportunity to build infrastructure and shed poverty; for the State of North Dakota, the opportunity to be relevant and to attract businesses and jobs; for communities, the opportunity to attract people and make needed investments; for the federal government, an opportunity to become a major player as an energy exporter and shed dependence; for businesses the opportunity to make billions of dollars. Everybody would profit except two entities—the environment and the people living with it. As a commodity, the environment does not have any rights or voices, though, and the people would have to be convinced.

In August 2012, I was at the Energy Impact Solutions Conference in Minot.[1] This event followed four symposia in 2010 and 2011, at Minot State University and Dickinson State University. The series had been funded through a grant from the U.S. Department of Energy, secured by the three members of the North Dakota congressional delegation (at that time all Democrats). The Solutions conference was seen as a capstone, investigating five larger issues through focus groups and other methods in several communities, and presenting the findings back to community leaders. The goal was to assist communities in preparing for coming challenges and opportunities. Of the five speakers, four were faculty at Dickinson State, and one was faculty at Minot State. The audience were mostly town and county leaders from the region. The five issues addressed were community culture, education, emergency preparedness, leadership, and public health. Without a question, these were important topics faced by communities, although a glaring absence was the environment as a topic of discussion. The

1 Beckman 2012.

presentations brought together a lot of facts, especially on education, health care, and emergency responses. What struck me most, though, as I was listening, was the absence of critical voices. For example, the presenter on community culture approached the subject from the perspective that communities had to change, and forward-looking change was acceptance and adaptation to the boom. Resistance to change, thus, was an obstacle to be overcome, and in order to welcome newcomers, communities should partner with businesses. Examples of ways to integrate newcomers given were community theater groups, book clubs, car shows, art shows, bingo nights, and so on; activities that struck me as not necessarily working very well in a population of young, single men who were mostly transient and worked three weeks on, one week off or similar schedules.

Underlying all the presentations were predictions by the State of a sustained population growth even after the boom was over. McKenzie county, for example, was projected to see a population three times higher than 2009 levels at least until 2050. These were the projections for which counties and communities were to prepare and plan. The initial boom population would bring their families and stay in North Dakota for the long term. These population projections relied on projections for jobs created by the oil industry, which were also seen to be sustained at a high level—one graph that was always shown when people talked about the oil boom predicted that production jobs in McKenzie County would stabilize at seven to eight times the number in 2010. The message sent to the public by the State was threefold. First, the boom was unavoidable. Nothing could be done about it. Second, it was a great opportunity. The State and the communities were going to be revitalized and join modernity writ large. Third, these changes were here to stay, and to make sure the development was sustainable, the State and communities had to improve infrastructure.

This message was so consistent and constant that very few people—none at the conference—questioned the underlying data. Projections were taken as fact. Ideas for changes or slowdowns were taken as resistance. The hegemony of the dominant narrative was not to be, and could not be questioned. The best example for this came when the presenter on emergency preparedness talked about threats to the region:

> I know, people look at me like I'm crazy when I talk about terrorists, and we are becoming more of a terrorist target in this country, right now, uh, for a couple reasons. We have two groups that don't want to see a

> lot of things going on here. One are the environmentalists, and, trust me, you read the blogs, and I mean they would just as soon close down the coal and everything else we have. The EPA is a good example of that, uhm … and, sorry, Senator Conrad's office, but, uhm … they passed a rule last year that said any power plant that uses coal will be fined unless it changes to a new biodegradable fuel.[2]

In other words, those who were trying to bring the environment into the discussion were perceived to be against extraction and were therefore equated with terrorists. This included the Environmental Protection Agency because they proposed changes to burning coal, another North Dakota resource. Nobody in the room batted an eyelid. This was the narrative built around the boom.

## Power and transformation

Power, as we know at least since Michel Foucault, is in the hands of those who control the discourse; in fact, controlling the discourse is the definition of power. Although many people decry Foucault and his theories, this observation—which dates back to long before Foucault—has been widely accepted. It is, perhaps ironically and somewhat paradoxically, used today mostly by right-wing conspiracy theorists and politicians. Public relations was born of it. Since the advent of mass media, revolutionaries' first targets are radio stations and newspapers. Reading Cicero demonstrates that the Roman senate was dominated by those with oratorical skills.

Yet, there is another aspect to power, which is its actual exercise. In the modern state, this falls to the government, which has a monopoly on power and the violence to enforce it. In a liberal state, this power is curbed by limitations and regulations, although Carl Schmitt pointed out that in actuality, power is in the hands of those who decide on when to declare these limitations to be obsolete, unnecessary, or temporarily an obstacle. That is how liberal democracies transform into autocratic structures. Since the government has all the power, it can of course delegate it. This has been a very important function under conditions of expanding frontiers. Expansion is costly, and governments have often entrusted these expansions to corporations, in return for

2 Minot State University and Dickinson State University 2012.

economic rewards. England used this method extensively, from the colonization of Ireland to the Hudson Bay Company, from the East India Company to its colonies on the North American Atlantic seaboard and to its privateers attacking the Spanish treasure fleets. The United States used this method to build transatlantic railroads and secure the plains with homesteaders, to expand and enforce capitalism in Central America and Iraq.

Because the expansion of frontiers is often imagined as an imposition of order onto wilderness, this exercise of power is often imagined to effectuate a transition from a void of government, or at the very least from a rudimentary, incompetent governance, to a full-fledged, real, competent government. In a 1956 article on extraction industries in South America, these relations are described:

> The government may eventually take over responsibility for public health, education, and transportation, but it is not prepared at the outset to assume these responsibilities on the scale that the new community requires. Under these circumstances, management inevitably assumes a large degree of responsibility for community needs. Furthermore, management finds that, however much it does, community residents and local and federal government officials are naturally inclined to suggest that new needs be met also by the company. Once the paternalistic relationship is established, these natural pressures generate to extend it farther.[3]

It is important to point out not only the analysis of the process, but also the discourse used. The assumption of governmental duties by companies on an extraction frontier, with the encouragement of the state, is described as inevitable and natural. What is described here is the takeover of government power—in a liberal democracy at least theoretically controlled by the people—by corporations, accountable to their shareholders. Because the state itself is interested in this takeover under frontier conditions, at least initially, it often also creates conditions favorable to it. "North Dakota has an abundance of legislation regarding leasing and other things connected with the industry, but the control of the production," the governor of North Dakota said in 1951, at the time when the first commercial oil well was developed

3 Whyte and Holmberg 1956:22.

in the State, "is in the hands of the state industrial commission, which was set up as a business board rather than a regulatory board." Without regulation, with a state that is actively encouraging industry to take over state responsibilities, and with the assumption that whoever and whatever is in place already is wilderness that needs to be disciplined and is open to extraction, the conditions are set for what is often referred to as the "wild west." A run on resources will follow, regardless of the local people. Their appeals are not heard by the State, which has relegated power to companies.

In the Bakken, state and industry told a story of the unfolding boom that compared North Dakota to Saudi Arabia. Like the historical narrative of that area, this story was that of a more or less undeveloped and unpopulated region becoming transformed into a modern state ready for contemporary civilization. Just like in Saudi Arabia, where the Arabian American Oil Company (Aramco) operated like a state, so did, in many ways, oil extraction companies in North Dakota. The State, interested in extraction and without the resources to regulate a vast area with a myriad of well sites, allowed the industry to write its own rules and enforce them. Industry and state crafted a narrative in which, like in Saudi Arabia, the industry brought economic modernity and the State delivered the infrastructure to transform the region from a desert into a civilization.[4] The boom conditions were the frontier of transition into something better.

Neither the state nor the industry are, of course, interested in chaos or disorder. Every boom phase is a transition to an integrated system, which replaces a short-lived initial openness with a structured order. If the boom seems chaotic to people in communities, it is for two reasons. First, they do not recognize the plan because they are not privy to the planning and do not have access to the information. Second, because it is the industry that takes the lead, their needs go unmet until either the state has the means to address them or the industry does so itself. When the boom is over, the state steps in because industry pulls out. During the boom though, the state assures the fundamental aspects of its monopoly, in the United States law enforcement and property rights, while the industry is trusted to follow the rules as a valued partner in development. It is this collaboration and "alliance between big business and the state" that should, according to this story, bring

4 See Parker 2014.

about a symbiotic relationship between not only these two actors but also a third, which are the communities that do not share in this power but are nevertheless impacted.[5]

In North Dakota, the partnership between the three entities was fostered by the combined narrative of the boom's inevitability and of the need for modernity. This narrative was also carried by a third party, presumably independent, a consortium called Vision West ND. In reality, Vision West ND was and is a collaboration between state, county, and industry leadership that aims to fully develop the Bakken, but in an organized, structured, planned manner. Vision West ND developed a comprehensive Regional Plan for Sustainable Development.[6] This plan departed from a specific set of assumptions:

> If there is one thing that that is certain in western North Dakota, it is this: change. While much of rural America seems to stand still, the 19 counties in the Vision West ND region are experiencing nation-leading change and growth. The people of the region must act effectively and strategically to shape such change positively. Otherwise, as is evident throughout parts of the region, development may occur without the long-term interests of the local population in mind.[7]

While this vision asks the local communities to get involved, it is also clear that some parameters are set. The state will not slow down or stop the boom; communities can either get involved or face chaos. The goal of getting involved is to shape developments in a positive way, but what this means is already decided. Positive change is to avoid chaos, not to limit the boom.

The plan's recommendations centered around building infrastructure and capacity. For example, in its recommendations on water, the plan identifies two primary issues: "the continued importance of regional water systems and the need to access Lake Sakakawea for recreational purposes."[8] Not a word was written about clean water, for example, and in fact there was no other mention of the environment in the plan summary. The emphasis was on building an economic environment where the state provided infrastructure, the communities

5 Rajak 2011:94
6 Vision West ND 2015
7 Vision West ND 2015:5
8 Vision West ND 2015:16

created educational, economic, and recreational activities, and the industry provided jobs while extracting resources. Keeping within the predominant discourse on modernity, progress, and civilization—all assumed to be unavoidable and desirable—neither the state nor the industry asked whether local people wanted the modernization. Conversations between state, industry, and communities focused on how projects would be managed and implemented, not whether they should be.

## Corporate Social Responsibility

Such projects like Vision West ND, structured to appear collaborative, yet driven by definitive state-industrial-business agendas, are ways in which the state can take influence without being seen as the State; nominally, the project is driven by a third party. Yet, industry also often engages communities directly, not in efforts to structure a boom and make it more orderly, but in order to create a better relationship with communities the industry ultimately depends on. In the twenty-fist century, this ascribed role of industry as responsible for community well-being is called Corporate Social Responsibility (CSR). CSR is the bridge between the industry, to which the State has abrogated the responsibility, and the community, which will be the recipient of growth, development, and progress. It produces narratives of responsibility and is supposed to enact them. Through both the narrative production and as a virtue of being the deputy of the State in acting on responsibilities to communities, CSR is also an exercise of power.

It should not be surprising that there are many parallels between the delegation of social responsibility to industry and the collapsing of the state into private business. What Niobe Thompson describes in his account of the post-Soviet modernization campaign under oligarchs holds, in broad strokes, true for resource extraction areas in the northern plains. The modernization campaign in North Dakota was carried out by outsiders, "a two-pronged campaign of technological and cultural transformation, relying on an almost completely new administrative staff and the injection of massive capital investment."[9] CSR projects created patronage systems between companies and communities, who depended on donations of new equipment and expertise to deal with the consequences of processes set in motion by

9 Thompson 2008:145-207

the companies themselves. As seen in the Vision West ND efforts, the industry, of course, depended on communities and the State to offset some of their costs—in emergency response capability, in entertainment, and in housing, for example.

It would be a mistake to see CSR simply as donations to communities. As mentioned, they establish a patronage system, especially in the absence of large-scale state involvement. A 2010 publication by the International Finance Corporation on community investment makes the goal very clear. "The tendency to view community development as charity rather than as an investment linked to the business," it reads, "has resulted in vague objectives and a lack of direction and purpose." The publication admonishes businesses to not provide free services or goods to communities, as the government or communities themselves should work towards providing health care or education. On one hand, the critique of paternalistic development projects is taken seriously. Simultaneously, the costs for the consequences of industry presence are handed on, and social responsibility is reframed as community investment (CI). As such, the IFC points out that, "In the past, separating CI from business interests was done so that, in theory, CI programs could focus on 'doing good' without being seen as 'self-serving.' In practice, however, the separation from core business weakens CI in terms of its relevance, sustainability, and effectiveness." Returns on investments should of course be measured. After all, "it is quite possible to invest considerable resources in CI and yet have little to show for it (e.g., in terms of improved local support or less social risk)."[10]

Social risk in a globalized world is of course not only related to local communities, or the actual support these receive. Community investment or corporate social responsibility are also factors in public relations for shareholders and other investors.

> In the light of globalization and the internationalization of many companies in all sectors competitive edge has taken a new direction with a greater emphasis on the socially responsible behaviour of companies, and the sponsorship of the communities that they expand into. How companies *are perceived* to behave is possibly as important as how they behave, and the faith of stakeholders in, company conduct is essential.[11]

10 International Finance Corporation 2010:1, 13
11 Anderson and Bieniaszewska 2005:1

Of course, different companies can have very different objectives for their social investment programs. While some see them as photo opportunities, others might see themselves earnestly as problem-solvers for communities.[12]

What all modernization campaigns have in common is that they are predicated on quantitative achievements, that is, returns on investments. Modernization, by its own definition, needs to be measured. Construction projects—infrastructure, housing, oil wells, pipelines, roads, and so on—are therefore often yardsticks of modernization. They are visible, quantifiable, and manageable signs of modernization. They are clear demonstrations of modernization occurring. One guidance document for the oil industry posits that while companies should run opinion surveys in communities on how well they and their efforts are perceived, to measure community needs, fewer indicators are better than more. For example, it states, "weighted asset-based surveys are statistically proven to be a good proxy for measuring people's wellbeing."[13] Ownership of TVs, bicycles, radios, or modern roofing and toilets are cited specifically as good indicators of well-being. CSR initiatives are often standardized,[14] and focus on such visible and quantifiable projects, which also make for great media campaign backgrounds to improve the perception of community support.

## Public relations

Corporate Social Responsibility in the Bakken provided communities with much needed resources. A few years into the boom, new firetrucks appeared in community parades, for example. But companies also sponsored other infrastructure needs, recreational activities like fishing tournaments, and community picnics. With money and competition came industry magazines and newspapers financed through advertisements. There were quarterly or monthly special issues and supplements in regular newspapers, such as *Bakken Breakout* in the *Bismarck Tribune* or *Bakken Living* in the *Sydney Herald*, which also ran a supplement geared toward industry called *Tappin' the Bakken*. *Boom and Bloom* was a supplement that ran in 2011 in eleven small local newspapers, from the *Beulah Beacon* to the *Velva Area Voice*. The supplement for the *Tioga Tribune* was called *Boom Times*. There were industry publications such

12 IPIECA 2008:19
13 IPIECA 2008:41
14 See Sydow (2016):238

as the *Petroleum News Bakken*, the *Bakken Oil Business Journal*, or the *Bakken Oil Report*. The North Dakota Petroleum Council published *Oil and Gas TidBits* from 2007 on, distributed to policy makers, as well as *Talkin' the Bakken*, news releases geared toward the general public. The North Dakota Association of Oil and Gas Producing Counties published *Basin Bits*, and the North Dakota Pipeline Authority under the Industrial Commission of North Dakota published the *Pipeline Publication*. *The Bakken Magazine* was an example of a publication bringing together industry and stories for the public interest for a general audience. The first advertisement in the inaugural issue of *The Bakken* magazine was a full-page ad by the North Dakota Petroleum Council from its "North Dakota—Oil Can!" campaign. It highlighted the boom's impact on the economy (retail sales, royalties, and state and local taxes), direct and indirect job creation, and the 243 million barrels of oil produced in the state in 2012, amounting to eleven percent of the domestic oil—"20 million barrels per month toward energy independence."[15]

The inaugural issue of *Bakken Living* can serve as an example for the stories carried in the publications for the general public. A portrait of Alexander, ND, several stories on grocery shopping (where to buy fresh produce, whether to buy organic foods, a profile of the local grocery store chain in eastern Montana), and recipes for smoothies, strawberry pie, and home-made butter shared the magazine with lists of regional events and stories about a local woman's life, a newcomer's path to the area, and several stories about blogs, as well as stories about preparations for winter and life in campers. Other issues continued this line, highlighting fishing sites, small towns in the area, state parks, opportunities for children to join sports teams, small businesses, and the settler history of the region. These publications tried to build a sense of community and show newcomers that the towns were a good place to settle permanently. At the same time, they tried to show local residents the realities of life for newcomers to create good will and empathy.

Several stories contradicted the official version of booming and blooming, of a boom that would not end in a bust, of permanent population gain. *Boom Times* carried a story about life in mancamps, in which workers point blank explained that they were in North Dakota for the money, which they sent home to their families. The reality as

15 NDPC 2013

reported ran contrary to the predictions of lasting positive impacts and growth: "Workers, says [one interviewee], for the most part don't plan on staying long, only 'until we can go home'."[16] Similarly, also in 2011, *Boom and Bloom* carried a story about state senator and area farmer John Warner, who warned about several issues emanating from the boom, wondering "how best to withstand the impact of development." He was not against the development, but argued for first thinking about what residents wanted their communities to look like after the boom was over.[17]

Such counternarratives, though, often drowned in the slew of positive messaging about industry safety efforts, community growth, and the need to embrace modernity. Toward the end of the boom, *Bakken Living* published a story about lasting impacts. The author began the story with a look at the oil-dependence of Azerbaijan, warning that dependence on oil can lead to economic highs but also woeful crashes. He then explained that oil and gas only accounted for 8.6 percent of exports in the United States, not 90 percent as in Azerbaijan—never accounting for the percentage for North Dakota, though. Although expressing concern that the "fragile expansion" of the boom could quickly reverse itself, the author mentions analyses that acknowledged the unsustainability of the boom, but adds that, "I know this view will be controversial—it is the lifeblood of this region and responsible for the economic resurrection that has taken place thus far."[18] This sentiment expresses the essence of the hegemonic narrative. Because oil was bringing growth and modernity to the region, those who expressed doubt were in danger of being seen as akin to traitors and had to walk a fine line. It is telling that the author ends the text by regretting not being able to get any interviews on the issue, "as nobody wanted to go on record." The boom was over within a year.

The main messaging focused on overcoming challenges toward a great future. A short piece from 2011 by Ron Ness, president of the North Dakota Petroleum Council, can serve as an example. This was, in fact, a version of an almost ubiquitous narrative in North Dakota during the boom years, repeated in speech after speech, editorial after editorial, interview after interview. In the Bakken, Ness wrote and others said, "we encounter some unfortunate, but not unexpected

16 Orlowski 2011
17 Merry 2011
18 Arias 2014

growing pains." The national spotlight was "shining brightly on our state" for low unemployment, business opportunities, wealth creation, and infrastructure developments, but communities could not keep pace. Therefore, "appropriate investments to sustain the growth" had to be taken, so that "the stars will soon shine brighter."[19] This allegory was unwillingly ironic, as the oil boom development and the flaring of gas at the wells created so much light pollution that the stars were, in reality, no longer visible in western North Dakota. The narrative, however, was powerful, as those who knew the region were few and without voice, while those interested in its resources were many and influential.

In the same issue of *Bakken Breakout* as Ness' piece, Brian Kroshus, the publisher of the *Bismarck Tribune*, also made the case for the boom. The State, he wrote, "is prospering mightily," and the oil reserves calculated at the time would be sure to change upwards "as more efficient extraction methods are developed to meet the geology of the formation." He admitted that "the actual use or consumption of fossil fuels isn't a perfect proposition," but "societal desires for amenities" necessitate it. In fact, he wrote, "oil and gas companies along with their brethren in the coal industry typically lead the charge in keeping it clean," proactively reducing environmental impacts. He assured readers that the industry had "a flawless record in terms of groundwater contamination, or lack thereof, since hydraulic fracturing came into play in the 1940s," so that EPA regulations were political theatrics stemming from the agency's "lack of enthusiasm for the energy industry." In short, he wrote, "we're likely far from the end" of the boom, and it was "entirely possible that there really isn't [an end] for this ever changing story, only more history in the making."[20] It is not a far stretch from Kroshus' text to the assertion, quoted earlier, that the EPA is a terrorist organization. In contrast to that sentiment, as I will show there are many people then and now who, for good reason, would strenuously object to the assertion that hydraulic fracturing has never contaminated any groundwater. By sidelining environmental concerns as political theatrics and simultaneously putting public trust for self-regulation into the industry, however, objections were delegated to politically motivated naysayers. In order to work toward

19 Ness 2011
20 Kroshus 2011

the culmination of the boom—or toward making the boom sustainable—the state had to trust the industry, communities had to make the investments needed for the industry, and interference had to be precluded.

The industry sent the same message as the state and the media. Don Eberhart, CEO of Frontier Energy Group, for example, assured readers that "we're invested in the local communities in which our employees live and work." The roles of these communities were clear: "The communities will provide housing, entertainment, and good resources—all of those things are really important to what Frontier is."[21] Companies in return provided public help to communities. The North Dakota Petroleum Council's Oil Can! Program, for example, established the Pick up the Patch! Program, under which companies adopted highways to clean up the trash, included the message in employee trainings and in daily briefings, and scheduled cleanup days in communities. Unfortunately, while efforts by volunteers were organized, not many people listened; human waste, tires, and other trash lined the roads. In April 2012, over one hundred volunteers cleaned fifteen miles of road around Watford City, filling a hundred garbage bags per mile and hauling away three truckloads of tires. Three days later, the trash was back.[22]

Companies sponsored town halls, concerts, and other events. One of the mainstays in these efforts were yearly Bakken Rocks CookFests. These events were large, community-wide barbeques. For example, in 2013, two CookFests were held, one in Crosby and one in Watford City. Crosby saw eight company-sponsored BBQ teams, and Watford City saw sixteen teams compete for the "Best Oilfield BBQ Experience." With the barbecue came informational stands from the industry and educational sessions on safety, drilling, regulation, and impacts. In addition to community events, donations, and volunteering efforts, and in addition to efforts to establish the media narrative, outreach efforts included attempts to bring an industry-friendly message to the educational system as early as possible. As one part of this effort, currciula were developed for schools, and teacher seminars offered on these curricula. These efforts, in other words, often organized not by the industry directly but by the North Dakota Petroleum Council, served to project the industry as good neighbors and trustworthy

21 Schettler 2011
22 Cashman 2012

collaborators. In a state like North Dakota, outreach efforts are usually welcomed, and in the absence of consistent alternative narratives in the media, the messaging worked for many people.

## Resistance

The first really powerful challenge to this messaging in North Dakota came in 2016, when protesters gathered on and off the Standing Rock Sioux Reservation in southern North Dakota to try and prevent the completion of the Dakota Access Pipeline. This was a follow-up from earlier efforts against the Keystone XL pipeline, but it was the first time that North Dakota had seen massive expression of public opposition to the extraction and its consequences. An editorial in *The Bakken* reacted as follows:

> Activities and outreach efforts by several industry groups have already done so much for the Bakken and created, for the most part, a state well-educated, well-versed and in favor of the amazing impact of the Bakken, and, on a larger scale, unconventional oil development and the efforts necessary to make it happen. However, even with so much accomplished, more needs to be done. [...] In a time when information—true or not—is available and updated by the minute, providing constant, accurate and important information is no longer an option, it is a must. Tell your story, or let someone else tell it for you.[23]

That several thousand protesters would gather in North Dakota shocked the State and the industry. Rob Lindberg, who led the Bakken Backers, a coalition of industry and state leaders in support of the oil development, thought that the protesters were organized by organizations with an anti-industry agenda that was hard to find in North Dakota because of the consistent educational efforts. While the oil industry "tend to just want to go and get the job done without a lot of fanfare," these organizations had "professional operations to put misinformation out and create their own stories." Kathy Neset, president of a consulting firm in Tioga and chair of the State Board of Higher Education, thought that the Oil Can! campaign and groups like the Bakken Backers had succeeded because of their "effort to reach out to

23 Geiver 2016

communities, teach people and hold forums and town halls and such." She felt that while the messaging in North Dakota was successful, in the national context, there were too many voices with alternative narratives. The industry had to step up: "Nobody knows the story better than we do. We are the ones who live it, eat it, and breathe it. No one person can do this. It has to be a united effort."[24]

These responses clearly demonstrate several issues at play. First is the effort to include all local people in the effort. This re-emphasized that no one could step out of line. Second, they show that there was a systemic intermingling of political leadership, industry, and opinion makers that resulted in a consistent, concentrated, and ultimately successful messaging to the public. This narrative connected to existing narratives about national security and environmental concerns as largely unfounded and anti-state as well as anti-industry. It was further supported by the political demands to the education system to support this narrative. Because North Dakota as a society worked largely on an informal basis, such demands were also informal, although the message was clear to everybody. People working for the State, its agencies, or for industry began to self-comply; after all, it was oil money that paid for their jobs, they were told. It was this creation of a hegemonic message that left two groups to raise concerns: farmers and ranchers and Native people. Yet, because both groups had nowhere near the supposed expertise or prestige the State and the industry held, and had nothing close to those entities' power, their voices could not compete.

One of the concerns around the Dakota Access protests was that the message from the protesters might spread into North Dakota. These concerns were justified; almost all successful campaigns against energy development on the Plains have seen coalitions of Native people and ranchers. This has been true for the resistance against coal development around the Northern Cheyenne reservation in Montana, for example, or for the movement against the Keystone XL pipeline. Lindberg, the Bakken Backers leader, pointed to another factor with the Dakota Access protests. "The situation of different governments at this pipeline site [...] really has allowed the whole action to happen. You have a tribal government, the federal government [...] and then you have private land surrounding it all that's largely governed by the county and the state."[25] The State—and, by implication, the alliances

24 Miller 2016
25 Miller 2016:17

with industry—in other words, was no longer solely in control of the territory. If the existence of different governments allows protests to happen, it is because opinion can no longer be controlled by one government entity.

## Consultation and sovereignty

The triangular concept of state, industry, and community is often more complex because the state divides into state or provincial and federal governments. These entities often do not have the same priorities. On the northern Plains, an important fourth or fifth actor is present: indigenous nations have tribal governments, and while industry as well as federal and state or provincial governments often assume that tribal governments are simply communities, they are not. They are sovereign nations with communities. Internally, these communities might have different interests from their national government just as is the case in states or on a federal level. Externally, however, indigenous nations control territories and resources, regulating the extraction of oil and gas differently from the states surrounding them.

Over the past few decades, the extraction industry has developed standards of working with indigenous communities. These efforts have developed what is known as Free, Prior, and Informed Consent (FPIC) policies. Many international agencies and finance corporations now require the industry to adhere in some form to this concept.[26] These standards were mostly arrived at through public relations pressures. Direct and indirect resistance against mining and oil operations are social risks that can negatively impact extraction companies. Over recent years, just as more attention has been shifted to community investment, companies have noticed that "it is in the financial interest of project sponsors and their financial backers to ensure that local communities have certain rights to provide or withhold their consent."[27] Business for Social Responsibility (BSR), a global business consulting firm, remarks that without FPIC, "opposition by indigenous peoples may result in a *de facto veto*" that would damage the company's reputation and protract project development.[28]

There are, of course, also attempts to create a legal framework for requiring consultations with indigenous peoples. The International

26 IPIECA 2011:8-10
27 Herz, La Vina, and Sohn 2007:1
28 BSR 2012:15

Labor Organization (ILO) Convention 169 from 1989 and the UN Declaration on the Rights of Indigenous Peoples (UNDRIP) from 2007 are at the forefront of these efforts. In the context of the northern Plains, neither the United States nor Canada have ratified ILO 169. Both countries also voted against UNDRIP. Canada passed Bill C-15 in 2021, which brought Canadian law into alignment with the declaration. In the United States, then President Obama announced in 2010 that the country would lend its support to UNDRIP, while making clear that the declaration had no legally binding character, but was a moral, aspirational document. Several presidential memoranda require federal agencies to regularly consult with tribes on federal policies that might impact Native peoples. How and whether these consultations are actually conducted, however, depends on political parties in charge and on the individual agencies.

It is worth emphasizing that there are no guidelines on consultations or FPIC processes with local communities that are not officially indigenous. The fact that states have defined who is indigenous often also leads to assumptions that other local communities are not seen to have relations with the land that would be worthy of protection. The FPIC process usually follows a political acknowledgment of communities deserving some form of protection. FPIC is thus an exceptional process, not the normal model for how to engage communities.

While indigenous nations are sovereign and have specific rights regarding their lands and their governments, consultations with indigenous peoples on extraction projects in so-called settler states (especially the United States, Canada, Australia, and New Zealand) are often seen in the context of public relations and social risks. Legal frameworks holding extraction industry to the task of respecting indigenous sovereign nations are usually weak. It is often up to indigenous nations themselves to defend their rights against an extraction industry that mostly works in agreement with the federal and state governments. Those government agencies in charge of protecting the cultural rights of indigenous peoples often try to convince the industry to respect them through a business argument. One example is a publication by Australia's Department of Industry Tourism and Resources that "provides guidance for resource developers on how to work effectively with Indigenous communities." It then identifies three goals, the first of which is to "identify key issues affecting sustainable development in the mining industry."[29] In this and other documents it is clear that consultations, FPIC efforts, community investment, and other projects are primarily aimed at reducing social risk for companies, pointing toward ways in which these companies can best deploy corporate social responsibility efforts, not to establish and enforce firm regulations on how companies can and must operate in indigenous communities.

Similarly, the Australian Ministerial Council for Mineral and Petroleum Resources (MCMPR) crafted a vision in 2003 that mentioned sustainability, competitiveness, and indigenous relations as three key components. "The industry's social credentials are as important as its economic and technical ones," said the chair of the meeting. The vision aimed at having Australia "recognised as a world-class location for mineral and petroleum exploration and development, with a competitive resources industry valued for its contribution to the sustainable development of the nation, and the world" by 2025. Such a recognition would come from, among other things, a "high level of community engagement and community appreciation of the industry's contribution to a sustainable future."[30] The goal of community investment is obviously to gain the community appreciation, while the sustainability mentioned several times is the sustainability of the industry, of economic development, and of modernity. With the government extremely interested in supporting mineral and oil extraction, its appeals to the industry to respect indigenous rights, cultures, and concerns amount to not much more than a moral reminder. It is not surprising, then, that a 2018 report on hydraulic fracturing in the Northern Territory, for example, found that "there has been a gross absence of FPIC in the process of issuing petroleum exploration permits in Northern Territory."[31]

There are energy industry standards that include versions of FPIC protocols. The Initiative for Responsible Mining Assurance (IRMA), for example, emphasizes the necessity for full FPIC rights and the

29 Commonwealth of Australia 2007:1; see also Commonwealth of Australia (2006).

30 Government of Western Australia 2003; MCMPR 2005

31 Jumbunna n.d.:5; I am working from Australian documents here because Australia at least takes the FPIC process seriously enough to publish guidelines. Even if they amount to mostly moral guidelines, the publications make the moral stance of the government explicit.

obligation for mining companies to adhere to human rights standards.[32] Most mining companies by now also have their own commitments. For example, one of the largest mining companies in the world, Rio Tinto, has a commitment to protecting cultural heritage. "Wherever we can, we avoid disturbing cultural heritage sites," the company states. "Where we have to disturb land, we consult with those for whom the cultural heritage site has significance. We work with them to preserve its value—for example by relocating artefacts—and we make sure we rehabilitate the land the right way afterwards."[33] While this reads really well, there are two central questions in all these commitments, including the oil and gas extraction industry: when does a company "have to" disturb lands, and what does "consultation" mean? In the North American context, Rio Tinto, together with BHP Billiton, for example, has plans to develop a mine in Arizona that would destroy an Apache sacred site, Oak Flat and Apache Leap. As of January 2025, Apache Stronghold, the main group resisting the mine, has launched a last effort to stop the destruction in form of an appeal to the Supreme Court.

That example also shows the collaboration of industry and government. The mine is only possible through a land swap with the federal government because the site is on National Forest land. The companies lobbied Congress, which agreed to a swap, and the first Trump administration relaxed the requirements for environmental impacts. The reasons for this agreement, and the rhetoric of development aimed at communities become obvious in remarks by then Commerce Secretary Wilbur Ross in 2020:

> It is great to be here with all of you, at one of the largest untapped copper deposits in the world. And my thanks to Mayor Mila Besich for joining us this morning. Your work has been instrumental to ensuring your community's prosperity over the next 60 years of this future mine's expected copper supply. A warm welcome also to the members of the White Mountain Apache Tribe and the United Steel Workers. I look forward to hearing your feedback during our discussion today as you work together with community leaders to move this project forward and provide

32 IRMA 2018
33 Rio Tinto 2021

> jobs for your communities. [...] The U.S. has a special appreciation for global enterprises like Rio Tinto [...]. I well remember when [you] met with me in 2017 and explained the 10-year challenge you already had endured as you sought the permits to enable you to make this huge investment. That was one of the major reasons why President Trump moved so aggressively to reduce the red tape involved in such projects.[34]

These comments obviously mirror the tenor of the rhetoric deployed around the Bakken boom in North Dakota, and can largely applied to extractivism in general. The government needs investments by private companies. Communities need jobs. Tribes, who might object to the destruction of sacred sites, are reduced to working with communities in economic endeavors. The time frame for success is the lifespan of the project, not the life expectancy of the community. What will happen after the community's prosperity will be ensured for the next sixty years is not addressed, and prosperity is clearly defined as economic prosperity: the availability of wage paying jobs.

While many of the discussions about collaboration with indigenous peoples focus on mining, the oil and gas industry has its own industrial standard, EO100, developed by Equitable Origin. The standard requires the industry to conduct "meaningful community engagement and consultation" about risks, to conduct a "human rights impact assessment," and to identify community concerns and to respond to them. Free, prior, and informed consent is required from indigenous peoples for storage or disposal of hazardous materials, transport and injection of wastewater, and the extraction of water.[35] There is no FPIC required for extraction sites or operation. The guidelines for community engagement by the American Petroleum Institute similarly do not ask for FPIC.[36] During the study of a potential location and initial lease acquisition, it is suggested that informational packets are distributed "that inform stakeholders about potential impending operational activities." During exploratory operations, companies should conduct meetings with landowners and other stakeholders on traffic concerns and to introduce key personnel; they should also engage "with elected officials, local authorities, regulatory agencies, commissioners,

34 Ross 2020
35 Equitable Origin 2020
36 ANSI/API 2014

and other key government stakeholders to confirm understanding of respective rights, where appropriate." Community investment, collaboration with local agencies, and 'good neighbor' policies are suggested for the lifespan of the project, but while the community would be engaged and consulted, it has no right of consent.

Free, prior, and informed consent is usually brought to the forefront in the context of indigenous peoples in the global south. This is especially true for places in which indigenous peoples might hold or claim traditional territories but do not have formally established land rights over them. Crown lands in Canada and Australia might fall under this category. In essence, FPIC processes resemble those of treaty negotiations, with some of the same goals. First is a clear legal assessment to land ownership or resource claims:

> The lack of clear indigenous legal title to land and the dearth of written records of land usage and its cultural significance creates additional challenges for companies that seek community agreement based on the principles of FPIC. The use of experts who are trained to understand indigenous cultures and map their land use will facilitate the process significantly. When groups disagree about who has traditionally used the land, and available evidence does not help solve the quandary, the company may best manage this risk by requiring the indigenous groups to resolve it themselves as a precondition to entering into negotiations with the company.[37]

In part because land ownership is already largely settled in the United States, FPIC processes are usually not applied here. The United States does not accord Native peoples the same rights on federal lands as Canada or Australia do on Crown lands. FPIC in the United States exists only in the much-weakened version of consultations with federal agencies and through cultural resource management regulations such as the National Historic Preservation Act. Most of these protections fall to the wayside when the activity takes place on private lands. The permission of the landowner, in many places, makes it impossible for the community to prohibit extraction activities. This, of course, is a

37 Lehr and Smith 2010:27

direct consequence of American property rights, the commodification of land, and the fragmentation of landscapes into distinct parcels discussed previously.

## Fort Berthold

Where consent from indigenous peoples is needed, however, is where they control resources and territories directly. In the United States and Canada, this is the case mostly on American Indian reservations and First Nations reserves.[38] As sovereign nations, but unilaterally declared under the protection of the federal governments, these territories follow federal law, but not state law. Entities which engage in business with a reservation government—a tribe—accept this sovereignty and also accept to some extent the tribe's jurisdiction. From the perspective of companies, this often creates heightened social, legal, and political risks. This was one reason why the Fort Berthold Indian Reservation did not immediately see oil development on its territory when the Bakken boom started.

When the boom began, the Three Affiliated Tribes of the Fort Berthold Reservation had a new chairman. Marcus Levings had beaten the politically very experienced Tex Hall, who had also served as president of the National Congress of American Indians for two election periods. The oil industry was reluctant to work on the reservation because of concerns over sovereignty and taxes. Only one well was completed on Fort Berthold between 1988 and 2008. The regulation of oil on Indian lands is indeed cumbersome when compared with lands within states; because Native trust lands are held in trust by the federal government, federal agencies regulate extraction. This also means reviews to federal standards. While states can alleviate the regulatory burden on non-federal lands, they cannot do so on American Indian lands. They also cannot speed things along. On Fort Berthold, oil leases went from zero to over 2,500 in only a few months in 2007. Yet, there was only one agent in the Bureau of Indian Affairs (BIA) to oversee all the leases. The federal government was absolutely overwhelmed. Federal reviews of oil leases on Indian land also take longer

38 For the purposes of this text, I will not get into a detailed discussion of sovereignty over off-reservation trust lands, but presume them under reservation status.

because the BIA is responsible to collect lease moneys and distribute them to mineral rights owners. By 2008, the situation was improved through the creation of new structures for lease approval.

A more stringent regulatory environment with a land bureaucracy under the federal government was one hurdle for companies. The other was a potentially very different tax environment. Because tribes are sovereign, they have the right to impose taxes. However, on Fort Berthold, both the State and the tribal government claimed the right to tax oil production on trust land, and the State claimed exclusive rights to tax production on private fee lands on the reservation. Companies balked at potentially being taxed twice and at walking into a situation where tax disputes between Tribe and State might have to be resolved in federal courts. Yet, both the State and the tribal government wanted to encourage production, and companies were pushing for a solution. In this situation, the State and the Tribe negotiated a regulatory and tax agreement, which went into effect on July 1, 2008. In the next eighteen months, 120 new wells were completed on fee lands on the reservation, and forty on trust lands.[39] The agreement specified that tax revenues from trust lands would be evenly divided between the State and the Tribe, while the State would keep eighty percent of the tax revenue from fee lands on the reservation. Trust lands carried a uniform production tax rate of 5% and an oil extraction tax rate of 6.5%, while non-trust lands carried the same production rate but no extraction rate. The Tribe obliged itself to not charge any other taxes or fees on production, but could charge two fees for wells on trust lands: a $60,000 fee for the Tribal Employment Rights Office (TERO) and a $40,000 Tribal Application Fee.

The tax agreement jump-started oil development on Fort Berthold. Until December 2009, the State received $13.3 million, while the Tribe collected $4.9 million in taxes from the agreement. Chairman Levings, pointing to the increased activity, said, "I think it speaks for itself," and promised the money would go toward tribal roads, health care, and law enforcement. Governor Hoeven argued that the agreement was beneficial to both parties. "We share revenue, we share jobs and we share economic activity," he said.[40] This perspective from the State ignored the fact that although the two parties shared a market and a boom, the Three Affiliated Tribes are sovereign, and do not share

39 North Dakota Legislative Council 2010
40 MacPherson 2010

their national economy with the State of North Dakota. From the perspective of many tribal members, the agreement represented a partial surrender of sovereignty to the State.

In 2010, Tex Hall was re-elected as tribal chairman; he also became president of the Fort Berthold Allottee Land & Mineral Owner's Association. The two functions could be seen as representing a conflict of interest, as the Tribe and the individual mineral rights owners were often in conflict over mineral rights. This was the case, for example, as mentioned under Lake Sakakawea. Being in both positions consolidated Hall's power. Hall immediately critiqued the tax agreement. In 2012, for example, he gave testimony before the Subcommittee on Indian and Alaska Native Affairs in Congress. "Of all of the challenges," he said, "the biggest issue we face is the inequitable division of tax revenues with the state. Under current law, states can tax energy companies on Reservation lands. Because of these state taxes, we cannot raise enough of our own tax revenue to provide the infrastructure needed to support and regulate the growing energy industry." The reservation, he contended, was "forced into a lopsided tax agreement with the State."[41] The state law specified that the revenues from the reservation taxes would be divided between state, county, and local governments. This meant that these revenues from the trust lands would not be flowing back to the reservation. Hall pointed out that in 2011, the State raised over $60 million from reservation taxes, but spent less than $2 million on the upkeep of state and county roads within reservation boundaries.

The tax agreement was amended several times over the next years, but it was still causing problems between the State and the Tribe in 2021. By then, the total combined tax revenue for State and Tribe since 2008 amounted to $3.5 billion. One of the stumbling stones was how off-reservation wells that extend lateral lines under tribal lands were taxed. When the Biden administration halted new drilling on federal lands, the Three Affiliated tribes received an exemption. The State then approached the Tribe and offered a deal. If the Tribe would get an exemption for federal lands off the reservation that could only be accessed from tribal lands, the State would agree to amend the agreement so that the off-reservation wells reaching under the reservation would count as reservation wells. When the state legislature

41 Hall 2012

put new requirements on the deal, however, chairman Mark Fox, who was the tribal tax director under Tex Hall, withdrew his support. He threatened instead to levy a tribal tax on the wells.

One state legislator showed the difficulty of negotiations when the state does not understand or does not accept tribal sovereignty. Reminiscent of former governor Hoeven's one-economy comment, he said of the Tribe, "They're also citizens of the State of North Dakota" and should be trying to help the State out anyway.[42] In general, the energy industry has a long history of opposing tribal sovereignty. One example is the foundation of One Nation in 2002, "a privately funded organization, the first and only advocacy-focused effort in Oklahoma and the U.S. created to 'push back' against the massive expansion of tribal authority and the various disruptions and inequities created by sovereignty-based policies," according to its then website. The two co-founders of the organization both worked for Harold Hamm, owner of Continental Resources, and a few years later most famous developer of the Bakken boom.[43]

## Political economies

In 2008, a report from Headwaters Economics, an independent economics research group in Montana, warned that United States counties focused on energy extraction saw slower economic growth than other counties in the long term.[44] These findings match the "resource curse" in countries around the world: countries rich in natural resources, and with economies dependent on their extraction, have seen less economic growth than others.[45]

The global oil industry has been trying to posit itself as a driver of sustainable economic growth. For example, a 2002 report from Ipieca (formerly the International Petroleum Industry Environmental Conservation Association) and the International Association of Oil and Gas Producers (OGP) held that the industry's aim "is to provide safe, accessible and economically viable fuels that are essential to economic growth, environmental protection and social progress."[46] The beginning axiom for the industry, globally and in the Bakken, is this:

42 Willis 2021
43 Brown 2021
44 Headwaters Economics 2008
45 See, for example, Sachs and Warner (2001).
46 IPIECA and OGP 2002:5-7

> It is impossible to overestimate the social and economic impact of the global oil and gas industry. For example, recent World Bank figures show annual oil and gas incomes of around $35 billion for Mexico, $30 billion for Venezuela and $22 billion for Nigeria. Such incomes bestow enormous potential for good—and equally immense temptations for abuse.[47]

In light of this statement, it is interesting that Sachs and Warner, commonly seen as early proponents of the resource curse concept, directly contradict the implications of this statement. They write that "Nigeria, or Mexico and Venezuela, have not experienced sustained rapid economic growth."[48] In other words, nobody denies that large amounts of money from oil developments flow into economies. The question is whether these monies can offset the expenses necessitated for and created by the development. Counting the money flowing in without taking a look at the costs and whether or not the money coming in is used to cover the costs, is equivalent to a rather cheap magic trick. It is a trick that we have become used to—the social and ecological costs of globalization are often ignored in favor of focusing on cheap consumer prices—but it is but a trick, anyway. I will return to this at the end of this text. A 2015 study of economic impacts of the recent oil and gas booms on counties and municipal governments across the United States found mixed results. Overall, though, it saw negative impacts on Montana and North Dakota counties' and municipalities' finances. The same held true for local governments in western Colorado and Wyoming during the heights of the booms.[49]

As should be expected, economists have come to point toward institutional quality as a determinant for success, rather than resource abundance or resource dependency. This follows in general the concept that economic success is tied to the modernization and democratization of institutions and economic failure (especially under conditions of resource abundance) is tied to corruption and nepotism. Extractivism as a political-economic system is not to blame, in other words; rather, bad actors hijack the potential for economic success. Oil extraction does "bestow enormous potential for good," but only if individuals'

47 IPIECA and OGP 2002:7
48 Sachs and Warner 2001:828
49 Newell and Raimi 2015

"temptations for abuse"[50] are held in check by modern institutions. If this is true, "suggestions that countries [and states or provinces] should turn their back on resource wealth to lower resource dependence and not jeopardize economic growth may have to be reconsidered."[51] As long as institutions hold temptations in check, the theory goes, oil creates wealth, and whether or not they do is an internal political issue; the industry provides opportunities.

Under this theory, the question is not resource dependency, but good institutions. In North Dakota, the State developed an intricate system to distribute oil revenues to counties and communities across the state. While there were objections, it seemed that most counties felt that this system was fair. However, it also gave the State the opportunity to point to the revenues flowing into the local governments, shifting responsibilities for infrastructure costs, and blaming inefficiencies or incompetence as the reasons why counties and towns might still have seen net negative financial outcomes. Some literature points to the potential that "countries with better developed institutions [...] have economies that are less biased towards lower-growth sectors (such as natural resource extraction and export) irrespective of their relative resource abundance."[52] Tying institutional quality back to resource dependency raises the question whether resource dependency itself could be seen as a sign of worse institutional quality. This would put resource dependency back into the primary spotlight for economic woes. It is true that a concentration of political and economic power is associated with resource curse states, which also see a blurring of the public and private (and of state and business), as well as a dominant strategy of seeking resource rents as a wealth creation strategy.[53]

A main issue in squandering oil resource wealth is policy design. The more power is concentrated within a smaller circle of people—for example, presidential or majoritarian systems compared to parliamentary or direct democratic systems—the more successful lobbying for special interests is.[54] Resource curses show up more in presidential systems or in non-democratic countries. In these cases, "sectoral lobbying pressure from resource firms is more relevant for policy design than

50 IPIECA and OGP 2002:7

51 Brunnschweiler and Bulte 2008:261

52 Brunnschweiler and Bulte 2008:258, fn 21

53 Karl 2007:7

54 See, for example, Persson, Roland, and Tabellini (2000).

electoral pressure through geographically defined constituencies."[55] In the Bakken, state and industry worked very closely together to convince the public that the industry could regulate itself, that government interference was not only unnecessary but would be harmful, and that federal agencies and rules were one of the main obstacles to the economic success of the industry, which was equated to the success of the state and of the public. This was also, with some differences, true for tribes.

Both states and tribes were, to some degree, correct, if the only criterion for success was temporary economic expansion. Under the model that governments build infrastructure for industry to use, both states and tribes immediately became dependent on oil rent money—fees, taxes, and royalties—to finance the infrastructure development necessary for the industry to operate. To be fair, those moneys now also financed other projects. That is, they allowed the State and the Tribe to tackle projects they had not addressed or could not address. In 2021, the Three Affiliated Tribes earned up to ninety percent of its revenues from oil fees, taxes, and royalties.[56] The State of North Dakota received around fifty percent of all its taxes from oil production and extraction taxes alone.[57] This money went into the general funds. However, such dependencies create powerful dynamics in which industry agendas can trump local concerns. If a state is dependent on an industry, will it really fine the industry for infractions, will it enact stringent regulations, and will it enforce them? The example of the Bakken boom demonstrates that the answer to all three questions is most probably "No."

I have tried to show how the State worked with the industry. As I mentioned in the beginning, around 2011 the motto for the Tribe became "Sovereignty by the Barrel." Just like the many state leaders, some people in the Tribe also saw the boom as primarily a huge opportunity to better the situation in which they found themselves. Creating sustainable tribal economies is an enormous struggle for most tribes on the northern Plains. Underdeveloped for decades, without critical infrastructure, without final power over their land, and with a federal government that controls every aspect of the political and economic situation, most of these tribes are burdened by massive unemployment, poverty, educational inequity, and the resulting social and health

55 Brunnschweiler and Bulte 2008:250

56 Deaton 2021

57 Western Dakota Energy Association 2021

issues.[58] The prospect of being able to solve some of these issues was as tempting to the Tribe as it was to the State, and as it has been for most cash-poor but resource-rich countries globally.

In the United States, tribes have had an opportunity to expand the practical exercise of sovereignty since the 1970s. As mentioned, the Indian Self-Determination and Education Assistance Act of 1975 and its various amendments provide tribes the opportunity to contract with federal agencies in order to manage themselves the programs these agencies deliver. Over the years, economically successful tribes have improved housing, health care, policing, child welfare, and other programs in this way, while also reclaiming practical sovereignty.[59] While some tribes—most famously those with large, economically successful gaming operations—have resources to put into these programs, others remain largely without such avenues. Finding a resource that promises wealth thus opens doors not only for economic improvement, but also for diminishing the dependence on the federal government, distinguishing the tribe from state government, and thus increasing practical sovereignty. One example I mentioned earlier that realized some of these ambitions early on was the new clinic in New Town.

The shift of administrative responsibility from the federal government to the tribal government comes also, however, with a shift in responsibility and internal and external scrutiny.[60] Tribal governments are held responsible when they have the power to enact policies; they cannot shift the blame for perceived and real failures to the federal government. The tax agreement with the State was one such action that received a lot of scrutiny. Signed by the tribal government, it made the participation by the Tribe in the boom possible. On the other hand, it was seen as giving up sovereignty to the State. The next tribal administration, under Tex Hall, inherited the monetary harvest of the agreement (although Hall sharply criticized it). Now, the scrutiny shifted from the consideration of a balance between sovereignty and wealth to the decisions on how the money was spent.

58 Pickering 2000; Braun 2008

59 All federally recognized tribes are inherently sovereign nations but declared to be dependent on the federal government. Should that political dependence be lifted, they would automatically be fully sovereign nations. In practice, a reduction of economic sovereignty can result in the ability to administer sovereign decisions. See, for example, Delaney (2017).

60 Washburn 2017:224-231

The modern state in the form of liberal democracies—the form of government generally seen as possessing the highest institutional quality—works through transparency. It is often assumed that transparency prevents corruption, while the absence of transparency is often in itself seen as a sign of corruption. Transparency, in resource economies, holds the temptation for abuse of the incoming wealth in check. For example, an excerpt of an International Monetary Fund (IMF) report on Angola, a resource curse country, reads: "[A]n effective policy response is urgently needed to make public finances transparent, strengthen institutions, establish a system of institutional checks and balances, and improve procurement practices."[61]

Tribal governments are often defined by the absence of strong, independent institutions, such as a non-politically controlled court system, of institutional checks and balances, and of transparent public finances. The Hall administration was immediately accused of corruption.[62] Corruption is a term coming from the global imposition of modernity on non-modern societies, and an expression of the critique by rational bureaucracies of "localized notions of kinship, exchange, reciprocity and solidarity."[63] As in many societies brought into modernity by colonialism, industrialization, and capitalism, in many Native societies two parallel moral, political, and economic systems coexist. Traditional society operates on some variety of a patron-client system that obliges those who attain power or wealth to take care of those who helped them achieve. Positions of prestige or power can only be reached with the support of a large, influential, and supportive family. In societies where, in some sense, "corruption" or "nepotism" is normal, however, bringing up corruption still serves a purpose: it "constitutes a profound critique of social hierarchies and power."[64] In that sense, wealth creation without reciprocity to supporters is corruption in a patron-client system.

## Sovereignty by the Barrel

Upon reelection in 2010, Tex Hall, as mentioned before, led both the Tribe and the allottee association. He also kept control of Maheshu Energy, a company he had founded in 2007, which seemingly covered

61 In Hodges (2004):121.
62 See, for example, a summary in Todrys (2021):32-36.
63 Stronen 2017:284
64 Stronen 2017:285

every aspect of the oil business. Companies with tribal member ownership were very important on Fort Berthold because of Tribal Employment Rights Office (TERO) regulations. The tribal TERO ordinance reads:

> [All private employers subject to the Nation's jurisdiction] for all employment that is subject to the jurisdiction of the Nation, shall give preference to qualified Indians, with the first preference to local Indians, in all hiring, promotion, training, lay-offs, and all other aspects of employment.

In addition, "No Covered Employer shall employ a non-local Indian or a non-Indian without first providing the TERO with no less than 72 hours to locate and refer a qualified local Indian," and "All Covered Employers shall comply with the goals and timetables established by the TERO specifying the minimum number or percentage of Indians a Covered Employer must hire, by craft or skill level."[65] On contracts or subcontracts in relation to oil production, exploration, or services related, contractors who "are 100% owned and controlled by enrolled members of the Three Affiliated Tribes" have preference.[66] The TERO keeps a list of certified firms and contractors; tribal members and their companies can thus apply to become certified to get preference for work on the reservation:

> Every Covered Employer engaged in any business activity within the exterior boundaries of the MHA Nation, including, but not limited to, construction, minerals development, supplies, and service shall give Preference to firms and services certified by TERO in any contract or subcontract to be performed on the Reservation, so long as there are Certified Firms that are technically qualified and willing to perform the work at a reasonable price.

To make sure that tribal members would be qualified, especially over time, the TERO regulations requested that employers have training programs "to assist Indians in becoming qualified in the various job classifications used by the employer." When the economy contracted, no "Local Indian worker shall be terminated so long as a non-local

65 MHA TERO Ordinance
66 MHA TERO Regulations

Indian or non-Indian worker in the same craft is still employed." Working on the reservation thus required working with tribal companies and hiring tribal members. Almost guaranteed contracts, many tribal members founded companies related to the oil industry.

However, a company wholly owned by a tribal member had preference even if the company did not employ any local tribal members, and there was the possibility of having an outside company fronted by a tribal member to receive preference. The existence or rumored existence of such practices as well as the non-transparency of the TERO process created a lot of frustration, suspicions, and lawsuits. At least two members of the tribal council were indicted in federal court for accepting bribes and kickbacks to help contractors gain business on the reservation.[67] If a person controlled the TERO and had a company that provided all those services, they, of course, had the best position to benefit. Rumors and accusation of corruption finally resulted in a New York Times article that reported on murders associated with the oil boom and, indirectly, Tex Hall.[68]

While these processes remained largely unexplored, however, possibly the largest symbol of corruption and excessive spending without real plans was not even the helicopter the Tribe bought to access Minot airport more quickly. It was the yacht the Tribe acquired for pleasure cruises on Lake Sakakawea. The Tribe had no captain for the boat, and it mostly sat on land right by the casino at the Four Bears Bridge across the lake from New Town. Temptingly named *Island Girl*, it very quickly was called *Textanic* by locals.

Nontransparent business practices, regulative processes, and political deals aside, the Tribe did work toward more practical sovereignty. The TERO regulations and the new clinic were two examples; the idea to diversify into tourism, as with the *Textanic*, was another. The concept here was to take the money from the oil and invest it into projects that would turn an extraction economy into a service economy. Adding value to the oil before it left the reservation would also have increased the economic position of the Tribe. The proposed solution for this was a plan to build a tribal refinery. The planning for the refinery predated the boom. It was supported by a BIA grant in 2002.[69] The final Environmental Impact Statement for the project was granted in 2009, and

67 DOJ 2020
68 Sontag and McDonald 2014
69 BIA 2002

in 2012, the Department of the Interior approved a land-into-trust application to build the refinery on the northeastern corner of the reservation, near Makoti. A groundbreaking ceremony was held in 2013. However, when the boom slowed down decisively in 2015, neighboring refineries had to drop production, and the new tribal administration under Mark Fox no longer pushed the project forward very quickly. In 2016, the plan was to complete some oil storage components. The refinery was not built.

The push for oil development by the Tribe was a gamble to leverage the money from the oil to increase sovereignty in order to save the homelands without destroying them in the process.[70] For many tribes on the northern Plains, economic and political sovereignty has to take precedence over conservation. The idea is to first assure independence and then redirect efforts to the environment and culture.[71] In his remarks at an oil meeting in New Town, the environmental resources chairman of the Crow Nation mentioned how he drove to town the night before. Seeing all the flares burning off the gas from the oil wells made him happy, he said: "No more are you gonna have to beg and borrow." For many tribal leaders, the responsibility to take care of the people economically had to take precedent over other responsibilities. The problem is whether the achievement of political and economic sovereignty on the conditions of modern extraction capitalism will not already destroy traditional environments and cultures.

## Differences

Overall, the income from the oil development allowed the State and the Tribe to make investments into infrastructure, education, health care, and other projects that are commonly seen as quality-of-life indexes. On the other hand, the oil development necessitated these investments. Modernity demands what is called progress; often, those who advocate for progress as a necessity do not take into account that perhaps people are better off without it. In the case of the Bakken, both in the State and the Tribe, the overarching question might not be whether the State or the Tribe achieve their goals, one of modernity, the other of sovereignty, but whether the communities can bear the burden placed on them in the process.

70 See, for example, Todrys (2021):220-221.

71 See Braun (2008).

In order to achieve their goals, the State, the Tribe, and the industry had to contend with one other actor, with yet a different agenda: the federal government. Federal agencies were seen by all three as imposing regulations that impeded their achievements. The State opposed federal regulations on air and water pollution, the Tribe opposed the bureaucracies of the BIA and other agencies controlling trust lands and mineral rights. In the political rhetoric of the Obama administration era, the federal government was seen as squarely opposed to extraction, and was therefore perceived by some as standing in the way of progress—alternatively, it was perceived as championing the conservation of the environment and the rights of people against the destruction of the landscape.

"Who's in power," Katherine Todrys writes in referencing Barack Obama, "makes a difference."[72] She refers to differential decisions by the Obama and Trump administration about the Dakota Access Pipeline; one could also mention the differences between the Obama, Trump, and Biden administration on the Keystone XL pipeline, or on opening the Alaska National Wildlife Refuge to oil development, or on Bears Ears National Monument, and so on. However, thinking back to my experiences in the Bakken, I wonder if these are not the perceptions of larger philosophical differences rather than actual practice. It seems that federal oil and gas policies have a lot in common with federal Indian policies: while the rhetoric differs from administration to administration, neither one changes too much in practice. In the context of free, prior, and informed consent or land rights, or the rights to preserve sacred landscapes, one could think of the United Nations Declaration on the Rights of Indigenous Peoples (UNDRIP). While the Obama administration adopted it as a moral, aspirational guideline, the difference between that and the outright rejection by the previous Bush administration are hard to determine in practice. In similar ways, the aspiration by some administrations to curb fossil fuel extraction is not the same as ending it.

At a tribal oil conference in 2012, the representative from the Office of Indian Energy Policy presented the administration's perspective. She emphasized that the top priority was energy security, and that clean energy for then President Obama included "clean gas" and "clean coal." She also remarked that some people were talking about "peak oil"—the idea that oil will at some point run out. However, she said,

72 Todrys 2021:7

to the applause of the audience, peak oil was a myth, and the Bakken was here to prove it. There was always more oil to be found, and with new technology it would be extracted. There was not much difference between that statement, made in the name of the president, and the chants of "Drill, Baby, Drill" at the rallies of his opponent in that year's election.

There are differences in policies between federal administrations. The question is whether or not they are different enough to positively affect the lives of people in communities.

# Chapter 6
# **Water**

"*Mni Wiconi*—Water is Life"
Standing Rock
Water Protectors

In the summer of 2015, I knew the boom was over. Earlier that year, I had been in Dickinson, where, outside of the city, about twenty drilling rigs sat idle in a large lot, waiting for better times again. The reduction in drilling all over the Bakken was a sure indicator for the end of the boom's first phase, but I really knew when I got gas at the new travel plaza in New Town. The attendant asked me how I was doing, and I politely asked him the same. "Okay," he said. "It could be worse. I could be out of a job." That notion was unheard of during the boom. It shocked me. At that moment, I knew the boom was done. Development continued, of course, and would not reach its height until 2020 or 2021. But it was clear that this new phase of development, when it would restart, would follow different rules. It would no longer be the overwhelming, chaotic, pulsating boom. The frontier would be controlled by the institutions that had caught up and channeled their energy.

I was on Fort Berthold for two reasons in 2015. The first was to attend the first meeting of Fort Berthold Protectors of Water and Earth Rights (POWER). I ran a demonstration of the GIS website we had developed, which led to great discussions about specific incidents on the landscape. Most of the conversation centered around spills—oil spills and "produced water" spills from pipelines and well sites as well as the illegal dumping of produced water and sewage. The second reason was to say goodbye because I was moving to Iowa. As I was leaving, Theodora Bird Bear mentioned that I would probably be hearing about the Bakken in Iowa, too, as she was hearing that some people on the Meskwaki Settlement were gearing up to oppose the Dakota Access Pipeline. I had never heard of the pipeline. A bit over a year later, I was in Minneapolis at the American Anthropological Association (AAA) meetings, on the panel of an emerging session about "Taking a Stand at Standing Rock."

The focus of attention had shifted from the oil boom itself to the transportation of the oil and its potential impacts on water. Water is life, as one of the slogans of the protesters at Standing Rock said. The larger conversation about oil shifted away from the boom itself to pipelines. In part, this was why leaders of industry and state in North Dakota lost partial control of the narrative, as mentioned previously. The local narrative was overtaken by a global discussion about climate change, access to clean water, and pollution. These discussions were not new in the Bakken. Because of the global attention, though, they now had the potential of finding a voice that could be heard.

These local and global discussions overlapped, but did not really engage each other. As the mostly Native panelists spoke at the 2016 AAA meetings, we tried to disentangle rhetoric from actions, referring back to community needs and agendas on Standing Rock, on Fort Berthold, and on the Crow reservation. Energy, sovereignty, and environmental protection are complicated issues, and so are the wishes and needs of tribal councils, we pointed out while we warned that local voices ran a danger of being ignored by those coming to communities with their minds already made up, not listening to the communities. As we spoke, a donation bucket made the rounds in the audience, for "standing with Standing Rock"—and without explanation as to where the money was going or how it would benefit the Tribe.

During the recurrent, relentless heatwaves in the summer of 2022, I was traveling through western Kansas, Colorado, and Wyoming. Even in the mountains, the old warnings of John Wesley Powell were coming true. Climate change and overuse reduced water to a premium. Reservoirs were two-thirds empty, campgrounds had run out of water, and the follies of building megacities into deserts were becoming glaringly obvious. "The lands have no value without water," Powell had realized in the late nineteenth century. As a solution, he proposed a scheme of careful irrigation and water management.[1] Climate change is now proving to us that such plans are hubris. Powell also warned against the commodification of water. "If the land titles and water rights are severed," he wrote, "the owner of any tract of land is at the mercy of the owner of the water right;" if water was to be commodified, "eventually the monopoly of water rights will be an intolerable burden to the people."[2] Water is life. It is easy to forget this when the

1 Powell 1879
2 Powell 1879:40

water comes out of the faucet. When water has to be carefully fetched, is in short supply, or in danger of running out, the ties are much more obvious.

The record on water management is not good. In the Sacramento Valley, the ground has subsided—sunk—over thirty feet in some places since irrigation started. On the Plains, the Ogallala aquifer is in danger of drying out in some places. In 2005, a report from the Canadian Senate pointed out that "summer flows in many of Alberta's rivers are already down by about 40% when compared to what they were a century ago."[3] The choices between watering lawns or golf courses and having water to drink, between flushing toilets and providing water to crops or livestock are not yet, or not anymore, on the minds of most Americans. For many, though, these choices will be a reality in the near future. What is a reality for many Americans, is that the water that is available to them might or might not be safely drinkable. Bottled water is on one hand a luxury branding business. On the other, however, it is how many people have to consume water. Apart from the dangers that potentially leaking pipelines present to water, hydraulic fracturing is creating dangers for both water supply and also clean water.

For many Americans, access to oil and its refined products is a more important question than access to water, only because access to water is taken for granted. This might be a sign of the times. The bottom line, however, is that oil is a luxury and water a necessity. Even though it is hard to imagine a life without oil for Americans in the twenty-first century, it is possible. Life without water, though, is impossible.

## New water wars

Hydraulic fracturing uses water to fracture the oil- and gas-bearing geological layers, hence its name. How much water is exactly used is a question that is hard to determine from public data. The *Texas Observer* wrote in 2013, after finding that the state estimates for water consumption were about two thirds the actual numbers compiled from data sources, "Getting the numbers right is critical. It's remarkable that journalists and independent scientists are having to do the work that the state government should be doing. It's almost as if they don't want to know."[4] One way to find water consumption for specific wells was

3 Canada Senate 2005:2
4 Wilder 2013

to look them up on fracfocus.org;[5] however, water needs differ widely from well to well, and with hundreds of wells in each county, the data quickly overwhelms an individual.

How much water is used to fracture a well depends on the specific geology and the length of the well. In the Horn River Basin in British Columbia, for example, between 6.5 million and twenty-six million gallons of water are used per well.[6] In the Marcellus Shale gas fields in the eastern United States, between two and nine million gallons of water were used to fracture one well in 2010.[7] According to a calculation from 2014, over its life stage, a gas well in the Marcellus Shale directly consumed between 11,000 $m^3$ (2.9 million gallons) and 13,000 $m^3$ (3.4 million gallons) of water on average.[8] Between 2005 and 2014, more than 2100 Marcellus Shale wells were drilled in West Virginia alone. Using the average numbers, that means 6.7 billion gallons of water were consumed for this purpose in West Virginia during this time. In Colorado, Chesapeake Energy estimated its need per well in the Niobrara formation at over four million gallons of water. For 2011, that would have meant the almost three thousand wells drilled and fractured used around 12.8 billion gallons that year alone.[9]

In 2013, the nonprofit Ceres, which works to inject sustainability into capital markets, delivered an assessment of water use by hydraulic fracturing operations. Analyzing data for over twenty-five thousand wells drilled in 2011 and 2012, it found that about 65.8 billion gallons of water were used to fracture these wells. Forty-one percent of the wells were located in areas with extremely high water stress, especially in Texas, Colorado, Wyoming, and Oklahoma.[10] According to the Ceres data, neither Pennsylvania nor North Dakota showed high or extremely high water stress at the time. Of most concern in terms of numbers of wells in extremely high water stress areas was Texas, although percentage wise, Colorado had ninety-two percent of its wells in extremely high water stress areas during this time.

In Texas, the town of Barnhart literally ran out of water in 2013. There was a drought, farming used a lot of water, but the burgeoning

5 There is a contention that fracfocus underreported water use. See WORC (2013):12-13.
6 Uwiera-Gartner 2013:2
7 Carluccio 2010:28
8 Jiang, Hendrickson, and VanBriesen 2014:1915
9 WORC 2013:29
10 Freyman and Salmon 2013

water market for hydraulic fracturing for sure did not help. While the town went dry, those with private wells continued to sell "fresh water" that was non-potable to the oil companies. "People use their water for food and fibre," one water seller said, "I choose to use my water to sell to the oil field. Who's taking advantage? I don't see any difference."[11] In a 2002 report on the privatization of water by the Pacific Institute, the authors had warned that governments "have a fundamental duty" to deliver basic needs to their people. "The failure to satisfy such basic needs, or at least enable the means for them, must be viewed as irresponsible," they wrote.[12] Their words mirror the old warnings of John Wesley Powell. Commodified water, however, is not only a reality, but also a measurement stick to see what is more important—the development of oil fields or the survival of communities.

It might be ironic, but hopefully understandable in light of what has been mentioned so far, that municipalities, cities, and rural water systems with water allocations sold water to energy companies. In part, because there were no accessible water data to access—neither on water use by the industry nor on water availability or depletion—governing bodies had no real way to assess potential damage to groundwater reservoirs. They could, however, assess the economic benefits of the industry. In places where residents were more alienated from water, potential consequences might also not have been so obvious. The city of Greely in Colorado provided over 580 million gallons of water to energy companies in 2013, for example.[13] Depleting groundwater levels to ensure economic benefits or to ensure the continued existence of communities has been a normal practice in many places that rely on irrigation agriculture in the West. Now, energy use and agriculture came into direct competition over water in many places, and energy companies began to outbid the farmers downstream.

Resistance began to spread in places where people took climate change seriously—several cities in the East, and eventually the state of New York banned hydraulic fracturing, starting with Pittsburgh in 2010—as well as in places where people lived with the land. In 2013, Mora County in northern New Mexico became the first county in the United States to ban hydraulic fracturing. The county was relatively poor, conservative, and energy rich, making it a prime suspect

11 Goldenberg 2013
12 Gleick, Wolff, Chalecki, and Reyes 2002:29
13 WORC 2013:29

for energy development. Conservative, however, meant that people were also interested in conserving their future on their land. Reliant exclusively on well water, their concerns were directly tied to water depletion.

While differences between Mora County commissioners involved in the decision emerged (one voted against the ban, in favor of strict regulation, as other counties had enacted),[14] the overall motivation for the ban seems very clear. John Olivas, in 2013 the chairman of the county commissioners, explained that during the process of trying to regulate extraction, people "began to learn the hard fact that the oil and gas laws were written to elevate the 'rights' of oil and gas companies to access Mora's resources above the rights of residents to stop that drilling."[15] Indeed, after the county enacted the ban, directly challenging "the anti-democratic system of law that we have,"[16] a federal judge ruled that the ban was unconstitutional and violated state laws.[17]

A look at the county's ordinance reveals several important issues for the context of this discussion. The language frames the kind of resistance that extraction states, including North Dakota, became worried about: alternative ideas that would disturb the education delivered to the state residents about the positive impact of oil development. The ordinance is also one example of the developing coordination and collaboration between these alternative voices, as it was crafted with support from the Community Environmental Legal Defense Fund, a Pennsylvania entity working in support of rights of nature and decolonial community rights. While it was hard to organize resistors and find them a voice in North Dakota, around the United States, the resistance to hydraulic fracturing grew. The same was true around the world. In fact, France banned hydraulic fracturing for gas extraction in 2011, a ban that was upheld in 2013. In the discussion about the ban, France's environment minister, Natalie Kosciusko-Morizet, drew explicit lessons from the United States: "I'm against hydraulic fracturing," she said. "We have seen the results in the U.S. There are risks for the water tables and these are risks we don't want to take."[18]

The Mora County ordinance reminds of a long history of water and land conflicts in the American West. In the face of pressures from

14 Garcia 2018; Olivas 2018
15 Olivas 2018
16 Olivas 2018
17 Matlock 2015
18 Patel 2011

outside entities trying to control resources, local communities tried to define these resources as their own. The extraction of these resources put their communities at risk while benefiting others. In many ways it was a demonstration of how the tragedy of the commons is the tragedy of outsiders trying to appropriate resources for free, not of residents trying to best each other. These issues are also reminders of the precursors to the sage brush rebellion mentioned in the beginning, or resistance to eminent domain rulings over rural communities who carry the risks while others benefit. The Mora County ordinance reads in part:

> We the People of Mora County declare that all of our water is held in the public trust as a common resource to be used for the benefit of Mora residents and of the natural ecosystems of which they are a part. We believe that industrial use of water supplies in this county placing the control of water in the hands of a corporate few, rather than the county would constitute abuse and usurpation; and that we are therefore duty bound to oppose such abuse and usurpation.[19]

The ordinance cites as one of its authorities the county's land use plan, which, in language paralleling that of John Wesley Powell read:

> Water is a vital link, which, if severed from the land, will also fragment our people from their land. The allocation of our limited water resources must recognize traditional subsistence agricultural and grazing activities as a priority over other types of more profitable land uses. Water is not just a commodity to be bought and sold, or exploited for short-term gains. Water is the lifeblood of Mora County's traditions, culture and land use. A sustainable future for Mora County requires protection of the most valuable resource for our communities—the Water![20]

It is not a coincidence that the fight against water commodification and appropriation that, in the West, goes hand in hand with the fight against industrialization is also a fight to remain living with the land.

19 SWEPI v Mora County 2015:5
20 SWEPI v Mora County 2015:7

As I have argued before, this is a struggle against the frontier as a harbinger of industrial capitalism and a commodified modernity. The language and the concepts used in this struggle thus mirror those used by other communities. Culture, and the recognition that culture is tied to the land, seems very important to this struggle. "We are one of the poorest counties in the nation," Olivas said, in a statement that one can hear at almost any public speech in indigenous communities on the northern Plains, "but we are money-poor, not asset poor. We've got land, we've got agriculture, we've got our heritage and we've got our culture."[21] "As a historically colonized community," he wrote, the county was used to a system that does not listen to the people. "But it doesn't mean we have to accept it. It doesn't mean we have to continue to live on our knees."[22] Resistance against outsiders is more easily organized when a community already distances itself from those others. A culture that already uses the concepts of dwelling on the land and is generally perceived to do so is also better mobilized to fight against deterritorialization. The people in Mora County defined themselves as indigenous with the land. While some people in North Dakota lived with the land, most defined themselves as settlers. Growing resistance against development was therefore much harder.

## Regulation

North Dakota, as mentioned, has been in the enviable position of not facing high water stress. Although the state has seen its share of drought years and the depletion of some aquifers, this is due primarily to the Missouri River. According to the State Water Commission, in 2013, the state used about 5.5 billion gallons of water for the oil industry.[23] The numbers reported by the commission seem to be on the low end. Each rig drilled on average about thirteen wells in 2013,[24] and there were 184 rigs active on June 14, 2013 according to official numbers. That would mean about 2,400 wells were completed in 2013. The North Dakota Department of Mineral Resources estimated that for two thousand new wells, between eleven- and twenty-two million gallons of water were needed for fracturing. Calculated with a median of sixteen million gallons, this lower number would indeed

21 Cart 2013
22 Olivas 2018
23 SWC 2016:24
24 KLJ 2014:10

result in 5.8 billion gallons of water for the year. However, already in 2010, the then director of the commission's Water Appropriation Division expected the industry to use 7.2 billion gallons of water, a demand that would have been impossible for the groundwater supply to meet.[25] The Department of Mineral Resources also calculated that forty thousand existing wells would require around twenty- to twenty-five million gallons water each day for maintenance. Maintenance water use almost never shows up in well statistics; if we assume that only 10,000 wells needed maintenance water in 2013, that would add about another 2 billion gallons of water use, and the estimate of over seven billion gallons seems much more correct.

The major, and only reliable aquifer in western North Dakota is the Fox Hills-Hells Creek aquifer, and it has been in decline or under significant pressure for the past decades. Because it supplies most water for ranching, the state hesitated to put more pressure on the aquifer. A 2010 report by the State Water Commission warned that it "is important that water in the FH-HC aquifer be conserved for future use by its cities, towns, ranches, and small industries." More pressure on the aquifer would "likely cause a hardship for many water users." Many of the state's shallow aquifers, the report pointed out, were already fully or almost fully appropriated. These shallow aquifers are also more susceptible to drought conditions; their viability is dependent on climatic conditions that are difficult to predict.[26]

While it was hoped that new efficiencies would reduce the water needed per well, the opposite seems to have happened. According to a 2022 brochure from the Department of Water Resources,[27] fracturing a well in the state used on average 8.5 million gallons of water. The number of wells completed per year hit the high in 2014 with about 2540, and in 2021 only 830 wells were completed. However, that number still adds up to seven billion gallons of water used. Despite lower numbers of wells drilled and fractured, then, the consumption of water has stayed about the same—if maintenance water is left out of the equation. The Department of Water Resources reported a lower number of total usage than these calculations (around 6.8 billion gallons of water),[28] but it arrives at its numbers in different ways.

25 WORC 2013:16

26 Schuh 2010:ES17-ES18

27 DWR 2022a. The North Dakota Department of Water Resources was formed in 2021, as a successor to the State Water Commission.

28 DWR 2022b:32-39

The department reports water use based on water taken from water depots. Water depots are places that are licensed to sell water to the oil industry. Often, they are simply a small shack with a hose; during the height of the boom, they were readily identifiable because a long line of water trucks was usually waiting to load. Everybody selling water to the extraction industry in North Dakota needs a permit to do so. The state examines the application, runs an assessment on water resources, and either approves or denies. The permit, if approved, results in a legal water depot. It has been obvious that some water sellers operate without a permit, while some users take water from wherever they can. While the state is trying to enforce the regulations, there seems to be a gap between the water reportedly used for the extraction industry and the water actually needed to complete the wells. Keeping that gap in mind, the highest water usage for the oil industry in the state, according to the State Water Commission, came in 2018, when it needed 12.7 billion gallons of water.[29]

While the regulations on water depots are well thought out, enforcement is difficult, although the agencies have issued assureances that violations "are heavily fined to assure compliance."[30] The Water Commission, now the Department of Water Resources, prefers to settle violations through administrative consent agreements to avoid lengthy and costly lawsuits. In 2017 and 2018, twenty-nine violations of the water depot regulations were resolved; $700,000 in fines were spoken. Of these fines, $129,000 were paid, and the rest suspended.[31] In the time span between 2010 and 2015, $3.5 milllion in fines were agreed, of which $2.3 million were paid.[32] The commission provided no data as to how many violations were investigated but not resolved; its public statements about avoiding lawsuits are geared to assure the state that it does not want to spend tax money, but might also serve as a signal to violators that they might get away with not abiding by regulations. During the boom years I heard a lot of anecdotal evidence that some water truck drivers simply backed up to a remote part of Lake Sakakawea and filled up. Whether or not that was widespread fact, what is true is that the state was forced or forced itself to largely leave compliance with regulations up to self-enforcement by companies.

29 SWC 2019:36
30 SWC 2016:24
31 SWC 2019:36
32 Lin et al. 2018:236

In order to assure the public about the industry's water use, the state has always compared the water use by industry to other uses; by far the largest consumer of water in North Dakota has been agriculture, which consistently has used about half of all the water. In 2014, irrigation used about 52.8 billion gallons of water in North Dakota.[33] In 2021, it used about sixty-two billion gallons.[34] There are two issues with this comparison, however. First, in the four main oil producing counties in the Bakken area, fracturing represented over 40% of water use in 2014—in 2007, it represented three percent.[35] Even though agriculture used by far the most water in the state as a whole, then, the situation became much more even in the Bakken counties. This additional usage placed a lot of stress on the system. Based on the calculations and estimates of water needs for the extraction industry, the 2010 report for the State Water Commission came to the conclusion that "the only plentiful and dependable supply of water for the oil industry in western North Dakota, at projected rates of extraction, is the Missouri River system."[36] The commission therefore rejected water depot applications for water from the aquifers,[37] and favored applications that were based on water diverted from the Missouri River, which mostly meant Lake Sakakawea.[38] The commission came to the understanding that "Lake Sakakawea will play an increasingly important role in North Dakota's oil development for decades to come."[39] The reality was that without water from the lake, oil development would have to be severely limited.

## The lake

Lake Sakakawea is managed by the U.S. Army Corps of Engineers. The Corps manages the lake for many different purposes, among them to reduce flood threats and keep a navigational channel open downstream. States below the Pick-Sloan Plan's mainstream dams, especially Missouri, thus have sometimes very different priorities for the water in the Missouri River from states further upstream. North Dakota has historically fought for federal authorities to retain water

33 SWC 2016:21
34 DWR 2022a
35 Lin et al. 2018:231
36 Schuh 2010:47
37 WORC 2013:16
38 Schuh 2010:47-50
39 Fridgen 2010:17

in reservoirs, arguably for recreational use. One author calls the state's stance on this water "schizophrenic," as recreational water use in North Dakota carries the lowest priority.[40] Be that as it may, the result is a history of conflict over water between the states.

In 2011, the Corps published a study investigating whether the lake carried any surplus water, and at what cost the Corps would agree for users to access it.[41] The recommendation from the report was that 100 thousand acre feet or about 32.6 billion gallons of water would be made available per year for five years, with an option for another five years. The Corps asked for users to pay $20.91 per acre foot.[42] The price calculated out to about one dollar for every 15,500 gallons of water. A quick survey of current water prices from water depots shows that prices vary, but some examples are charges of around 2 cents per gallon, $8.25 per one thousand gallons, or $50 per twenty thousand gallons. In 2011, when the Corps proposed its pricing, the city of Parshall was selling water for $15 per one thousand gallons and made $2 millions in revenue from these sales.[43] The Corps' price point was incredibly cheap, in other words. This was due, in part, to the fact that the Corps actually could not sell the water—instead, it proposed to charge a storage fee for the convenience of making the water available.

Because water rights are so fundamental to all other issues, the conflict that followed over Lake Sakakawea water illuminates essential standpoints from which states, tribes, and the federal government approached oil development and, in fact, the historical and contemporary concepts at play in discourses surrounding it. Neither North Dakota nor Missouri nor the tribes were amused by the Corps' proposal. Their responses all showcase longstanding issues with the Pick-Sloan dams and with their larger situations.

Missouri opposed the plan because it was interested in water flowing downriver. It asserted that these allocations would be permanent, not temporary as the Corps had said; that the Corps needed congressional approval for the decision; that there was in fact no surplus water available; and that the Corps had not complied with the National Environmental Policy Act (NEPA) in its assessment of

40 Beck 2011:514
41 USACE 2011a
42 USACE 2011a:iii
43 Boom and Bloom 2011:5

potential environmental consequences.[44] The Standing Rock Sioux Tribe, also opposed, asserted that it had never been invited to consult by the Corps, although the Corps then counterargued that the Tribe had declined to participate in consultations.[45] Such issues with consultation would be mirrored in future conflicts over the Dakota Access Pipeline. Standing Rock was also concerned that the Corps did not seem to have any action plans for consultation or for a determination of cultural resources at potential intake sites, and that erosion from resulting changing water levels at downstream lakes (including Lake Oahe) would result in damage to culturally significant sites. Like Missouri, the Tribe thought the Corps was in violation of NEPA because it had not completed a formal Environmental Impact Statement for the project.[46] Again, this would be a focus in the dispute over the Corps permit for the Dakota Access Pipeline to cross Lake Oahe five years later. The Tribe also raised the issue that the cumulative impacts from the proposed allocation of water were much farther reaching than simply building access points for water intake. The Tribe insisted that the cumulative impacts from this project would be truck traffic to haul the water, housing developments, well pads, flares, and other impacts on the environment and cultural resources associated with oil development in general.[47]

Similarly, the Mandan, Hidatsa, and Arikara (MHA) Nation asserted that Corps had never begun consultations over the plan.[48] It was opposed not to take water from the lake, but having to pay for it. The MHA Nation pointed out to the Corps that Lake Sakakawea had destroyed communities, wildlife habitats, agricultural lands, and aspects of traditions and culture. "For USACE to now propose to charge the Tribe to access the very waters which destroyed the heart of the MHA Nation, and caused the present-day poverty and economic distress the MHA Nation is struggling to defeat,"Tex Hall pointed out

44 Letters from the Attorney General of Missouri and the Missouri Department of Natural Resources in USACE 2011b

45 Letter from Standing Rock Tribal Historic Preservation Office in USACE 2011b

46 Letter from Standing Rock Tribal Historic Preservation Office in USACE 2011b

47 Letter from Standing Rock Tribal Historic Preservation Office in USACE 2011b

48 Letter from the Office of the Chairman, MHA Nation in USACE 2011b

in his letter, "is not only illegal, it is morally reprehensible." He asserted that the Corps' report did not address the sovereign rights of the tribe to its territory, which by treaty include the Missouri, and its rights to make decisions about the resources on this territory. He pointed to the fact that the Bureau of Indian Affairs could permit intakes from the lake, which the Corps never acknowledged, and stated that the Tribe had plans to build irrigation infrastructure for some of its lands, for which it would use this water. He then argued that the Corps, under the Flood Control Act of 1944, which established the Pick-Sloan Plan, has the authority to make water supply agreements with "states, municipalities, private concerns and individuals," but therefore neither with tribes nor with federal agencies.[49]

If the Tribe asserted its sovereignty over Lake Sakakawea, the state of North Dakota, not surprisingly, saw things very differently and in turn asserted its own perceived sovereignty over the lake. It has to be remembered that the state has been fighting the Tribe and the federal government over mineral rights under the lake, among other things. North Dakota took the position that "the entire surplus storage initiative" by the Corps was "an illegal taking of state water rights by an agency of the federal government." The state referred to its constitution by which all flowing streams and waterways are a property of the state.[50] This argument, like in many other states with similar language, set up a conflict with the tribes, of course. However, in this instance, the state also chose to integrate what it deemed the tribal argument within its own argument, without mentioning tribal sovereignty. "The upper Missouri River Basin states and tribes have sacrificed greatly in loss of land and resources and suffered personal hardship for the Missouri River Basin. Most of the promised benefits for the upper basin states and tribes have never been realized," the state argued. The Corps, it said, now wanted to charge for access to natural flow "simply because those flows lie within the boundaries of the reservoirs."[51] In other words, the state argued that it owned all the water in natural flowing streams, and even if the flow was dammed, the water in the lakes still came from the flow. The Corps, North Dakota asserted,

49 Letter from the Office of the Chairman, MHA Nation in USACE 2011b

50 Letter from North Dakota State Engineer and Secretary of the Water Commission in USACE 2011b

51 Letter from North Dakota State Engineer and Secretary of the Water Commission in USACE 2011b

"continues to cause harm to the state's citizens by denying their timely access to the waters of North Dakota and holding water uses hostage to surplus storing fees."[52] The state saw the federal government as actively endangering the oil development, and therefore a hostage taker. This is a very similar argument to the ones made about other federal agencies, such as the Environmental Protection Agency being positioned as environmental terrorists.

Under pressure, the Corps enacted an addendum to the report in June 2012. While the availability of 100 thousand acre feet of surplus water and the finding of no environmental impact were left standing, the fees were put on hold until a nationwide policy could be enacted.[53] In December 2012, the first new water agreement was signed for lake water to be piped to the oil patch. Congress, however, preempted the review for the new policy by passing the 2014 Water Resources Development Act, establishing that no fees were to be paid for surplus water.[54] In 2012, the MHA Nation had passed a resolution asking the Corps to refrain from issuing permits until formal consultations had been held with the tribe.[55] Because the findings were left intact, neither the downstream states' concerns nor the relevant objections by tribes over missing consultations and environmental impact statement were addressed. Again, consultations with tribes did not take place.

## "Produced water"

I mentioned above that there are two issues with comparing the water use for fracturing with other water uses such as irrigation or household consumption. The first was that a statewide comparison is misleading because fracturing takes place in mostly arid counties and because in these counties, the percentage of water use for fracturing is much higher than statewide. The second issue is much more fundamental. Water that is used for irrigation, households, municipalities, or other needs is usually cleaned and reenters the water cycle. In contrast, the water that is used for hydraulic fracturing in North Dakota and other places cannot be allowed to get back into circulation. It is so salty and toxic that it needs to be permanently removed from the cycle.

52 Letter from North Dakota State Engineer and Secretary of the Water Commission in USACE 2011b

53 USACE 2012

54 Hearne and Fernando 2016:6

55 MHA Nation 2012

In a euphemism, the water that has been used for fracturing wells and comes back up with the oil and gas is called "produced water." Its quality depends on the geological formations in which it has been used as well as on what exactly specific companies have added to it, other than sand, to increase the pressure and efficiency of the fracturing process. Each company has its own formula, which is usually a trade secret. In many states, North Dakota included, companies do not have to disclose what chemicals they add to the fracturing mix. One of the consequences from that has been that if a fire breaks out at a rig, the responders usually are not aware what kinds of chemicals they will encounter. Companies now have to disclose chemicals on fracfocus.org, but many states, North Dakota included, allow for exceptions. Hydraulic fracturing is also exempt from the Safe Drinking Water Act and the Clean Water Act, although spills of hazardous chemicals do have to be reported.

In general, produced water in North Dakota is about ten times saltier than sea water.[56] Anybody who has watered plants understands that most plants cannot withstand that level of salinity. In part because of the salinity, the produced water is also highly conducive. Pure water has no electrical conductivity, but as soon as ions are dissolved in the water, conductivity increases. Conductivity is measured in Siemens per meter, or derivatives from that, such as deciSiemens per meter (dS/m) or microSiemens per centimeter (uS/cm). Drinking water typically carries a conductivity of about 0.5 dS/m; 2.5 dS/m to 3dS/m is the tolerance limit for consumption by humans. Above about 0.8 dS/m, care needs to be taken in irrigation, while some extremely salt-tolerant plants can withstand water of up to 6 dS/m.[57] Produced water in the Bakken carries an electrical conductivity of up to 200 dS/m.[58] In fact, the electrical conductivity of produced water (or, as is now clear, more accurately brine) contributed to the danger of lightning strikes on brine storage sites. Infamously, in several instances, brine storage tanks at injection well sites caught on fire from lightning strikes. Seawater has a Total Dissolved Solids (TDS) concentration of about 35,000

56 Benko and Drewes 2008:240-241

57 There are many sources on limits of electrical conductivity (as a measurement of salinity) for uses of water; their exact numbers differ slightly. The numbers mentioned here come from Australian government and non-governmental sources, but a perusal of other sources shows that these numbers are largely shared and agreed upon.

58 McDevitt et al. 2022:4

mg/L. While some produced water samples from other oil and gas basins show TDS levels below that (for example, from the Niobrara in Colorado and Eagle Ford in Texas), samples from the Bakken show TDS levels between 257,000 mg/L and 304,000 mg/L.[59] Some samples showed over 380,000 mg/L.[60] Contamination of water or soil with brine thus has catastrophic consequences. Without remediation, there is a potential for the soil to retain high salt concentrations for decades or longer, prohibiting plant growth. In the Williston Basin, the most common response to a brine leak from a well, storage site, or pipeline is to remove the contaminated topsoil and deposit it in an approved landfill, and then to replace it with new soil.[61] Communities were more afraid of brine spills than of oil spills because the potential consequences were more drastic.

In the beginning of the boom, the brine was kept in so-called reserve pits. A reserve pit is a lined earthen pit dug next to a drilling rig. The waste from the drill and fracturing operation is then put into the pit. Following the completion of the well, the equipment is removed, leaving the full reserve pit behind. The liquids are allowed to evaporate, and the remaining contents are then covered up with lining and buried under earth. Depending on what state regulations apply, reserve pits have to be buried within between a month and a year. One of the issues with reserve pits is that they often leak through the lining.[62] They may also contain all kinds of other waste that is disposed in the pit to save time and effort. Especially in a state like North Dakota, which lies in the flyway of migrating bird populations, another issue is that birds cannot distinguish between produced water and actual water. They land in the pit and then get entrapped in the brine or die from exposure to toxins.[63] The Fish and Wildlife Service estimated in 2017 that around 750,000 birds died in reserve pits every year.[64] Reserve pits could be made more secure for birds with netting and other measures that would prevent birds from landing. In North Dakota, however, yet another issue led to a policy change. During the spring floods in 2011, around fifty reserve pits overflowed, washing the brine away downstream. In 2012, the state phased out the pits, requiring that brine be

59 McDevitt et al. 2022:4
60 Preston et al. 2014:29
61 Green et al. 2020
62 Ramirez 2009:4
63 Ramirez 2009:9-12
64 USFWS n.d.

disposed of immediately. The fact that such oil waste sticks around for a long time becomes obvious now and then. In 2015, a reserve pit from 1966 began to erode in the bluffs along the Little Missouri River, for example. In other cases, contaminants from pits rose to the surface. The state had only begun to require that the pits were lined in 1981.[65]

Under some circumstances, produced water can be treated or recycled. Several companies have been working on developing mobile solutions to treating the brine. Many states allow the use of produced water on roads for de-icing or dust control, among them North Dakota. In some states, like Wyoming, produced water can be released for beneficial uses. The literature on treatment for beneficial use is vast,[66] perhaps reflecting the economic incentives to find a treatment method. Nevertheless, most produced water is not recycled or reused, other than being used for secondary or enhanced recovery. In these applications, the brine is injected into the oil or gas-bearing formation, which increases the pressure in the ground and displaces and drives more oil toward the production well. A review of 2017 federal and state data showed that 1.3% of produced water was re-used outside the industry, and 5.5 percent was discharged to surface water. The overwhelming majority of produced water was injected back into the earth. 43.6 percent was injected for enhanced recovery—this officially constitutes recycling—and 47.9 percent of all produced water was injected through non-commercial and commercial disposal wells.[67] In North Dakota, all of the produced water was injected. Only eight percent was used for secondary or enhanced recovery, mostly for conventional wells. Ninety-two percent of North Dakota produced water was injected through saltwater disposal (SWD) wells, ninety-five percent of it into the Dakota Group sandstone formation.[68]

## Brine injection

The Dakota formation spans almost all of the Williston Basin, at a depth between 1800 and 6220 feet. It is about seven hundred feet

65 Nowatzki 2015:127

66 A few samples must suffice to prove an overview of the diversity of approaches. See, for example, Sirivedhin, McCue, and Dallbauman (2004); Brown et al. (2007); Ma, Geza, and Xu (2014); GWPC (2019); McDevitt et al. (2020).

67 Veil 2020:8

68 Veil 2020:95-96; EERC 2020:vi

thick, and lies under the Pierre formation, which has a low permeability. This should not allow the injected brine to rise through the Pierre formation and into the Fox Hills formation, which hosts the aquifer of the same name mentioned above as the major reliable aquifer in western North Dakota.[69] The Bakken shale itself lies several geological layers below the Dakota formation. The Dakota sandstone formation is also home to an aquifer, but because it is not used for consumption, it has been allowed to be used for water disposal, thereby precluding any future use.[70] It also seems that the Dakota formation is reaching its capacity for injection. Pressure rates in the formation have gone up significantly, and increasingly salt-water disposal has to be done further away. One consequence of pressure in the formation increasing is that oil wells drilled in those areas—which have to be drilled through the formation to reach the Bakken shale—have had to be reinforced so that the increased pressure does not impact their integrity.[71] A 2020 report forecast that the "one-size-fits-all solution to produced water management" that salt water disposal into the Dakota represents might become economically much less advantageous because of increased brine volumes, shrinking capacity in core areas, and resulting needs to truck the brine to other areas and to find different formations for injections. All of this will result in additional costs for producers.[72]

Wells used to inject produced water and other waste from oil and gas developments are classified as Class II wells by the Environmental Protection Agency (EPA). There are six categories for the more than 740,000 underground injection wells in the United States.[73] Class II wells are for the disposal of fluids from oil and gas activities, and most fall into two groups: disposal wells and recovery wells. According to the 2019 Underground Injection Control Inventory by the EPA, there

69 EERC 2020:18

70 Mall and Troutman 2020:12

71 EERC 2020:21-25

72 EERC 2020:26-29

73 This number is based on the 2019 State and Tribal UIC (Underground Injection Control) Inventories by the EPA. It relies on numbers declared by states and is approximate because several states did not report. Especially the number of Class V wells (used for injection of non-hazardous waste) might be under-reported. Actual numbers might be more than double (see the estimates from GWPC n.d.:5, which notes 1,500,000 Class V wells).

were about 37,650 disposal wells operating in the United States, and about 122,000 enhanced recovery wells. North Dakota had 674 disposal wells, and there were fifteen on the Fort Berthold reservation. The number of disposal wells, however, can be deceptive because the actual number of wells can differ dramatically from the number of wells that are permitted and active. 537 salt water disposal (SWD) wells were active in North Dakota in 2019.[74] In states with historically established oil and gas plays, the difference between existing and active disposal wells can be stark. Pennsylvania, for example, had 1,855 Class II wells in 2010, but only eight were active and licensed. Ohio had over two thousand disposal wells, but less than two hundred that were permitted to operate.[75] Another difficulty in interpreting potential impacts comes from the fact that not every well injects the same amount of water by far. For example, in 2008, while there were three hundred salt water disposal (SWD) wells in North Dakota, forty percent of the disposed water went through only twenty-three wells. In 2019, two hundred of the about six hundred SWD wells in the state disposed of 80% of the brine. By that time, each one of these wells disposed of over one million barrels of brine (forty-two million gallons).

Injection is expensive, and people looked for alternatives. During the early days of the boom, when law enforcement was absolutely overwhelmed, it was not uncommon to see produced water trucks driving the rural roads on Fort Berthold while letting the brine run out the back. Drivers simply did not close the hoses, leaving a trail of brine on the road behind them. A few years later, when the practice had become too obvious, some drivers drove around in a mist of brine—they poked holes into the hoses on the outside of the truck from where the brine was sprayed out. Perhaps people thought that the brine was not that harmful, since it can be legally used to melt ice on roads in the winter and for dust control on gravel roads in the summer. Dumping waste on the reservation was not uncommon, though. According to anecdotal evidence, some people simply drove onto the rural parts and dumped raw sewage.

Just as is the case for volumes of produced water, the numbers for the volume of SWD injection in the United States are almost impossible to calculate. "Due to what are sometimes significant differences in the types of data collected and the mechanisms, formats, and definitions

74 EERC 2020:21

75 Hammer and VanBriesen 2012:20

used," the EPA concludes, "data cannot always be directly compared from state to state."[76] According to numbers from the North Dakota Industrial Commission, however, a total of 683.4 million barrels (28.7 billion gallons) of brine was injected in 2019 in the state. In 2008, it had already been 106.8 million barrels (4.5 billion gallons). While these numbers are almost impossible to comprehend in size, according to data from the Texas Railroad Commission, which oversees oil and gas development in its state, on average, Texas injected about the same amount in every single month in 2021. In total, Texas disposed of over 8.2 billion barrels, or about 348 billion gallons of produced water that year.[77] Injecting that amount of brine, most of which should never come into contact with an aquifer again, represents not just the loss of a huge amount of water, but also a large risk. Disposal wells are known to have leaked.[78] A 2015 review found that existing practices and data collection is insufficient for the detection of long-term effects from wastewater disposal on water quality in the United States.[79]

Spills and leakages from oil and brine pipelines, wells, and transport trucks are a threat to freshwater. In 2014, a brine pipeline leaked about one million gallons over five days north of Mandaree, on the Fort Berthold reservation. The brine reached a creek, and about ten thousand gallons flowed into Lake Sakakawea. Many other leaks and spills, smaller and larger, have happened. However large their consequences are, they would be small compared to injected brine reaching an aquifer of drinking, irrigation, or livestock water. As mentioned, the Dakota formation, into which most of the brine is injected, is covered by a low permeability layer, which should provide some protection. Early studies on drinking water contamination focused especially on the Marcellus Shale, where multiple incidents occurred.[80] Fears about migrations of hydraulic fracturing liquids from the fractured formations

76 EPA 2016:8-8

77 These numbers are from the Injection Volume Query on the H10 Filing System website of the Texas Railroad Commission at http://webapps.rrc.state.tx.us/H10/h10PublicMain.do. Accessed in July 2022.

78 See, for example, Lustgarten 2012

79 Bowen et al. 2015

80 See, for example, Ramudo and Murphy 2010; Myers 2012; Warner et al. 2012; Jackson et al. 2013.

to aquifers were dismissed by a series of articles whose research was sponsored by Haliburton. Such scenarios, the authors assured, were "not physically possible" and "not a realistic expectation."[81]

Most of the studies looking into migration of fluids to aquifers assume a route between a deep fracturing zone and a shallow aquifer. Models for such migration, depending on the geology and the presence of permeable pathways, assume a potential time frame of a few decades to a few thousand years.[82] Without overestimating the potential risks, it might be extremely valuable to run models instead on migration of brine from salt water disposal formations into aquifers, as the amount of brine injected by far exceeds the volume of hydraulic fracturing fluids pumped into active wells. As one study points out, the issue of brine injection "raises the question of the time frame of water resources management and the ethical time frame to be considered when actions are taken to prevent groundwater contamination."[83] In other words, the question is this: are we ready to sacrifice the groundwater aquifers of a region and thus prevent functional life there if the contamination will happen in a hundred, five hundred, or a thousand years, so that we can access oil now? This is the fundamental question of the Anthropocene. Are we willing to risk (and by now witness) the disappearance of landscapes and communities?

## Risk management

There are four main risks factors for the migration of brine into aquifers: hydraulic fracturing in an upper portion of the oil or gas bearing formation, a highly permeable pathway such as a fault, a pathway along a production well, and overpressure in the formation.[84] Nobody is fracturing the Dakota formation, into which the brine is injected, or the overlaying Pierre formation. As mentioned, the pressure in the Dakota formation is growing to the point of doubts about how long it can used for brine injection. Production wells fail from time to time, and they have to go through the Pierre and Dakota formations to reach the Bakken shale. The assumption has been that the Pierre foundation acts as a barrier to the brine injected below it into the Dakota formation.

81 Flewelling, Tymchak, and Warpinski 2013; Flewelling and Sharma 2014
82 See, for example, Gassiat et al. (2013), Birdsell et al. (2015), and Wilson et al. (2017).
83 Gassiat et al. (2013):8326
84 EPA 2016; Gassiat et al. (2013)

As an example of the risks involved, a Statement of Basis from an application for a salt water injection well on the Fort Berthold reservation will serve our purposes. Previous submissions had been withdrawn because the Tribe had noted that they had been located over the New Town Aquifer. The third location was approved, and the hydrogeological setting, prepared by a geologist working for the company that submitted the application, notes that "Faulting is rare and of minor (< 5 feet) displacement in this area, as evidenced by the many horizontal wells drilled without fault complications."[85] The assumption that only minor faults exist in the Pierre formation has been taken generally as fact, although there do not seem to be many studies on this. One, however, completed in the context of potential $CO_2$ storage in depleted oil fields or the use of $CO_2$ for enhanced recovery, notes that in "the Dakota sandstones" and in formations below, "evidence suggests that faulting and fracturing are quite prevalent." Finding the faults surprised the investigators, as they had assumed a very simple geological stratigraphy. On top of the Dakota formation, the study notes, "is approximately 1000 meters of Cretaceous Pierre, Greenhorn, and Mowry Shales which should act as a good stratigraphic seal as long as the faults and major fractures in these layers are closed to fluid flow. More work and testing would be necessary to determine the location and transmissibility of these faults and fractures."[86] In other words, while the industry (and the State that relies on the industry) take the absence of data to the contrary to mean that there are no risks, a closer look reveals that the absence of data to the contrary is simply the absence of data. In reality, two or three of the major risks for migration from the Dakota formation to the Fox Hills-Hells Creek aquifer might actually be present. That does not mean that a migration of brine to the aquifer is imminent. It does seem to indicate, though, that it is possible.

Mistaking the absence of data indicating risks for proof that there are no risks seems to be a recurrent theme in the industry, and one that matches the discourse by state and industry on the oil boom as a whole. As discussed above in the context of other impacts, when risks or negative impacts are acknowledged, they have been minimized in comparison to positive, foremost economic impacts. Obviously, a real risk of contamination of drinking water with brine would be hard to

85 EPA n.d.:5
86 Gorecki et al. 2009:2893

outweigh by economic factors. The industry celebrated a draft EPA report on the risks. The draft proposed that the EPA "did not find evidence that these mechanisms [of potentially contaminating drinking water] have led to widespread, systemic impacts on drinking water resources in the United States."[87] Upon critique by the EPA's own scientific advisory board, however, the final report replaced this language with statements expressing the impossibility of reaching conclusive assessments because the data was either lacking, was inconsistent, or impossible to be aggregated.[88]

It is revealing to read the responses from the industry to this change. One example is a report from the Fraser Institute, a Canadian libertarian think tank associated with the Economic Freedom Network and the Atlas Network, two initiatives in support of free markets and individual economic freedom and opportunities against regulations and limitations. "As far as we can tell," the report reads,

> the full EPA 2016 study does *not* contain evidence of widespread, systemic impacts, nor does it update the number of identified cases of contamination such that they are no longer "small" compared to the total number of fracked wells. In short, the original 2015 EPA draft language still seems appropriate, as does its assessment in *Managing the Risks of Hydraulic Fracturing: An Update* (Green and Jackson, 2015). Although there have been some documented problems with fracking, the extreme claims from some activists that it represents a widespread and serious threat to the quality of drinking water is not borne out by the evidence, at least as covered in the 2016 EPA report.[89]

Again, while the EPA pointed out that it could not reach any conclusions because the data is lacking, the report claims that because there is no widespread data to the contrary, hydraulic fracturing represents no risks to drinking water. I hope it is obvious that these two statements are not the same. If there is no data on how many pedestrians are being killed by cars, that does not amount to the fact that no pedestrians are being killed by cars.

87 EPA 2015:10-1
88 EPA 2016:10-24 through 10-28
89 Murphy 2020:8

One 2015 study maintains that "there is only one confirmed case of HF fluids migrating to drinking water aquifers via subsurface pathways (which occurred in Jackson County, West Virginia in 1982)."[90] However, to see what a contamination of drinking water from hydraulic fracturing brine looks like, one does not have to travel to West Virginia from the Williston Basin. Instead, within the basin lies the Fort Peck Indian Reservation, which has struggled with just such a contamination for decades.

First discovered by landowners in the 1970s, it was obvious to researchers ever since the first investigation in 1984 that what contaminated the water was brine from oil production. The produced brine was injected through at least twenty injection wells, active at different times. In 1997, three of the four active disposal wells injected into the Dakota sandstone formation.[91] The injected brine then actually reached aquifers. The contamination in the East Poplar oil field traveled down the Poplar River valley in underground brine plumes. At the end of the valley lies the city of Poplar and the Missouri River. The Poplar River and private water wells became contaminated through the 1980s and 1990s. The oil companies active in the oil field were ordered to supply bottled water to the residents in 1999, and then to build a freshwater pipeline from Poplar to the rural houses affected. While it is unclear which exact wells started to leak when, the nearest leaking well to the city is known. After leaking for about twenty years, it was finally plugged in 1997. In 2007, a remediation system was started.[92] This remediation system, voluntarily built by Pioneer Natural resources, has been operational since 2008. It pumps the brine from one plume around the Mesa Biere #1-22 well through thirteen removal wells and then injects it through five enhanced recovery wells and one deep injection well.[93]

In 2000, Congress mandated the Assiniboine and Sioux Rural Water Supply System, which delivers water to rural residents in northeastern Montana from an intake in the Missouri River. The edge of one brine plume hit the public wells of Poplar in 2010. These wells were the only source for drinking water for the 3,000 people in and around Poplar. Finally, Poplar got connected to the rural water system

90 Birdsell et al. 2015:7159

91 Thamke and Craigg 1997; see also Thamke and Smith (2014).

92 Thamke 2008

93 Jacobs, Smith, and Tyrrell 2013

in 2011,[94] receiving its first water in 2012. What remains to be seen is if and when the brine plumes will reach the Missouri River and how that will affect water quality and life in the river.

## Pipelines

It is important to understand this background in the context of tribal resistance against projects threatening their water supply. The Bear Den brine spill on the Fort Berthold reservation mentioned above reached Lake Sakakawea upstream of a water intake for Mandaree. In 2011, a pipeline burst near Billings spilled over sixty thousand gallons of oil into the Yellowstone. In 2015, another spill from a pipeline near Glendive sent forty thousand gallons of oil to the river and contaminated the city's water supply. While barely anybody pays attention to Poplar, Montana, or the Fort Peck Tribes, tribal governments on the northern Plains know and understand the danger emanating from brine and oil, and for many tribes in South Dakota from old and current mining in the Black Hills. The Missouri is not only the only realistic source of water for the oil industry. It is also the main source of drinking water for the tribes. While that holds true for most towns and rural areas in the region, recent plans for oil pipelines saw routes cross the river upstream of water intakes for reservations. Narrowly avoiding reservation boundaries, the Keystone XL pipeline was supposed to cross the Missouri right below the Fort Peck Dam spillway. The Dakota Access Pipeline is crossing Lake Oahe just north of the reservation boundary from Standing Rock Sioux Reservation. In both cases, water intakes were a few miles downstream.

It is fascinating that the risk assessment for the proposed Keystone XL Missouri River crossing, literally missing the reservation boundary by a few hundred yards, never mentions the Fort Peck Tribes or the reservation in over a hundred pages. In fact, even the maps included in the assessment, although coloring the territory of the reservation differently, never indicate that there is a reservation, the territory of a sovereign nation.[95] Similarly, one of the main issues surrounding the Lake Oahe crossing of the Dakota Access Pipeline was the missing collaboration and consultation with tribes.[96] The tribes surely remembered the Corps of Engineers' lack of consultation on

94 Dutton and Thamke 2021
95 Stantec 2017
96 See Braun (2020):14-17.

the use of water from Lake Sakakawea. There seems to be a general trend in recent decades, that the individuals who have been directly working on projects with, in, and around Native (and rural) communities value collaboration and understand its many advantages. On the managerial level, however, many federal agencies, despite directives for consultation from the federal government, seem to not thoroughly engage in collaboration. This could have many reasons. In the case of energy-related projects, however, it seems pretty clear that they are stuck between energy companies and their political power, trying to push the projects through as fast as possible, and a realization that tribes have specific concerns that would create obstacles in a thorough consultation. Within the discourse of economic development, national security, a denial of tribal sovereignty, and eminent domain, it is hard to resist energy companies that are supported by members of Congress and the federal government. Tribes, on the other hand, see a continuing trend to ignore their existence, their sovereignty, and their futures. Unless they can bring massive pressure to bear on the state, the state, it seems, favors oil and gas extraction.

While the Keystone XL pipeline permit was revoked by the Biden administration in 2021—after the Obama administration had denied it in 2015, and the Trump administration revived it in 2017—the Dakota Access Pipeline (DAPL) is operating. In 2016, massive protests against the pipeline construction erupted on the Standing Rock Sioux Reservation and north of it along the Cannonball River. This very rural area became the flashpoint for protests for several reasons. One was that the Standing Rock Sioux Tribe opposed the pipeline and that there was a prayer camp against the pipeline on reservation territory. Prayer camps had been used in the fight against Keystone XL. Another reason was that to cross Lake Oahe, the pipeline needed a permit from the U.S. Army Corps of Engineers. The pipeline was largely built on private lands, with landowners either agreeing to it or, especially in Iowa, being forced to agree to it through eminent domain actions. Here, however, the federal government had to issue a permit. The Corps of Engineers thus played a key role: without the permit, the pipeline could not be finished. Although the pipeline started operating in 2017, a long history of court battles has since been ongoing.

Courts are nominally independent of the political process in the United States. Supreme Court decisions, however, have long been used to enact, legitimize, and enforce political decisions over land rights, jurisdiction, and sovereignty. In a Native context, federal courts are thus almost always a part of the political process. They wrote and write the rules they then refer to as law. European discovery leads to title and therefore Native nations have only rights of usufruct and occupation, but no title; that native nations are not truly sovereign but "domestic dependent nations," like wards to the federal guardian; that the federal government can change any treaty once it has decided it is in the best interests of Native peoples; that the illegal acquisition of land is not illegal if enough time has passed; or that reservations are really parts of states[97]—all of these decisions and more were not derived at through an interpretation of law (some of them directly contradict established law), but through a unilateral imposition, a political process. When tribes look at decisions related to energy extraction, especially pipelines, they see a continuation of the pattern. As a federal judge wrote in a memorable opinion in an unrelated case in 2005, "After all these years, our government still treats Native American Indians as if they were somehow less than deserving of the respect that should be afforded to everyone in a society where all people are supposed to be equal." The state, he wrote, "has time and again demonstrated that it is a dinosaur—the morally and culturally oblivious hand-me-down of a disgracefully racist and imperialist government that should have been buried a century ago, the last pathetic outpost of the indifference and anglocentrism we thought we had left behind."[98]

In 2020, the U.S. District Court for the District of Columbia came to the conclusion that the Corps of Engineers had, after all, violated the National Environmental Policy Act (NEPA) in permitting the Dakota Access Pipeline, and should have prepared an Environmental Impact Statement (EIS) for the crossing.[99] As mentioned above, the same issue was brought up by downstream states and tribes when the Corps tried to sell Lake Sakakawea waters to the oil industry a few years earlier. The court in this case, a few months later, decided that since the Corps could not issue a permit, the easement for the pipeline was revoked and the pipeline should be shut down.[100] Immediately, the company appealed. After an immediate stay was given against

97 Johnson v McIntosh 1823; Cherokee v Georgia 1831; Lone Wolf v Hitchcock 1903; Sherrill v Oneida 2005; Oklahoma v Castro-Huerta 2022

98 Cobell v Norton 2005

99 Standing Rock v Corps of Engineers 2020

100 Standing Rock and Cheyenne River v Corps of Engineers and Dakota Access 2020

having to empty the pipeline, the Court of Appeals for the District of Columbia took up the case. In 2021, the court decided that, indeed, the Corps' permit was illegal without the EIS. It then discussed at length whether the pipeline should be forced to shut down while the EIS was being prepared. "If, when an agency declined to prepare an EIS before approving a project, courts considered only whether the agency was likely to ultimately justify the approval," the court argued, "it would subvert NEPA's purpose by giving substantial ammunition to agencies seeking to build first and conduct comprehensive reviews later." Typically, courts would shut down a project. However, while the appeals court agreed that the Corps must prepare an EIS and that the easement for the pipeline was vacated, it also decided that the pipeline can continue to operate based on a technicality.[101] The pipeline has since operated without a permit, on land for which it has no easement.

It may be that it makes legal sense to allow an industrial operation a court deems risky enough to require an EIS continue to operate without a permit and while it is trespassing on federal lands. However, given the background, tribes also may be excused to look at the process with great frustration. In 2022, new Standing Rock Chairwoman Janet Alkire decided to withdraw the Tribe from serving as a cooperating agency on the EIS. The Corps had given the contract for the EIS to Energy Resources Management. The contractor is a member of the American Petroleum Institute, which had filed amicus briefs for DAPL in lawsuits. The Standing Rock, Cheyenne River, and Oglala Sioux Tribes had protested against this situation in a letter to the Corps in 2021.[102] In that letter, the tribes complained that the Corps was holding key documentation secret from them, asserted that the draft EIS ignored technical and cultural materials shared by the tribes, and assessed that it was "an advocacy document that appears to be prepared by the proponent for a single purpose: to justify issuance of a new easement of the pipeline at its present location." After Standing Rock withdrew, the Corps halted the process to make the draft EIS public.

In all of this, the Williston Basin was intimately involved. The Dakota Access Pipeline was after all built to transport Bakken oil to refineries and market. This put the MHA Nation in a very delicate position. On one hand, the stereotypical expectations of Native communities have

101 Standing Rock v Corps of Engineers 2021

102 Faith, Killer, and Frazier 2021

been that they protect the environment at all cost. On the other hand, as a sovereign nation that owns considerable oil and gas reserves, and as the owner of oil extraction businesses, the tribe has an interest in oil production and in bringing that oil to market. That interest is tied to an economic dependence on oil extraction and thus does not differ substantially from the interests of the state of North Dakota. Both North Dakota and the MHA Nation, for example, requested meetings with the Corps over concerns that a potential shutdown of the Dakota Access Pipeline would present economic losses for them. What does differ between the state and the Tribe, though, is that because of public expectations, when the Tribe pursues its economic interests, it meets with criticism that the state does not encounter.

One of the manifestations of this complex situation was the Sacagawea pipeline, designed to carry oil from eastern McKenzie County across Lake Sakakawea and the reservation to facilities and a rail terminal in Sidney and Palermo. The pipeline thus crossed the Missouri just as the Dakota Access Pipeline did. In 2015, the Tribal Business Council approved rights of ways for the pipeline on tribal tracts.[103] Sacagawea Pipeline Company is an affiliate of Paradigm Midstream, but twelve percent of it is owned by Gray Wolf Midstream, which is an affiliate of Missouri River Resources, the MHA Nation's tribally chartered oil company. In other words, the tribe owned part of the pipeline. Despite this, as the pipeline was being built in summer 2016—at the same time that DAPL was being built further south—the Tribe served a cease and desist order, claiming that the company needed a tribal permit for crossing Lake Sakakawea. The MHA Nation also rescinded its permission to use its lands. The Tribe said the company had agreed in discussions to gaining tribal consent before beginning to bore under the lake, and that such a consent had been refused.[104] The Tribe argued that because it owns the mineral rights under the lake, boring through the subsurface required not only the Corps' permission, but also the Tribe's. During the resulting trial, however, undisputed testimony pointed to the Tribe simply seeking more value from the project, perhaps in the context of the building tension around DAPL. Allowing a pipeline to be built had become a much more valuable proposal. Both the Tribe and the company, in

103 MHA Nation 2015

104 MHA Nation 2016a; MHA Nation 2016b; The Tribal Business Council minutes do not show any discussion of needed consent before boring under the lake.

which the Tribe had a financial interest, actually wanted the pipeline to be built.[105] Once the court found in favor of the company, the pipeline was indeed finished.

The Sacagawea pipeline does not demonstrate that tribes are especially hypocritical or greedy. It demonstrates, especially in the context of the simultaneous Dakota Access protests and narratives, that tribes, like states, and like the federal government, pursue their own economic interests. It also shows that these economic interests are extremely powerful and often outweigh other considerations.

## Politics

The sticking point in the Dakota Access fight has been that the Corps of Engineers based its decision to issue a permit on an Environmental Assessment instead of an Environmental Impact Statement. In the Sacagawea case, the decision to provide the permit was also based on an Environmental Assessment. Here, before the Corps could reach a decision, the Bureau of Indian Affairs (BIA) had already signed off on a Finding of No Significant Impact, necessitating the Corps to appeal that decision and issuing an addendum, which reached the same conclusion. In its initial reaction to the BIA's assessment, the Environmental Protection Agency (EPA) pointed out that, "If the BIA finds that this project poses a substantial risk to drinking water supplies and other resources of Lake Sakakawea, the EPA would recommend that the BIA consider completing a full environmental impact statement (EIS)." It then, perhaps somewhat unintentionally ironically, given it addressed this to the Bureau of Indian Affairs, further noted that,

> Because Lake Sakakawea supplies drinking water and recreation to tribal communities, any impacts from spills to this lake may disproportionately affect environmental justice (EJ) communities. An EIS process would typically include additional opportunities for public input and consideration of a broader range of alternatives. We recommend that this document identify and evaluate an alternative that would reduce or avoid disproportionate impacts to EJ communities.[106]

105 Paradigm v Fox and Heart 2016
106 SWCA 2016

In its response to the Corps' addendum, the EPA leaves out any reference to an EIS. It does note, however, that although the BIA and the Corps saw "a low probability of a significant spill reaching the lake, the proposed pipeline location of only four miles above the Mandaree drinking water intake would allow for a very short notice if a discharge occurs." The water intake is closer than the one for Standing Rock is to the DAPL crossing.

The only difference between the Sacagawea crossing and the DAPL crossing is that on Fort Berthold, the Tribe did not sue the Corps over the lack of an EIS. Because oil and gas development is seen as critical to the economy, the default notion by people who live in areas that are not directly affected is to support it. Local political entities—the state and tribes—try to find a balance between potentially positive economic and potentially negative ecological impacts. Because they see themselves as dependent on growing the economy, that usually becomes a one-sided argument. It is places like Standing Rock or Fort Peck, which face a reality where they would carry the risks for negative ecological impacts without any positive economic impacts, that resist. There are, of course, people in North Dakota and on Fort Berthold who benefit from the oil development yet are very aware of the ecological risks and weigh them higher than economics. However, in a culture that celebrates the primacy of economic growth and relegates the environment to commodity status, they will usually be in a minority.

Organizations that lobby for oil and gas development and for pipelines have been warning against what they portray as politicizing the regulatory process. As an example, we can to turn to GAIN (Grow America's Infrastructure Now) a group that has been vigorously advocating for pipelines. It notes "the rigorous and thorough nature of the U.S. regulatory process," reminding courts not to usurp the findings and to "trust the career professionals and experts who oversee critical infrastructure development, rather than second-guessing their analysis." To do this, courts must do their work "free of political pressure," to reach "straightforward, fact-based decisions." In the case of the Dakota Access pipeline's EIS, "the Corps—if allowed to follow facts and science—will validate previous findings that Dakota Access presents no significant impact or risk." Yet, what the two cases clearly demonstrate is that decisions over permits are political first, and then scientific. If there are considerable legal and political hurdles to overcome before an EIS is allowed and required to be performed, if that process is completed in a context where key data remain secret, and if the assessment is contracted out to parties that carry at least the suspicion of a conflict of interest, it is difficult to see the regulatory process as rigorous or scientific.

The key argument in calling for a scientific process seems to rather rely on the intermingling of the state and industry in the regulatory process that assures the outcome. This outcome cannot be in question because, as GAIN itself asserts, it serves a larger purpose:

> Encouraging the development of renewable energy sources is important, but denying the facts and reality of our energy needs aren't doing the American people any favors. Calling for DAPL's shutdown and its accompanying shortsighted rhetoric is irresponsible. DAPL, and more broadly, American energy production and capabilities, is key to fueling the American economy and achieving our national security and foreign policy goals.[107]

Even here, though, there is no scientific, factual, thorough review of conclusions. The facts and reality of energy needs are exactly what lead others to the conclusion that oil pipelines should be stopped. Fueling the American economy, achieving national security, and achieving foreign policy goals are all rather vague concepts, that could potentially be achieved by different means depending on how they are actually defined. What they mean is already predetermined in this discourse, however; it thus becomes obvious that the whole discourse itself, while calling for a process free from politics, is in fact political.

Because they are the critical link between extraction and the market, pipelines have become a flashpoint of resistance to oil and gas development. Keystone XL, Dakota Access, Line 3 in Minnesota, Line 5 in Wisconsin, Coastal GasLink in British Columbia, and other pipeline projects have faced resistance from communities that see themselves endangered. The media often focuses on these protests when they are led by indigenous peoples. The reality, however, is not that other communities are not concerned. Native nations can organize better because state governments are often downplaying local concerns over the economic benefits for the regions not directly affected.

107 The quotes are taken from entries over several years on https://gainnow.org/blog/. Accessed 8/5/2022.

One issue with the balance between potential economic benefits and potential ecological risk is that the benefits are more or less immediate while the risks are delayed. The people who reap the benefits can also work to shift the risks onto others. Many people benefiting from the boom, for example, left the Williston Basin while keeping their mineral rights or companies. Most people benefiting from jobs were not residents and did not plan to settle in the area permanently. Environmental justice is always an issue when those who have the means to avoid an environmental disaster profit from practices that raise risks for those who are vulnerable. These risks are highest in the case of water. Nobody knows whether or not the injected brine, for example, will eventually reach aquifers or rivers. In many areas, it has not happened, or has not happened yet. If it ever does, though, the landscape will truly disappear.

# Epilogue
# Legacies

A few years ago, I was visiting with a tribal historic preservation officer, and we came to talk about the oil boom and the Dakota Access Pipeline. He said something in the line of, we all know oil will run out eventually. I wish it would run out now, though, so we would not destroy everything in the meantime.

We will not be able to work ourselves out from under peak oil, no matter how many times people declare it to be a myth. Technological advances cannot make new oil. It might be that they push back peak oil, but it does not take a mathematical genius to understand that a limited resource that meets unlimited demand will run out at some point. In the meantime, we are burning through fossil fuels as if we do not care that we are destroying the planet and ourselves. This is not a controversial idea in the slightest. It is simply scientific fact. A geologist I know pretty closely has kept telling me that the earth used to be a lot hotter. That is true. It is just as true that there were no humans around then. In geological time, we do not have to worry about the planet. It will exist without us. In human time, we should not only worry, but also take action.

Tim Ingold writes that the question of anthropology is "How should we live?"[1] For humans, as he points out, this is a choice. It is perhaps a consequence of the general hubris of humankind that those who live in relative security think that it is a choice without consequences, or that we can mitigate any consequence. That idea has certainly become adhered to by specific cultures. How we should live is, of course, a moral question. In order to answer it, we have to take into account the consequences. What I should do, in the absence of an extreme adherence to an invariable code of conduct, is predicated on what my actions create. When cultures decide how they should live, in other words, they consider their potential legacy.

No culture can consider potential consequences on everything. There are too many variables. In order to not be paralyzed, then, we consider first those we are most closely related to—those to whom we

1 Ingold 2018

feel a close relationship. Because kinship is a cultural classification, this can be anything, or anyone, to whom we extend relations. Cultures that are almost totally alienated from the environment thus do not concern themselves with what they consider to be "nature" because most often nature is a commodity. The mistake, of course, is that humans ourselves are not actually disconnected from nature, but dependent on it. We are animals. We just pretend that we are not, which is both to our own advantage and to our own peril.

The question of our legacy is significant because we have the power to destroy the planet as we know it. Humanity's legacy is thus not simply a matter of different options. It is a question of survival. If we want to survive, or want our children to survive, the question of how we should live might not turn into the question of how we must live, but definitely into how we cannot live. Humanity cannot engage in a lifestyle that is unsustainable, otherwise we write ourselves out of existence. We all know this. What seems to be difficult is that the cultures that are currently dominant prioritize the well-being and choice of the individual and define well-being primarily through immediate access to goods. This has given rise to a system that relies heavily on individual mobility, the mobility of goods, and the primacy of immediate returns. Coupled with an economic system that demands growth, profits, and efficiency, and which postulates that everything (except, at least in theory, humans) is a commodity, we have created a society that is heavily dependent on oil. If we want to use oil, we need to extract it, transport it, refine it, distribute it, and burn it. If we do not want to do any of these things, we cannot use oil. This is the fundamental choice.

## Sustainable development

In the context of the 1992 Earth Summit in Rio de Janeiro, then U.S. President George H.W. Bush famously remarked that "The American way of life is not up for negotiations. Period." Although he did not define what the American way of life was, it seems clear that the idea was tied to the consumer economy that drives the United States. President George W. Bush was much more explicit when he addressed the Kyoto Protocol in 2001. "Kyoto is," he said, "in many ways, unrealistic. Many countries cannot meet their Kyoto targets. The targets themselves were arbitrary and not based upon science. For America, complying with those mandates would have a negative economic impact, with layoffs of workers and price increases for consumers."[2] Such ideas have become commonplace critiques of environmental protection policies. As discussed, the absence of specific data regarding negative impacts is often misinterpreted as proof that there are none. Even now that much more specific data has been generated, some people simply make up "alternative facts."

President Bush did not deny that climate change was a developing problem. He even laid out the fundamental premise: "There are only two ways to stabilize concentration of greenhouse gases. One is to avoid emitting them in the first place; the other is to try to capture them after they're created." The first option, however, does not show up as a solution. "We all believe technology offers great promise to significantly reduce emissions -- especially carbon capture, storage and sequestration technologies," Bush said. "Our approach must be flexible to adjust to new information and take advantage of new technology. We must always act to ensure continued economic growth and prosperity for our citizens and for citizens throughout the world."[3]

It would not be fair to see President Bush, or Americans, as the only ones who prioritize economic growth over climate change. The Brundtland Report of 1987 identified two problems with how humans lived: poverty and environmental degradation. These were intertwined, as "many present development trends leave increasing numbers of people poor and vulnerable, while at the same time degrading the environment."[4] Both of these issues, the report assured readers, could be addressed by a new concept—sustainable development. The report explicitly stated that, "Sustainable global development requires that those who are more affluent adopt life-styles within the planet's ecological means—in their use of energy, for example." But it also reads, "But technology and social organization can be both managed and improved to make way for a new era of economic growth." President Bush's thoughts show how the requirement to reduce resource use was mostly overlooked in hopes that technological innovations would allow us to pursue more growth. This matches to a large degree the narratives present in the Bakken and other resource booms.

Sustainable development—to have both growth and an intact planet—has been the sought after panacea, or cure-all, ever since.

2 Bush 2001
3 Bush 2001
4 United Nations 1987

The problem with the term is twofold. First, sustainability carries different meanings dependent on its context and the applied timeframe.[5] Second, development has been practiced and narrated in a neoliberal context, emphasizing the role of industry as caretaker and the need for commodification and privatization of resources. At the very least in this context the term sustainable development without the technological solutions the Brundtland Report dreamed about is an oxymoron.[6] In his early writings about capitalism, the anthropologist Marshall Sahlins explained how the "market industrial system institutes scarcity." Because "production and distribution are arranged through the behavior of prices, and all livelihoods depend on getting and spending, insufficiency of material means becomes the explicit, calculable starting point of all economic activity." In a consumer society, "every acquisition is simultaneously a deprivation, for every purchase of something is a foregoing of something else."[7] While this system has been convincing us that prosperity lies in (never achievable) choices—infinite needs—another kind of prosperity can be found in "an objectively low standard of living," that, is in reducing choices and needs but having them easily attainable.

Since John Stuart Mill, and probably earlier in thought, people have seen an "economic man" as the modern model for humans: it is rational that we should strive to possess wealth and develop the most efficient means to obtain it. Sahlins thus calls those who have never developed this cultural need "uneconomic man." Without the never-ending spiral of infinite needs, he argues, it is not rational to possess ever more wealth. Other anthropologists have critiqued the idea of rationality as a universal concept rooted in finding economic efficiency and growth. Bronislaw Malinowski defined Economic Man as

> the conception of a rational being who wants nothing but to satisfy his simplest needs and does it according to the economic principle of least effort. This economic man always knows exactly where his material interests lie, and makes for them in a straight line. At the bottom of the so-called materialistic conception of history lies a somewhat analogous idea of a human

5 Grober 2012:18; Boff 1997:67; Braun 2016b.

6 Boff 1997:66-67; Grober 2012:169-170

7 Sahlins 1972:1-37

> being, who, in everything he devises and pursues, has nothing but his material advantage of a purely utilitarian type at heart.[8]

He then expressed his hope that readers would agree with the need to "dispell such crude, rationalistic concepts" and to revise the ideas emanating from them. Clearly, however, the neoliberal imagination of Economic Man has survived its critics, buoyed in part by "winning" the Cold War.

It is no coincidence that the idea of Economic Man and of neoliberal capitalism has its most ardent supporters, and has found its most pure expression, within the United States. Apart from all political causes for this, one fact is that the underlying ideas are deeply enshrined in American culture. It is here that Economic Man, oil extraction, resource commodification, nationalistic denouncement of environmental advocacy, and the frontier come back together to reveal a whole. Considering Malinowski's formulation of the economic man as rational, efficient, materialistic, straightforward, and pragmatic, consider what Fredrick Jackson Turner had to say about the "striking characteristics" of American culture:

> That coarseness and strength combined with acuteness and inquisitiveness; that practical, inventive turn of mind, quick to find expedients; that masterful grasp of material things, lacking in the artistic but powerful to effect great ends; that restless, nervous energy; that dominant individualism, working for good and for evil, and withal that buoyancy and exuberance that comes with freedom—these are traits of the frontier.[9]

Turner was writing toward an American myth or creation story, and whether the frontier actually created the highest possible expression of Economic Man can at least be doubted. What is important, however, is that the idea of the frontier, underlying many origin stories of American culture, clearly aligns with the idea of Economic Man and catapults that concept into the model of a cultural hero.[10]

8 Malinowski 1966:516

9 Turner 1953:37

10 One of the best texts on the American hero is Sardar and Davies (2002), especially "The Burden of the American Hero" (171-191).

The fact that ravaging industrial extraction and environmentalism both find their source in the frontier myth is proof that it is foundational. It also demonstrates that many of the debates over extractivism in America are, as John Trudell once put it in a different context, "fighting over the lie." The frontier as wilderness, readily accepted by Puritan ideas of surviving in a desert and a continuous fight against the forces of evil inherent in a godless nature,[11] gave rise to the idea of the Ecological Indian,[12] and also stands at the beginning of modern environmentalism, which originated in part as a movement to preserve the frontier.[13] Thus the idea of the frontier underlies three separate ideologies, often at conflict with each other in the American West. The political evolution of these ideas in modernity sees them expressed as neoliberal extractivism, romantic settler guilt, and ecological activism. All three claim the land. While it is tempting to see these conflicts predicated upon whether people are indigenous,[14] the real issue is that they adhere to very different interpretations of the same myth, which they all use as the central text to their beliefs. Conflicts thus become unavoidable.

One of the government reports in response to the Dust Bowl shows the consequences of turning the myths of neoliberal freedoms into a hegemonic narrative dominating public discourse and policies. Simultaneously one of the beginnings of federal intervention in the West, an expression of American optimism to find technological solutions, and an example of early environmental concerns, the report by the Great Plains Committee sets out to find the issues that led to the Dust Bowl in order to secure the region's future. Portraying the Plains as wilderness before the coming of Americans, based on the widely-held (at the time) assumption that Native peoples were a part of nature, the report laid the blame at the feet of settler society: "Nature has established a balance in the Great Plains by what in human terms would be called the method of trial and error. The white man has disturbed this balance; he must restore it or devise a new one of his own."[15] Clearly,

11 Nash 2001
12 Krech 2000; Harkin and Lewis 2007
13 See, for example, Aldo Leopold's argument (Flader and Callicott 1991:134-142) that we should conserve the environment to preserve "the indigenous part of our Americanisms," which he takes straight from Turner.
14 Keeler 2021
15 Roosevelt 1937:2

the text embraces the ideas that Native peoples were part of nature. It partially follows a narrative of wilderness conservation and a romantic critique of civilization.

In addition to this social evolutionary framework, however, there is a reliance on resource balance. "The fact that even the relatively small population of the Great Plains cannot be sustained adequately under present conditions," reads the report, "has been demonstrated in recent years."[16] In order to build or rebuild a balance with nature (again, in exclusion of Native peoples' presence on the Plains), settlers in their colonial efforts have to take into account the limitations of the environment, even if only to improve upon them or to overcome them. As the Dust Bowl is often seen as a consequence of agricultural overuse of resources, one might expect a government report to stop there.

The report lays out, however, that it is not enough to change agricultural practices. Instead, "attitudes of the mind" must also change. The cultural assumptions that the report states need to be changed are then listed and explained. The list is revealing as it addresses some of the exact concepts that underlie what George H.W. Bush probably meant by the American way of life: "That Man Conquers Nature"; "That Natural Resources are Inexhaustible"; "That Habitual Practices are the Best"; "That What is Good for the Individual is Good for Everybody"; "That an Owner May Do with His Property as He Likes"; "That Expanding Markets Will Continue Indefinitely"; "That Free Competition Coordinates Industry and Agriculture"; "That Values Will Increase Indefinitely"; "That Tenancy is a Stepping-Stone to Ownership"; "That the Factory Farm is Generally Desirable"; "That the Individual Must Make His Own Adjustments."[17] In fact, the report is a condemnation of what might be called settler-colonialism: the ethnocentric, extractivist imposition of industrial capitalist practices onto landscapes. Insights from the report highlight that Americans have recognized the problems of sustainability and have identified solutions for a long time. Implementing these solutions, however, is difficult as long as cultural values oppose them. The fact that powerful economic interests defend these values does not help because it reinforces them as foundational myth and thus prevents actual sustainability.

16 Roosevelt 1937:39
17 Roosevelt 1937:63-67

## Economic resistance

As people were beginning to ponder strategies to slow down oil development—although some wanted to end it for good—they began to look at the tools of capitalism itself. The companies and the state could not be convinced to change. But in an economy that runs on debt, companies need capital, too. Changing the minds of those with capital to invest might be easier. After all, for those who invest, companies are also commodities. There is an investment market, and if one segment is perceived as unethical to invest in—and thereby the social risk of investment is elevated—there are others available to choose from. If fossil fuels are unethical to invest in, and solar or wind energy is ethical, then investors will invest in the latter if their actions are public. A new tactic was deployed in the context of oil and gas developments: convince the economic backers of pipelines to withdraw their funding.

Lenin is attributed with the quote that capitalists will sell the rope with which they will be hanged.[18] On the one hand, the rope can be oil; as long as there are profits to be made, oil will be extracted, but the very fact that fossil fuels are burned will condemn the world. "Damn the torpedoes," as Americans say, or perhaps more appropriately "après nous le deluge" in French. On the other hand, though, the rope can be the necessary capital. Because capitalists have made themselves dependent on investments, if the flow of capital is cut off, business comes to a halt. It is left hanging, so to say.

The threat of economic action on energy companies has long been a reality. I remember boycotts against Shell, for example, after the execution of the Ogoni Nine, including Ken Saro-Wiwa, in Nigeria in 1995. Because of Shell's alleged complicity in the Nigerian crackdown against the Movement for the Survival of the Ogoni People, protests erupted. After several years of facing protests over this and other issues, Shell publicly issued a report, *Profits and Principles*, in which it pledged to "better manage our social and ethical responsibilities." In a step that can be seen as a major contributing factor to the development of corporate social responsibility and the realization by environmental groups that businesses must respond to public pressure if their profits

18 In reality, this saying cannot be found in any of his works. It seems that it is of the same order as President Jackson's infamous reaction to Worcester v. Georgia—"The court decided, now let them enforce it." Nobody knows if he actually said it, but it fits into the context so well that he should have said it.

are at stake, Shell assured the world that "the basic interests of business and society are entirely compatible—that there does *not* have to be a choice between profits and principles."[19] This assertion is, of course, a mirror to the invention of "sustainable development." Present anti-capitalist campaigns have evolved to question and deny this very assertion, at least where fossil fuels are concerned.

Denying the flow of capital to specific portfolios is called divestment. Divestment is a strategy that can be applied to all kinds of situations, but the crux is that those who control the investment capital need to be convinced that the companies they should divest from have done something wrong. Divesting from oil companies in general can be risky, especially if these companies engage in great corporate social responsibility programs or portray their practices as either sustainable or on the way there. Harming the environment by contributing to climate change is not a crime in most industrial states. If communities are directly helped to balance the impact, it is difficult to find fault. However, over the past decades, public pressure has been rising to defend the rights of specific communities. No bank wants to be caught doing business with companies that tread on human rights. As discussed, the rights that have been defined for indigenous peoples include Free, Prior, and Informed Consent (FPIC). This is not the law in the United States, but a moral standard. Breaking the standard is thus seen as unethical. And so the "torch and spirit of this historic moment for water, life, and human rights broke through the doorways of banks and financial institutions seeking a reckoning, truth, and accountability from the economic powers behind destructive projects like DAPL."[20] Making financial transactions public and simultaneously taking the lenders to task for financing projects perceived as unethical can be very effective.

The downside to these efforts is that they work mostly for indigenous contexts alone. Native peoples have rights to FPIC. There are no such rights for non-indigenous peoples; they are supposed to be able to voice concerns through the democratic process. Standing Rock was not the only place where the Dakota Access Pipeline crossed a waterway controlled by the Corps of Engineers or where landowners did not want the pipeline passing under their soil. Yet, in Iowa, for example, at the crossings of the Des Moines or the Mississippi rivers,

19 Shell 1998:3
20 Cook 2019:132

protests did not get the same media attention by far, and landowners were forced to accept the pipeline under eminent domain rules. If environmental rights are tied to FPIC, non-indigenous peoples are out of options as long as the environment does not rule the vote.

Some voices in the industry prefer not to call this tactic divestment. Pipelines are critical infrastructure to national security and economic well-being, they point out. Now, however, "Across the nation and around the globe, banks are being besieged by these activists demanding that they breach their contracts to fund pipelines or face campaigns of mischief orchestrated to harm the banks' business and reputation." This, according to some, is illegal: "Sabotaging private funding commitments for pipeline development crosses [the] line from normal opposition to unlawful conduct."[21] Organizations supporting extraction, "wise-use," and privatization of resources often paint themselves and the industry as allies of local communities and all three as victims of well-funded urban elites.

This was, for example, the case in a lawsuit by Energy Transfer, the parent company of Dakota Access, against Greenpeace and others. That lawsuit followed on the heels of a mostly identical lawsuit brought by the same law firm against Greenpeace on behalf of Resolute Forest Products. Both argued that environmental organizations were exploiting indigenous peoples and that the companies enjoyed local support in contrast to the environmentalists who were outsiders.[22] The president of the Mountain States Legal Foundation, a law firm providing its services to pro-extraction, pro-wise-use, and anti-government causes, has argued that while lawyers for the National Wildlife Federation "fly in from Portland and Seattle" lawyers for the "ranchers fighting for their very survival" are "operating mostly *pro bono* (without pay)."[23] Of course, *pro bono* work does not mean a lawyer is not paid. It means that their client does not pay them; there is a huge gap between those statements. In the current climate, however, both sides work very hard at being perceived as standing with local communities of grassroots people and down-to-earth hard workers. Because that, too, is part of the frontier myth: real Americans are hard

21 Goldberg, Thompson, and Mott n.d.:2-3

22 Resolute v Greenpeace 2016; Energy Transfer v Greenpeace 2017; see Braun (2020):8-9.

23 Pendley 1995:10

workers who pull themselves up by their bootstraps against incredible odds, but especially against elites from the outside who are trying to tell them what to do while swimming in money.

## Boom economics

The irony of the hydraulic fracturing oil booms has been that they were built on debt, not profits. True, much capital was created even though oil price fluctuations affect the industry outside its control. Companies created jobs, although most of them disappeared, projected numbers were overinflated, and most of the money left communities almost immediately[24]. Infrastructure was built. Energy independence came closer and national security was enhanced. However, it seems much, if not most, of this capital and economic activity was financed not by a product—in this case, oil—but by, as two analysts put it, "debt, debt, and debt."[25]

The operating principle for this business model was that companies would acquire leases and drill until they found a high producing well. Then, the numbers from that well were used as an estimate for what all wells on the lease would produce. On that basis, the company would then borrow money to complete more wells and possibly look for a buyer to sell to with those estimates in hand. That is the debt was predicated on potential future extraction, which, however, was taken as the guarantee for the debt. Between 2015 and 2021, 274 oil and gas producers and 330 service companies declared bankruptcy, after having accumulated a combined debt of over $321 billion.[26] Granted, these were bad years for the shale fracturing industry. However, the debt does not cover all expenses—much of the infrastructure that enables the industry to do business, and on which the industry depends, was financed by the states and municipalities in which the companies operated, based on the promise of economic development and tax returns. Incentives, tax exemptions, regulatory exemptions, housing, roads, water, schools, health care facilities, emergency response, and law enforcement followed, provided by tax money and fueled by more debt.

The practice underlying the fracturing oil and gas booms between 2008 and 2015 was "reserve base lending." In reserve base lending

24 See, for example, ORVI 2021
25 Wethe and Crowley 2020
26 Haynes Boone 2022:2

(RBL), companies borrow money based on the oil to which they have acquired a lease and which they therefore predict they will extract. That money is spent on drilling wells, which are taken to prove that the company will be able to extract more oil, and on which basis the company then borrows more money. However, fractured wells have a very fast decline in production. After a year or two, production volumes can fall by eighty percent, unless the well is refractured. Thus, the borrowing develops into a cycle, and under these conditions companies aim to either drill as many wells as possible or buy out other companies with more wells, to increase the proven production rate against which their debt and their worth is evaluated. Between 2005 and 2015—during the boom years—aggregate debt of exploration and production companies in the United States climbed from $50 billion to $200 billion. During those years, low interest rates meant that it was cheap to acquire high debts, which were used to bolster market value because they seemingly proved that companies had money in hand to further expand.[27] Because industry, the federal government, and states wanted (or needed) the booms, nobody looked too closely. The public, starving for jobs after the financial crisis of 2008, was convinced unless they were directly affected by development.

The general understanding of the booms is that they were a consequence of technological ingenuity and innovation. As discussed, hydraulic fracturing has been around for a long time, and vertical drilling has a long history. Although the techniques were combined and improved, making them more efficient, the real cause for the booms was another: low interest rates after the 2008 economic crash meant that hydraulic fracturing became financially attractive. "The real catalyst of the shale revolution was thus the 2008 financial crisis and the era of unprecedentedly low interest rates it ushered in, driven by the US Federal Reserve Bank's monetary policy."[28] Once interest rates rose, borrowing became more difficult and more expensive, and the business model fell apart. Operating on an actual cash-flow model meant that fewer wells could be afforded.[29] With projections adjusted, borrowing became even more difficult.

27 Wharton 2018; Azar 2017; RAN 2020; see also the series of reporting on DeSmog, "Finances of Fracking: Shale Industry Drills More Debt than Profits" at https://www.desmog.com/finances-fracking-shale-industry-drills-more-debt-profit/. Accessed 8/9/2022.

28 Azar 2017:6; see also Kreps (2020):708-713.

29 Brower and McCormick 2021

One legacy of the debt-fueled boom is that companies which have declared bankruptcy cannot assume the costs for rehabilitation of wells and other impacted sites. According to EPA estimates, there are about 2.2 to 2.3 million abandoned oil and gas wells in the United States. Of these wells, it is almost impossible to say how many are plugged, even though the EPA has been in discussions about methodologies for estimates. However, the assumption is that around half of the abandoned wells remain unplugged.[30] Unplugged wells are a huge problem because, apart from potential leaks, they emit methane, one of the most damaging greenhouse gases. While the EPA estimates over two million abandoned or orphaned wells, states identified over 130,000 abandoned wells in 2021—twice the number of wells they reported in 2019, which was before the federal government allocated almost five billion dollars in grants to clean up the sites starting in 2021.[31]

Legally, companies have asset retirement obligations, or a responsibility to clean up abandoned wells. These are sometimes called reclamation obligations. However, older assets are often sold to weaker companies, which hope to still get the wells to produce. These companies are then left with the obligations. If they declare bankruptcy, they will not pay for the cleanup, which means that government has to do so. Even if companies are still active, the cleanup bonds they have to post to get a drilling permit are often absolutely inadequate to pay for reclamation. Most infamous are so-called "blanket bonds," for which companies pay a set amount for an unlimited number of wells. The average per well is sometimes as low as $80. In New Mexico, the oil and gas industry has a total bond coverage of about two hundred million dollars; estimated cleanup costs are over $8 billion.[32] When reclamation obligations are not enough to pay for the cleanup, governments have to step in to cover the costs. In other words, not only do tax payers pay for the infrastructure necessary for oil and gas development, they also pay for the cleanup when wells are abandoned.

## Energy returns

If all the costs of hydraulic fracturing for oil and gas were actually included in a calculation of costs and benefits, extraction might not be

30 EPA 2021

31 Budryk 2022

32 Carbon Tracker 2020; Zibel and Mitchell 2021; WORC 2021; Center for Applied Research 2021.

cost-effective at all. However, at least one benefit of the booms was not only economic. As discussed, domestic oil and gas production would support energy security and thereby national security, has been one of the main arguments for hydraulic fracturing development from the beginning to the second Trump campaign. "Drill, baby, drill" is just as associated with national security as it is with economic profits and jobs.

All other financial and climate factors aside, oil and gas production truly supports energy independence only if extraction requires less energy than what it produces. There is a term for this calculation: EROI (energy return on investment). Like other formulas used to calculate net energy returns, this is a deceptively simple concept for a vastly complex calculation.[33] Not only might the data for energy capture be incomplete, but the real question is what counts as energy invested. For example, does the necessary infrastructure count? Exploration, building access roads, transportation to market, refining—all these processes use energy. With hydraulic fracturing wells, truckloads of sand and water need to be brought to the well and then taken away from the well. Energy use will depend on how far the well is located from these resources' point of origin and from the disposal sites, as well as on the individual geology of the well. Often, unconventional fracturing wells are located next to conventional wells, and some of the infrastructure is already in place, which muddles the picture. Also, because fracturing wells decline in production very rapidly, refracturing has to be factored into the overall equation, but the time factor is also difficult to include into the equation.

EROI for hydraulic fracturing is thus difficult to assess. What is clear is that it is much lower than EROI for conventional oil and gas. When EROI numbers are high, a fall in efficiency is almost imperceptible for society. At a societal EROI of 100, a society spends one percent of its energy to harvest its energy, at an EROI of 80, it spends 1.25 percent of its energy to do so. When EROI numbers get low, however, the impact is dramatic. At an EROI of 2, half of the energy captured is used to harvest more energy, an EROI of 3 means that a third of the energy recovered needs to be reinvested, and at an EROI

33 For a discussion of the concept, see for example Lambert, Hall, and Balogh (2013): 5-13 and Murphy (2014):2-3.

of 5, twenty percent needs to be spent in capturing more energy. In general, EROIs around and under 3 are extremely taxing and are not sustainable for a modern industrial society.

Modern states have subsidized many processes that otherwise would not be profitable, of course. They do so when the services provide a benefit to people but would be too costly for individuals without state subsidies. Public transportation, education, health care, defense, or sewage infrastructure are just some of the projects most modern states subsidize. Of course, the determination about what constitutes a public good, or whether a state wants to or should subsidize a particular public good, are different in different societies. The United States, for example, famously does not subsidize health care or education in the same way other states do. What is important to remember in this context, however, is that efficiency, or the EROI of energy extraction, is different from production. Production volume says nothing about how much energy goes into the extraction and refining process. Agricultural output, for example, is not indication as to whether it is profitable. Subsidized energy extraction—as shown above a reality—is not an indication of energy surpluses created:

> Theoretically, fossil-fuel extraction could expand into more and more difficult areas and continue to grow until it was producing vast amounts of energy output that just equaled the energy inputs. In that absurd situation, fossil-fuel outputs would be at an all-time high, but the *net* outputs or usable energy surplus would be zero. Nevertheless, it is possible to operate individual projects with *negative* net energy (EROI less than 1) with an energy subsidy from elsewhere.[34]

While it is extremely difficult to determine the exact EROI of hydraulic fracturing for oil, it is clear that both overall EROI, and the EROI of oil extraction in particular, has been reduced dramatically over the past century. In the 1970s, the EROI for oil production in the United States still stood at about 25. Oil shale extraction (hydraulic fracturing) in general is assumed to have an EROI of about 7.[35] However, some reports assess the value for oil shale extraction is between 1 and 3.[36]

34 Kreps 2020:703
35 Lambert, Hall, and Balogh 2013:143
36 Cleveland and O'Connor 2010

One analyst comes to the assertion that "the shale revolution cannot produce a large net energy surplus for the United States, no matter how high total energy output might become."[37] If this holds true, several consequences emerge. First, the question of whether the boom was worth it needs to be reposed. If it can be assumed that oil companies usually like to extract oil at high EROI, there must be a dire need to get at oil with low EROI. The hydraulic fracturing booms might thus push back peak oil, but do so in a transitional capacity. In other words, landscapes are disappearing because we are just not ready yet to let go of oil. Second, as net energy harvest values fall, we need to urgently rethink society and how it works.

Modern society was built on the availability of cheap energy with high EROI values. Coal, when mined in open pits, still carries an EROI of around 50—unfortunately, energy efficiency is not directly related to emissions. We still consume as if we can throw energy out the window (and in some cases we literally do). As EROI values sink, though, we will not be able to afford this anymore. Regardless of emissions (which should not be ignored), it is not a good idea to drive a heavy-duty pickup truck to the grocery store when energy net returns are low because the practice is wasting energy, and energy is now costly. High prices for gasoline shocked Americans in 2022. For years, they have been told that oil will not run out, and that one reason is the production from hydraulic fracturing. It is true that large oil reserves remain. It is also true, however, that extracting that oil will become ever-more costly and will eventually not be worth it anymore. "Drill, baby, drill" will temporarily flood the market and bring prices down. The question is, for how long? Yet, the system is geared to specific parameters, and it is difficult to change it because that requires enough political will to break existing interests. Many people argue that this is proof of the free market at work. In reality, the opposite is the case. The system works because true costs and debts are hidden; it is heavily subsidized by society, although society does not know.

One of the best examples for this is ethanol production from corn, often touted to be a green energy. Ethanol from corn carries an EROI value between 0.8 and 1.3 according to most calculations.[38] In other words, ethanol from corn either uses more energy to produce than it delivers or returns just a little bit more. I write this in Iowa, which is

37 Kreps 2020:705

38 Hall, Dale, and Pimentel 2011:2417-2420

one of the main ethanol producers. Iowa also is one of the main pork producers, and astonishingly, biodiesel from swine fat has an EROI value of almost 3.[39] That is still very low, but it is two and a half times higher than ethanol from corn. Ethanol from switchgrass, however, carries an EROI value of about 4 to 6.[40] Some studies, in part because they grew switchgrass on established fields instead of on small plots, actually estimate a value of 13 to 17.[41] Ethanol yields from switchgrass about equal the yield from corn, but switchgrass uses much less energy to be grown. Even if the EROI of ethanol from switchgrass would come out to be merely 10, more net energy could be harvested from growing switchgrass than from extracting oil through hydraulic fracturing. Yet, resistance to switching from corn ethanol to switchgrass ethanol is great, largely because the existing subsidy system is geared directly at corn, and because an established industry profits greatly from farmers buying corn seed, fertilizer, and herbicides every year.

## Legacies

Sinking net energy returns indicate that humans need to seriously rethink how we live. Replacing fossil fuels with alternatives will not work. Instead, we need to use less energy. That will indeed interfere with the American way of life (and all other ways of life modeled on it). I am writing this as Russia is waging war on in Ukraine and Europe is forced to contemplate a near future without or with much reduced Russian gas and oil. Discussions are running high about whether people actually need streetlamps that are on all night or how energy could be saved by taking cold showers. Europe already has, in many parts, a functioning railway system and public transportation is not burdened by socio-economic stereotypes as it is in the United States. Humans should probably stop flying to New York City or London or Dubai for shopping trips. We should think about making things regionally instead of having them made across the world. Globalization is based on the premise of cheap energy and the assumption that costs to the environment are debts that come due after we are dead, so we will not have to pay them.

39 Chiriboga et al. 2020

40 Hammerschlag 2006:1749

41 Schmer et al. 2008:466; Hall, Dale, and Pimentel 2011:2421-2428; see also Larnaudie (2018).

The real question about bearing burdens of and for booms, or extraction in general, is what our legacy will be for our children. Driving through Sheridan Lake, Colorado (whose lake has long disappeared) in the summer of 2022, my son asked where communities in that area get their electricity from. A week later, we approached the massive coal power plant south of Craig, Colorado, and I told him that this is where electricity comes from. We need to understand the cost of energy. That cost is best seen in rural areas actively involved in energy extraction. They carry the cost, while others benefit. The question is whether we have enough solidarity to empathize with those onto whom we have shifted our long-term debts—or whether we ignore them so we can enjoy our near-term profits.

A lot has changed since the introduction of the national sacrifice area concept into our vocabulary. We now understand that this concept has real implications. We understand the social and environmental consequences of energy development. We understand the potential disastrous outcomes of water contamination. We know that extraction might not be economically profitable, and that net energy returns are becoming more questionable. Yet, for cultural reasons, we hold on to what we know, in part because not many people explain what all of this means. There are huge short-term incentives to keep to the status quo, so we ignore the compiling long-term debt. The newest pipelines across the plains are CO2 pipelines, going in the opposite direction of oil pipelines to pump gases into the geological formations that are now empty of oil. We are still looking to technological solutions to a problem we are creating so that we can continue to ignore the fact that we could solve the issue by stopping to create it.

The question is simply whether all this will be worth it. Aldo Leopold asked the same question. We "might be capable of squeezing a living even out of a ruined countryside," he wrote,[42] "yet who wants to be a cell in that kind of a body politic? I for one do not."

I agree.

Booms like the Bakken undoubtedly create wealth. So did booms before and since, on the Northern Plains and elsewhere. That wealth, however, can be deceptive. Those who profit from resource booms are often not those who live or continue to live in the areas where those booms take place. That alone is food for thought—it means that the

42 In Flader and Callicott (1991):217.

wealth, like the resources, are extracted. The question is what stays behind. I have argued here that much of what stays after booms are over is the burden to carry on in a place that is no longer the same.

The fur trade boom ended in dependency for Native nations after the commodified furbearing animals' populations were exhausted (and diseases had similarly ravaged Native communities). The land boom ended in dependency on railroad companies and the consolidation of land into bonanza farms and other industrial agriculture enterprises. The industrial agriculture boom ended in the dust storms of the Great Depression. The push to extract energy from the Plains, through dams and coal plants, turned fertile soil into lakes and farming communities into industrial labor towns. The oil and gas booms came and went, but most of the money left the area for investors far away. All those booms made some people in the area wealthy. They arguably built infrastructure that was both necessary for the economic activity but also benefited communities. Primarily, however, each boom drove the communities further into dependency and left communities with larger burdens. To alleviate those burdens, more outside investment became needed, which was available through further booms. The Bakken fits into this cycle.

What is different about hydraulic fracturing booms is two things—one quantitative and one qualitative. First, the Bakken boom is more intense. The scale of investment and of profits, of infrastructure needed and of devastation enacted, is greater than in previous booms. This opens up the hopes and dreams for greater benefits. It also creates greater dangers. The scale of this boom is such that the landscape and the communities might not be able to shake off the impacts once it is over. Mitigation will not be a question of having a few empty classrooms and a subdivision planned where nobody built houses, leading to a few decades of debt. The mitigation of these impacts will be an existential burden to carry for communities, and the burden might be too high for the landscape.

The qualitative impact, especially on water, is so much higher that it fundamentally endangers the future of the region. This was not the case in previous booms. Even the flooding of Lake Sakakawea left people with alternatives to continue living in the area. If the fracking brine gets into aquifers, there won't be alternatives. This is a steep price to pay. Those who profit from the boom will be able to leave. Those who carry the burden of the boom will not have that privilege.

I do not know how we should live, but investigating the Bakken oil boom from different sides leaves me with a vision of an alternative. What if the billions of dollars with which we subsidize the oil development that produces questionable net energy results would be spent differently? For example, this money and energy could be spent restoring railroad lines and building hydropower stations. They could be spent converting monocrop corn and soybean fields to switchgrass or prairie lands and for research on biofuels production that actually carry net energy returns. This would actually support rural communities and make them viable in the long term. Instead of localities of unsustainable extraction for profit maximization, they would become central to a vision of sustainability and long-term security. It would also provide for a change in the cultural understandings of farming from merely converting the rural landscape to an industrial production site to instead being stewards of the land. If, at the same time, lands would be opened to the public like they are in Europe, a real chance of reterritorialization, of reconnecting with the land, exists. This, in turn, would enhance an understanding of locality, of the land itself, and of our landscapes and our obligations to it.

The inimitable Vine Deloria, Jr. once pointed out that one of the issues of American culture and society is that it is a society based on individual rights. I have the right to do something, so I do it. There are no rights of nature recognized in American society because nature is a collection of resource commodities. What if a society would be based, instead, on the basis of obligations? The recognition of obligations based on relationships does not take away rights, but makes them secondary to the needs of others, including non-humans. It is difficult, if not impossible, to allow for every entity to have the same legal rights as us. However, a recognition that we live in landscapes we are dependent on, that our environment is not a collection of commodities, and that communities as a whole do have certain rights over landscapes that individuals should not be able to break, would go a long way to start real discussions about the value of land, water, and life.

A vision like this might be a crazy dream if the current situation actually worked toward a future of well-being or was sustainable. As has become clear during this discussion, however, it does not. It does not create real positive net results in the end. The American way of life as it is now currently leads straight to a net energy cliff and the actual destruction of itself. Realizing that, it might be time for a change. What is more American than understanding a problem, analyzing it, finding a solution, and then implementing that? The notion of the frontier spirit can stay alive. It just needs to be applied with an understanding of all the facts. Nobody survived the frontier as an individual insisting on their right to do whatever they wanted. Instead, what was needed was the formation of communities and listening to the land. That need is still here.

# Bibliography

Adams, Terry K., and Greg J. Duncan, 1992. "Long-Term Poverty in Rural Areas," in Cynthia M. Duncan (ed.) *Rural Poverty in America*, pp.63-93. Westport, CT: Auburn House.

Adhikari, Arjun, and Andrew J, Hansen, 2018. "Land Use Change and Habitat Fragmentation of Wildland Ecosystems of the North Central United States," *Landscape and Urban Planning, 177*, pp.196-216.

Agee, James, 1941. *Let Us Now Praise Famous Men*. Boston: Houghton Mifflin.

Allison, James Robert, III, 2015. *Sovereignty for Survival. American Energy Development and Indian Self-Determination*. New Haven: Yale University Press.

Allred, Brady W., W. Kolby Smith, Dirac Twidwell, Julia H. Haggerty, Steven W. Running, David E. Naugle, and Samual D. Fuhlendorf, 2015. "Ecosystem Services Lost to Oil and Gas in North America," *Science, 348*(6233), pp. 401-402.

Ambler, Marjane, 1984a. "Uncertainty in CERT," in Joseph G. Jorgensen (ed.) *Native Americans and Energy Development II*, pp.71-78. Boston: Anthropology Resource Center / Forestville, CA: Seventh Generation Fund.

Ambler, Marjane, 1984b. "The Three Affiliated Tribes at Fort Berthold - Mandan, Hidatsa, Arikara - Seek to Control Their Energy Resources," in Joseph G. Jorgensen (ed.) *Native Americans and Energy Development II*, pp.194-199. Boston: Anthropology Resource Center / Forestville, CA: Seventh Generation Fund.

Ambler, Marjane, 1990. *Breaking the Iron Bonds. Indian Control of Energy Development*. Lawrence: University Press of Kansas.

Anderson, Christina L., and Rebecca L. Bieniaszewska, 2005. "The Role of Corporate Social Responsibility in an Oil Company's Expansion into New Territories," *Corporate Social Responsibility and Environmental Management, 12*, pp.1-9.

Anderson, S. B., J. P. Bluemle, and L.C. Gerhard, 1982. "Oil Exploration and Development in the North Dakota Williston Basin," in *4th International Williston Basin Symposium*, pp.3-10. North Dakota Geological Society and Saskatchewan Geological Society.

ANSI/API, 2014. *Community Engagement Guidelines.* ANSI/API Bulletin 100-3. First Edition, July 2014. American National Standards Institute/American Petroleum Institute. Washington, D.C.: API Publishing Services.

Arboleda, Martin, 2020. *Planetary Mine. Territories of Extraction under Late Capitalism*. London: Verso.

Arias, Logan, 2014. "The State of the Bakken Oil Boom. Will it Last?" *Bakken Living, 1*(3), 54-57.

Ashabranner, Brent, 1982. *Morning Star, Black Sun. The Northern Cheyenne Indians and America's Energy Crisis.* New York: Macmillan/McGraw-Hill.

Augé, Marc, 1995. *Non-Places. Introduction to an Anthropology of Supermodernity.* Translated by John Howe. New York: Verso.

Azar, Amir, 2017. *Reserve Base Lending and the Outlook for Shale Oil and Gas Finance*. Columbia University, SIPA. Center on Global Energy Policy. May 2017.

Ballard, Chris and Glenn Banks, 2003. "Resource Wars: The Anthropology of Mining," *Annual Review of Anthropology, 32*, pp.287-313.

Barnes, T. R., 1952. "The Williston Basin – A New Province for Oil Exploration," in *Guidebook: Third Annual Field Conference, Black Hills, Williston Basin*, pp.96-117. Billings: Billings Geological Society.

Bateson, Gregory, 1958. *Naven*. Second Edition. Stanford: Stanford University Press.

Bateson, Gregory, and Mary Catherine Bateson, 1987. *Angels Fear. Towards an Epistemology of the Sacred.* New York: Bantam.

Baynard, Chris W., 2011. "The Landscape Infrastructure Footprint of Oil Development: Venezuela's Heavy Oil Belt," *Ecological Indicators, 11*, pp.789-810.

Baynard, Chris W., Ksenya Mjachina, Robert D. Richardson, Robert W. Schupp, J. David Lambert, Alexander A. Chibilyev, 2017. "Energy Development in Colorado's Pawnee National Grasslands: Mapping and Measuring the Disturbance Footprint of Renewables and Non-Renewables," *Environmental Management, 59*, pp.995-1016.

Beck, Robert E., 2011. "Water Resources and Oil and Gas Development: A Survey of North Dakota Law," *North Dakota Law Review, 87*, pp.507-533.

Beckman, Joanne (ed.), 2012. *Energy Impact Solution Models Project. Final Report.* Dickinson, ND: Dickinson State University and Minot State University.

Behrends, Andrea, Stephen P. Reyna, and Gunther Schlee (eds.), 2011. *Crude Domination. An Anthropology of Oil.* New York: Berghahn Books.

Benko, Katie L., and Jörg E. Drewes 2008 "Produced Water in the Western United States: Geographical Distribution, Occurrence, and Composition" *Environmental Engineering Science*, 25 (2), 239-246.

Berger, Thomas R., 1988. *Northern Frontier, Northern Homeland. The Report of the Mackenzie Valley Pipeline Inquiry.* Revised Edition. Vancouver: Douglas & McIntyre.

BIA, 2002. *BIA Supports Three Affiliated Tribes' Dream of Joining Oil Refining Industry Through Grant Award.* Bureau of Indian Affairs, September 20, 2002.

Birdsell, Daniel T., Harihar Rajaram, David Dempsey, and Hari S. Viswanathan, 2015. "Hydraulic Fracturing Fluid Migration in the Subsurface: A Review and Expanded Modeling Results," *Water Resources Research, 51*, pp.7159-7188.

Bismarck Tribune, 1946. "Off to Look at Indian Lands. Group Flies in Army Plane to See What Can Be Done to Relocate Folk at Elbowoods," in *Bismarck Tribune*, Jan. 10 1946.

Bismarck Tribune, 1951. "Would Have Landowners Keep Dam Area Oil Rights," in *Bismarck Tribune*, April 9, 1951.

Bodley, John H., 2008. *Victims of Progress.* Lanham, MD: AltaMira Press.

Boff, Leonardo, 1997. *Cry of the Earth, Cry of the Poor.* Maryknoll, NY: Orbis Books.

Boom and Bloom, 2011. "Parshall Adapts to 'Boom' Times" *Boom and Bloom.* A supplement to *Mclean County Independent, Underwood News, Leader-News, Mclean County Journal, McClusky Gazette, Velva Area Voice, Hazen Star, Beulah Beacon, Center Republican, New Town News* and *Mountrail County Record.*

Bowen, Zachary H., Gretchen P. Oelsner, Brian S. Cade, Tanya J. Gallegos, Aida M. Farag, David N. Mott, Christopher J. Potter, Peter J. Cinotto, Melanie L. Clark, William M. Kappel, Timothy M.

Kresse, Cynthia P. Melcher, Suzanne S. Paschke, David D. Susong, and Brian A. Varela, 2015. "Assessment of Surface Water Chloride and Conductivity Trends in Areas of Unconventional Oil and Gas Development – Why Existing National Data Sets Cannot Tell Us What We would Like to Know," *Water Resources Research, 51*, pp.704-715.

Branton, Nicole, 2009. "Landscape Approaches in Historical Archaeology: The Archaeology of Places," in Teresita Majewski and David Gaimster (eds.) *International Handbook of Historical Archaeology*, pp.52-65. New York: Springer.

Braun, Sebastian Felix, 2008. *Buffalo Inc. American Indians and Economic Development*. Norman: University of Oklahoma Press.

Braun, Sebastian Felix, 2013a. "Imagining Un-Imagined Communities. The Politics of Indigenous Nationalism," in Brian Hosmer and Larry Nesper (eds.) *Tribal Worlds. Critical Studies in American Indian Nation Building*, pp.141-160. Albany: SUNY Press.

Braun, Sebastian Felix, 2013b. "Against Procedural Landscapes," in Sebastian Felix Braun (ed.) *Transforming Ethnohistories: Narrative, Meaning, and Community*, pp.201-221. Norman: University of Oklahoma Press.

Braun, Sebastian Felix, 2013c. "Introduction. An Ethnohistory of Listening," in Sebastian Felix Braun (ed.) *Transforming Ethnohistories: Narrative, Meaning, and Community*, pp.3-21. Norman: University of Oklahoma Press.

Braun, Sebastian, 2016a. "Revisited Frontiers: The Bakken, the Plains, Potential Futures, and Real Pasts," in William Caraher and Kyle Conway (eds.) *Boom. Oil and the Changing Geographies in Western North Dakota*, pp.91-116. Grand Forks, ND: Digital Press at the University of North Dakota.

Braun, Sebastian F., 2016b. "Sustainability, Resiliance, and Dependency: The Great Plains Model," in H. Thomas Foster, Lisa M. Paciulli, and David J. Goldstein (eds.) *Viewing the Future in the Past: Historical Ecology Applications to Environmental Issues*, pp.133-146. Columbia: University of South Carolina Press.

Braun, Sebastian Felix, 2017. "Mourning Ourselves and/as our Relatives: Ecology as Kinship," in Ashlee Cunsolo Willox and Karen Landman (eds.) *Mourning Nature: Hope at the Heart of Ecological Loss and Grief*, pp.64-91. Montreal: McGill-Queens University Press.

Braun, Sebastian Felix, 2020. "Culture, Resource, Management, and Anthropology: Pipelines and the *wakan* at the Standing Rock Sioux Reservation," *Plains Anthropologist, 65*(253), pp.7-24.

Braun, Sebastian, 2025. "'Bad Anthropology.' Engagement in a Time of Crisis," in Jack David Weller (ed.) *Anthropology – History, Theory, Practice, and Engagement.* IntechOpen.

Briody, Blaire, 2017. *The New Wild West. Black Gold, Fracking, and Life in a North Dakota Boomtown.* New York: St. Martin's Press.

Brower, Derek, and Myles McCormick, 2021. "US Shale Oil: Can a Leaner Industry Ever Lure Back Investors?" *Financial Times*, January 31, 2021.

Brown, Alleen, 2021. "Inside the Oil Industry's Fight to Roll Back Tribal Sovereignty after Supreme Court Decision," *The Intercept*, March 10, 2021.

Brown, Terry, Carol D. Frost, Thomas D. Hayes, Lea A. Heath, Drew W. Johnson, David A. Lopez, Demian Saffer, Michael A. Urynowicz, John Wheaton, and Mark D. Zoback, 2007. *Produced Water Management and Beneficial Use: Final Report.* Office of Fossil Energy. Department of Energy Award No.: DE-FC26-05NT15549.

Brunnschweiler, Christa N., and Erwin H. Bulte, 2008. "The Resource Curse Revisited and Revised: A Tale of Paradoxes and Red Herrings," *Journal of Environmental Economics and Management, 55*, 248-264.

BSR, 2012. *Engaging with Free, Prior, and Informed Consent.* BSR (Business for Social Responsibility).

Buckland, Jerry, 2004. *Ploughing Up the Farm. Neoliberalism, Modern Technology, and the State of the World's Farmers.* London: Zed Books.

Budryk, Zack, 2022. "Interior: US has Twice as many Abandoned Oil and Gas Wells as Previously Thought," *The Hill*, January 5, 2022.

Bush, George W. 2001 *President Bush Discusses Global Climate Change.* The White House, Office of the Press Secretary, June 11, 2001.

Canada Senate, 2005. *Water in the West: Under Pressure.* Fourth Interim report of the Standing Senate Committee on Energy, the Environment and Natural Resources. November 2005.

Caraher, William, and Kyle Conway (eds.), 2016. *The Bakken goes Boom. Oil and the Changing Geographies of Western North Dakota.* Grand Forks, ND: Digital Press at the University of North Dakota.

Caraher, William R., and Bret A. Weber, 2017. *The Bakken: An Archaeology of an Industrial Landscape.* Fargo, ND: North Dakota State University Press.

Carbon Tracker, 2020. *It's Closing Time: The Huge Bill to Abandon Oilfields Comes Early.* June 2020. Carbon Tracker Initiative.

Carluccio, Tracy, 2010. "Will We Sacrifice Our Water for Gas?" *Outdoor America*, Spring, pp.27-33.

Cart, Julie, 2013. "New Mexico County First in Nation to Ban Fracking to Safeguard Water" *Los Angeles Times*, May 28, 2013.

Cashman, Kay, 2012. "NDPC launches trash clean up," *Petroleum News Bakken, 1*(2), p.3.

Catlin, George, 1841. *Letters and Notes on the Manners, Customs, and Condition of the North American Indians.* Vol. I. London: George Catlin (Egyptian Hall, Piccadilly).

Cawley, R. MacGregor, 1993. *Federal Land, Western Anger. The Sagebrush Rebellion and Environmental Politics.* Lawrence: University Press of Kansas.

Center for Applied Research, 2021. *An Analysis of the Adequacy of Financial Assurance Requirements for Oil and Gas Infrastructure Located on State Trust and Private Lands in New Mexico.* The Center for Applied Research.

Chamberlain, Kathleen P., 2000. *Under Sacred Ground. A History of Navajo Oil, 1922-1982.* Albuquerque: University of New Mexico Press.

Chance, Norman A., 1990. *The Iñupiat and Arctic Alaska. An Ethnography of Development.* Fort Worth: Holt, Rinehart and Winston.

Chapin, Mac, Zachary Lamb, and Bill Threlkeld, 2000. "Mapping Indigenous Lands," *Annual Review of Anthropology, 34*, pp.619-638.

Cherokee v Georgia, 1831. *Cherokee Nation v. Georgia.* Supreme Court of the United States. 30 U.S. 1. March 18, 1831.

Chiriboga, Gonzalo, Andres De La Rosa, Camila Molina, Stefany Velarde, and Ghem Carvajal C., 2020. "Energy Return on Investment (EROI) and Life Cycle Analysis (LCA) of Biofuels in Ecuador," *Heliyon, 6*, e04213.

Cleveland, Cutler J., and Peter O'Connor, 2010. *An Assessment of the Energy Return on Investment (EROI) of Oil Shale.* Final Report. Prepared for Western Resource Advocates.

Cobell v Norton, 2005. *Elouise Pepion Cobell et al. v. Gale Norton et al.* Civil Action No. 96-1285 (RCL). United States District Court for the District of Columbia. Memorandum Opinion. July 12, 2005.

Commonwealth of Australia, 2006. *Community Engagement and Development.* Leading Practice Sustainable Development Program for the Mining Industry. Australian Government, Department of Industry Tourism and Resources.

Commonwealth of Australia, 2007. *Working with Indigenous Communities.* Leading Practice Sustainable Development Program for the Mining Industry. Australian Government, Department of Industry Tourism and Resources.

Conway, Kyle (ed.), 2020. *Sixty Years of Boom and Bust: The Impact of Oil in North Dakota, 1958-2018.* Grand Forks, ND: Digital Press at the University of North Dakota.

Cook, Michelle L., 2019. "Striking at the Heart of Capital. International Financial Institutions and Indigenous Peoples' Human Rights," in Nick Estes and Jaskiran Dhillon (eds.) *Standing with Standing Rock. Voices from the #NoDAPL Movement*, pp.103-157. Minneapolis: University of Minnesota Press.

Council of Europe, 2000. *Rapport explicatif de la Convention européenne du paysage.* Florence, 20.X.2000. Série des traités européens - n° 176.

Cruikshank, Julie, 1992. *Life Lived Like a Story. Life Stories of Three Yukon Native Elders.* Lincoln: University of Nebraska Press.

Cunfer, Geoff, 2005. *On the Great Plains. Agriculture and Environment.* College Station, TX: Texas A&M University Press.

Curley, Andrew, 2023. *Carbon Sovereignty. Coal, Development, and Energy Transition in the Navajo Nation.* Tucson: University of Arizona Press.

Cushman, Frances, and Gordon MacGregor, 1948. *Harnessing the Big Muddy. The Story of the Missouri River Basin.* U.S. Indian Service, Education Division, Haskell Institute Print Shop.

d'Aujourd'hui, Rolf, 1998. "Zum Genius Loci von Basel. Ein zentraler Ort im Belchen-System." in *Basler Stadtbuch, 1997*, pp.125-138. Basel: Christoph Merian Stiftung.

Dalrymple, Amy. 2016. "Bakken Multi-Well Pads Getting Bigger," *Bismarck Tribune*, July 4, 2016.

Darrow, George, 1955. "The History of Oil Exploration in Northwestern Montana, 1892-1950" in *Guidebook: Sixth Annual Field Conference*, pp.225-232. Billings: Billings Geological Society.

Davidson, Carlos, 1998. "Issues in Landscape Fragmentation," *Wildlife Society Bulletin*, *26*(1), pp.32-37.

Davidson, Osha Gray, 1990. *Broken Heartland. The Rise of America's Rural Ghetto*. New York: Doubleday.

Davis, W. E., and R. E. Hunt, 1956. "Geology and Oil Production on the Northern Portion of the Cedar Creek Anticline, Dawson County, Montana," in *First International Williston Basin Symposium*, pp.121-129. North Dakota Geological Society and Saskatchewan Geological Society.

Deans, W. Stuart, Lee R. Scherer, and John Pulley, 1991. "A Study of Horizontal Drilling and the Bakken Formation Williston Basin, North Dakota," in William B. Hansen (ed.) *1991 Guidebook to Geology and Horizontal Drilling of the Bakken Formation*, pp.95-104. Billings: Montana Geological Society.

Deaton, Jeremy, 2021. "A Tribal Nation Made Dependent on Oil and Gas Got Little Relief When the Market Crashed," *Nexus Media News*, April 22, 2021.

Delaney, Danielle, 2017. "The Master's Tools: Tribal Sovereignty and Tribal Governance Contracting/Compacting," *American Indian Law Journal, 5*(2), pp.308-345.

Deloria, Vine, Jr., 1998. "Intellectual Self-Determination and Sovereignty: Looking at the Windmills in Our Minds," *Wicazo Sa Review, 13*(1), pp.25-31.

Deloria, Philip J., 2004. *Indians in Unexpected Places*. Lawrence: University Press of Kansas.

DeMallie, Raymond J., 1993. "'These Have No Ears': Narrative and the Ethnohistorical Record" *Ethnohistory, 40*(4): pp.515-538.

Department of the Interior, Office of the Solicitor, 2020. *Memorandum M-37056, Status of Mineral Ownership Underlying the Missouri River within the Boundaries of the Fort Berthold Indian Reservation (North Dakota)*. May 26, 2020.

Department of the Interior, Office of the Solicitor, 2022. *Memorandum M-37073, Opinion Regarding the Status of Mineral Ownership Underlying the Missouri River within the Boundaries of the Fort Berthold Indian Reservation (North Dakota)*. February 4, 2022.

Dickinson State University, 2011. *Energy Impact Symposium. Environmental and Workforce Impacts. Emergency Preparedness and Response. September 18-20, 2011, Dickinson, North Dakota*. 2 DVDs. With possession of author.

DOJ, 2020. *Three Tribal Officials Charged in Bribery Scheme*. Department of Justice, Office of Public Affairs, July 30, 2020.

Dokis, Carly A., 2015. *Where the Rivers Meet. Pipelines, Participatory Resource Management, and Aboriginal-State Relations in the Northwest Territories*. Vancouver: UBC Press.

Dolan, Catherine, and Dinah Rajak (eds.), 2016. *The Anthropology of Corporate Social Responsibility*. New York: Berghahn Books.

Donahue, Debra L., 1999. *The Western Range Revisited. Removing Livestock from Public Lands to Conserve Native Biodiversity*. Norman: University of Oklahoma Press.

Duncan, Cynthia M., 1999. *Worlds Apart. Why Poverty Persists in Rural America*. New Haven: Yale University Press.

Dussel, Enrique, 1998. "Beyond Eurocentrism. The World-System and the Limits of Modernity," in Fredric Jameson and Masao Miyoshi (eds.) *The Cultures of Globalization*, pp.3-31. Durham, N.C.: Duke University Press.

Dussel, Enrique, 2006. "Globalization, Organization, and the Ethics of Liberation," in collaboration with Eduardo Ibarra-Colado. *Organization, 13*(4), pp.489-509.

Dutton, DeAnn M., and Joanna N. Thamke, 2021. "Physical and Chemical Characteristics of Samples Collected in the East Poplar Oil Field Study Area, Fort Peck Indian Reservation, 1952-2016." U.S. Geological Service Data Release. https://www.sciencebase.gov/catalog/item/5f69328882ce38aaa2425591. Accessed 8/3/2022.

DWR, 2022a. *North Dakota Hydraulic Fracturing and Water use Facts. February 2022*. Bismarck, ND: Department of Water Resources.

DWR, 2022b. *Biennial Report, July 1, 2019 to June 31, 2021*. Bismarck, ND: Department of Water Resources.

Eagleton, Terry, 1990. *The Ideology of the Aesthetic*. Oxford: Blackwell

Edwards, Richard, 2015. *Natives of a Dry Place. Stories of Dakota Before the Oil Boom*. Pierre, SD: South Dakota Historical Society Press.

EERC, 2020. *Produced Water Management and Recycling Options in North Dakota. Final Report*. Prepared for North Dakota Legislative Management Energy Development and transmission Committee and North Dakota Industrial Commission Oil and Gas Research Council. Energy and Environmental Research Center, University of North Dakota.

Ellis, Stephen C., 2005. "Meaningful Consideration? A Review of Traditional Knowledge in Environmental Decision Making" *Arctic, 58*(1), pp.66-77.

Elwood, Sarah, 2006. "Critical Issues in Participatory GIS: Deconstructions, Reconstructions, and New Research Directions," *Transactions in GIS, 10*(5), pp.693-708.

Energy Development and Transmission Committee, 2012. *Presentation on behalf of Western North Dakota School Districts.* January 26, 2012, State Capitol, Bismarch, ND.

Energy Transfer v Greenpeace, 2017. *Energy Transfer Equity and Energy Transfer Partners v. Greenpeace International et al.* Case No. 1:17-cv-00173-CSM. Complaint, Jury Trial Demanded. US District Court for the District of North Dakota, Western Division. August 22, 2017.

England, J. Lynn, and Stan L. Albrecht, 1984. "Boomtowns and Social Disruption," *Rural Sociology, 49*(2), pp.230-246.

England, Lynn, and Ralph B. Brown, 2003. "Community and Resource Extraction in Rural America," in *Challenges for Rural America in the Twenty-First Century*, edited by David L. Brown and Lois E. Swanson, pp.317-328. University Park, PA: Pennsylvania State University Press.

EPA, n.d. *Statement of Basis.* Big Bend 1-5 SWD, Mountrail County, ND. EPA Permit No. ND22184-08837.

EPA, 2015. *Assessment of the Potential Impacts of Hydraulic Fracturing for Oil and Gas on Drinking Water Resources.* External Review Draft. EPA/600/R-15/047a. Washington, D.C.: Environmental Protection Agency.

EPA, 2016. Hydraulic Fracturing for Oil and Gas: *Impacts from the Hydraulic Fracturing Water Cycle on Drinking Water Resources in the United States.* EPA-600-R-16-236Fa. Washington, D.C.: Environmental Protection Agency, Office of Research and Development.

EPA, 2021. *Inventory of U.S. Greenhouse Gas Emissions and Sinks 1990-2020: Updates Under Consideration for Abandoned Oil and Gas Wells.* September 2021. Environmental Protection Agency.

Equitable Origin, 2020. *EO100™ Standard Technical Addendum. EO100.1: Shale Oil and Gas Operations.* Revision 2. Equitable Origin.

Esri, 2021. Petroleum and Pipeline. https://www.esri.com/en-us/industries/petroleum/overview Accessed 6/9/2021.

Euler, Robert C. and Harry L. Naylor, 1952. "Southern Ute Rehabilitation Planning. A Study in Self-Determination" *Human Organization, 11*(4), pp.27-32.

Faith, Mike, Kevin Killer, and Harold Frazier, 2021. *Re: Environmental Review of Dakota Access Pipeline*. Letter to Jaime Pinkham, Acting Assistant Secretary of the Army for Civil Works. September 22, 2021.

Fichtner, Uwe, 1988. *Grenzüberschreitende Verflechtungen und regionales Bewusstsein in der Regio*. Schriften der Regio 10. Frankfurt a.M.: Helbing und Lichtenhahn.

Fingerhuth, Carl, 1999. "Die trinationale Agglomeration Basel aus städtebaulicher Sicht" in *Basler Stadtbuch 1998*, pp.41-47. Basel: Christoph Merian Stiftung.

Fischer, Joern, and David B. Lindenmayer, 2007. "Landscape Modification and Habitat Fragmentation: A Synthesis," *Global Ecology and Biogeography, 16*, pp.265-280.

Fitzgerald, Timothy, Yusuke Kuwayama, Shiela Olmstead, and Alexandra Thompson, 2020. "Dynamic Impacts of U.S. Energy Development on Agricultural Land Use," *Energy Policy, 137*, pp.111-163. I

Flader, Susan L., and J. Baird Callicott (eds.), 1991. *The River of the Mother of God and Other Essays by Aldo Leopold*. Madison: University of Wisconsin Press.

Fleming, Andrew, 2006. "Post-processual Landscape Archaeology: A Critique," *Cambridge Archaeological Journal, 16*(3), pp.267-280.

Flewelling, Samuel A., Matthew P. Tymchak, and Norm Warpinski, 2013. "Hydraulic Fracture Height Limits and Fault Interactions in Tight Oil and Gas Formations" *Geophysical Research Letters, 40*(14), pp.3602-3606.

Flewelling, Samuel A., and Manu Sharma, 2014. "Constraints on Upward Migration of Hydraulic Fracturing Fluid and Brine" *Groundwater, 52*(1), pp.9-19.

Forbes, Gerald, 1939. "Southwestern Oil Boom Towns," *Chronicles of Oklahoma, 17*(4), 393-400.

Ford Foundation, 1974. *Rehabilitation Potential of Western Coal Lands*. Cambridge, MA: Ballinger Publishing.

Foster, John Bellamy, 2000. *Marx's Ecology. Materialism and Nature*. New York: Monthly Review Press.

Foster, John Bellamy, and Brett Clark, 2020. *The Robbery of Nature. Capitalism and the Ecological Rift*. New York: Monthly Review Press.

Fowles, Severin, 2010. "The Southwest School of Landscape Archaeology," *Annual Review of Anthropology, 39*, pp.453-468.

Frantz, L.F., 1952. "The Canadian Portion of the Basin – 1952" in Petroleum Information *An Introduction to the Williston Basin*, pp.45-46. Casper, WY: Petroleum Information.

Freyman, Monika, and Ryan Salmon, 2013. *Hydraulic Fracturing and Water Stress: Growing Competitive Pressures for Water*. Boston: Ceres.

Fridgen, Patrick, 2010. "Abundant Lake Sakakawea Water Becoming Focus for Oil Development," From the Oxbow, *North Dakota Water*, June, pp.16-17.

Fritz, Gayle J., 2019. *Feeding Cahokia. Early Agriculture in the North American Heartland.* Tuscaloosa: University of Alabama Press.

Fritz, Henry E., 2005. "Allotment of Mineral and Timber Lands on Indian Reservations and the Public Domain," *The Historian, 67*(4), pp.645-663.

Gabriel, Tezikiah, 2012. *Expansion of Quality Child Care in Williston North Dakota. A Solution-Based Plan.* Minneapolis: First Children's Finance.

Garcia, Paula, 2018. "A Retrospective on the Mora County Fracking Ban," *La Jicarita*, February 7, 2018.

Gassiat, Claire, Tom Gleeson, Rene Lefebvre, and Jeffrey McKenzie, 2013. "Hydraulic Fracturing in Faulted Sedimentary Basins: Numerical Simulation of Potential Contamination of Shallow Aquifers over Long Time Scales," *Water Resources Research, 49*, pp.8310-8327.

Gedicks, Al, 2001. *Resource Rebels. Native Challenges to Mining and Oil Corporations.* Cambridge, MA: South End Press.

Geiver, Luke, 2014a. "The Making of the Watford City Story." *The Bakken Magazine, 2*(10), p.6.

Geiver, Luke, 2014b. "The Heart of the Bakken," *The Bakken Magazine, 2*(10), pp.24-37.

Geiver, Luke, 2016. "Remember Parts of 2016," *The Bakken Magazine, 4*(6), p.4.

Ghazvinian, John, 2007. *Untapped. The Scramble for Africa's Oil.* Orlando, FL: Harcourt.

Gilberthope, Emma, and Gavin Hilson (eds.), 2014. *Natural Resource Extraction and Indigenous Livelihoods. Development Challenges in an Era of Globalization.* Farnham, UK: Ashgate.

Gleick, Peter H., Gary Wolff, Elizabeth L. Chalecki, and Rachel Reyes, 2002. *The New Economy of Water. The Risks and Benefits of Globalization and Privatization of Fresh Water.* Oakland, CA: Pacific Institute for Studies in Development, Environment, and Security.

Godoy, Ricardo, 1985. "Mining: Anthropological Perspectives," *Annual Review of Anthropology, 14*, 199-217.

Goldberg, Phil, Jamie Thompson, and Dalton Mott, n.d. *Vigilante Regulation: When Anti-Pipeline Activism Becomes Tortious Interference.* GAIN (Grow America's Infrastructure Now).

Goldenberg, Suzanne, 2013. "A Texan Tragedy: Ample Oil, No Water," *The Guardian*, August 11, 2013.

Gomez-Barris, Macarena, 2017. *The Extractive Zone. Social Ecologies and Decolonial Perspectives.* Durham: Duke University Press.

Goodin, Maury, 1952. "Oil and Gas Leasing in the Basin," in Petroleum Information *An Introduction to the Williston Basin*, pp.53-60. Casper, WY: Petroleum Information.

Gorecki, Charles D., James A. Sorensen, Edward Steadman, and John A. Harju, 2009. "$CO_2$ Storage Risk Minimization through Systematic Identification and Assessment of Faults: A Williston Basin Case Study" *Energy Procedia, 1*, pp.2887-2894.

Government of Western Australia, 2003. *National Vision for Mineral and Petroleum Sector Released.* Media Statement, 8/10/2003. https://www.mediastatements.wa.gov.au/Pages/Gallop/2003/10/National-vision-for-mineral-and-petroleum-sector-released.aspx Accessed 7/7/2021.

Great Plains Committee, 1937. *The Future of the Great Plains.* 75th Congres, 1st Session. Document No. 144.

Green, A., T.M. DeSutter, M.A. Meehan, A.L.M. Daigh, and P.L. O'Brien, 2020. "Produced Water's Impact on Soil Properties: Remediation Challenges and Opportunities" *Agrosystems, Geosciences and Environment, 3*:e20042.

Gries, John Paul, 1952. "History of Exploration in Williston Basin, North Dakota, South Dakota, Montana, and Canada: Abstract." *AAPG Bulletin, 36*(5), p.964.

Grober, Ulrich, 2012. *Sustainability. A Cultural History.* Totnes, UK: Green Boooks.

Grossman, Zoltan, 2017. *Unlikely Alliances. Native Nations and White Communities Join to Defend Rural Lands.* Seattle: University of Washington Press.

Groth, Paul, 1997. "Frameworks for Cultural Landscape Study" in Paul Groth and Todd W. Bressi (eds.) *Understanding Ordinary Landscapes*, p.1-21. New Haven: Yale University Press.

GWPC, n.d. *Injection Wells. An Introduction to Their Use, Operation, and Regulation*. Groundwater Protection Council.

GWPC, 2019. *Produced Water Report. Regulations, Current Practices, and Research Needs*. Groundwater Protection Council.

Hagmann, Daniel, 2006. "Kultort Basel. Beobachtungen zum Himmel über Basel heute," in *Basler Stadtbuch 2005*, pp.41-43. Basel: Christoph Merian Stiftung.

Hall, Charles A.S., Bruce E. Dale, and David Pimentel, 2011. "Seeking to Understand the Reasons for Different Energy Return on Investments (EROI) Estimates for Biofuels," *Sustainability, 3*, pp.2413-2432.

Hall, Charles A.S., Jessica G. Lambert, and Stephen B. Balogh, 2014. "EROI of Different Fuels and the Implications for Society," *Energy Policy, 64*, pp.141-152.

Hall, Tex G., 2012. *Testimony of the Honorable Tex G. Hall, Chairman, Mandan, Hidatsa, and Arikara Nation of the Fort Berthold Reservation*. Legislative Hearing on H.R. 3973, the Native American Energy Act. Subcommittee on Indian and Alaska Native Affairs, Natural Resources Committee, U.S. House of Representatives. February 15, 2012.

Hallowell, A. Irving, 1967. "The Backwash of the Frontier: The Impact of Indian on American Culture" in Paul Bohannan and Fred Plog (eds.) *Beyond the Frontier. Social Process and Cultural Change*, pp.319-345. Garden City, NY: Natural History Press.

Hammer, Rebecca, and Jeanne VanBriesen, 2012. *In Fracking's Wake: New Rules are Needed to Protect Our Health and Environment from Contaminated Wastewater*. NRDC Document May 2012 D:12-05-A. Natural Resources Defense Council.

Hammerschlag, Roel, 2006. "Ethanol's Energy Return on Investment: A Survey of the Literature 1990-Present," *Environmental Science and Technology, 40*(6), pp.1744-1750.

Harkin, Michael E., and David Rich Lewis (eds.), 2007. *Native Americans and the Environment. Perspectives on the Ecological Indian*. Lincoln: University of Nebraska Press.

Harries-Jones, Peter, 1995. *A Recursive Vision. Ecological Understanding and Gregory Bateson*. Toronto: University of Toronto Press.

Harvey, David C., and Emma Waterton, 2015. "Editorial: Landscapes of Heritage and Heritage Landscapes," *Landscape Research, 40*(8), pp.905-910.

Haynes Boone, 2022. *Oil Patch Bankruptcy Monitor.* January 31, 2022. Haynes Boone Energy Practice Group.

Headwaters Economics, 2008. *Fossil Fuel Extraction as a County Economic Development Strategy. Are Energy-focusing Counties Benefiting?* Bozeman, MT: Headwaters Economics.

Hearne, Robert R., and Felix Fernando, 2016. "Strategies for Community and Industry Water Management in the Oil Producing region of North Dakota," *Water, 8*, 331.

Hedges, Chris, and Joe Sacco, 2012. *Days of Destruction, Days of Revolt.* New York: Nation Books.

Herz, Steven, Antonio La Vina, and Jonathan Sohn, 2007. *Development Without Conflict. The Business Case for Community Consent.* Washington, D.C.: World Resources Institute.

Hetherington, Kregg, 2011. *Guerilla Auditors. The Politics of Transparency in Neoliberal Paraguay.* Durham, NC: Duke University Press.

Hicks, Celeste, 2017. *Africa's New Oil. Power, Pipelines and Future Fortunes.* London: Zed Books.

Hobsbawm, Eric, 1983. "Introduction: Inventing Traditions" in Eric Hobsbawm and Terence Ranger (eds.) *The Invention of Tradition*, pp.1-14. Cambridge: Cambridge University Press.

Hodges, Tony, 2004. *Angola: Anatomy of an Oil State.* Fritjof Nansen Institute, Oxford: James Currey, and Bloomington: Indiana University Press.

Hoelscher, Steven D., 1998. *Heritage on Stage. The Invention of Ethnic Place in America's Little Switzerland.* Madison: The University of Wisconsin Press.

Holdaway, Simon, Matthew Douglass, and Patricia Fanning, 2012. "Landscape Scale and Human Mobility: Geoarchaeological Evidence from Rutherfords Creek, New South Wales, Australia," in Sjoerd Kluiving and Erika Guttmann-Bond (eds.) *Landscape Archaeology between Art and Science. From a Multi- to an Interdisciplinary Approach*, pp.279-294. Landscape and Heritage Series. Amsterdam: Amsterdam University Press.

Holder, Preston, 1970. *The Hoe and the Horse on the Plains. A Study of Cultural Development among North American Indians.* Lincoln: University of Nebraska Press.

hooks, bell 1994 *Teaching to Transgress. Education as the Practice of Freedom*. New York: Routledge

Howard, G. C. and C. R. Fast, 1970. *Hydraulic Fracturing*. New York: American Institute of Mining, Metallurgical, and Petroleum Engineers.

Howett, Catherine E., 1997. "Where the One-Eyed Man is King: The Tyranny of Visual and Formalist Values in Evaluating Landscapes," in Paul Groth and Todd W. Bressi (eds.) *Understanding Ordinary Landscapes*, pp.85-98. New Haven: Yale University Press.

HUD, 2012. "New Oil and Gas Drilling Technologies bring Significant Changes and Challenges to Housing Markets," in *U.S. Housing Market Conditions*, Summer 2012.

Ingold, Tim, 2005. "Epilogue: Towards a Politics of Dwelling," *Conservation and Society, 3*(2), pp.501-508.

Ingold, Tim, 2018. *Anthropology. Why It Matters*. Cambridge: Polity.

International Finance Organization, 2010. *Strategic Community Investment. A Good Practice Handbook for Companies Doing Business in Emerging Markets*. Washington, D.C.: IFC.

IPIECA, 2008. *Creating Successful, Sustainable Social Investment. Guidance Document for the Oil and Gas Industry*. London: International Petroleum Industry Environmental Conservation Association.

IPIECA, 2011. *Indigenous People and the Oil and Gas Industry. Context, Issues, and Emerging Good Practice*. London: International Petroleum Industry Environmental Conservation Association.

IPIECA and OGP, 2002. *The Oil and Gas Industry from Rio to Johannesburg and Beyond. Contributing to Sustainable Development*. London: International Petroleum Industry Environmental Conservation Association and International Association of Oil and Gas Producers.

IRMA, 2018. *IRMA Standard for Responsible Mining, IRMA STD-001*. Initiative for Responsible Mining Assurance.

Jackson, John Brinckerhoff, 1994. *A Sense of Place, a Sense of Time*. New Haven: Yale University Press.

Jackson, Robert B., Avner Vengosh, Thomas H. Darrah, Nathanial R. Warner, Adrian Down, Robert J. Poreda, Stephen G. Osborn, Kaiguang Zhao, and Jonathan D. Karr, 2013. "Increased Stray Gas Abundance in a Subset of Drinking Water Wells near Marcellus Shale Gas Extraction," *Proceedings of the National Academy of Sciences, 110*(28), pp.11250-11255.

Jacobs, Meg, 2016. *Panic at the Pump. The Energy Crisis and the Transformation of American Politics in the 1970s*. New York: Hill and Wang.

Jacobs, Michael, Bruce Smith, and Christa Tyrrell, 2013. "Use of Electromagnetic Surveys to Monitor Removal of and Oil Field Produced Water Plume, East Poplar Oil Field, Eastern Montana," Paper presented at the SPE Americas E&P Health, Safety, Security and Environmental Conference, Galveston, TX.

Jameson, Fredric, 1998. *The Cultural Turn. Selected Writings on the Postmodern, 1993-1998*. London: Verso.

Jiang, Mohan, Chris T. Hendrickson, and Jeanne M. VanBriesen, 2014. "Life Cycle Water Consumption and Wastewater Generation Impacts of a Marcellus Shale Gas Well," *Environmental Science and Technology, 48*, pp.1911-1920.

Johansen, Bruce E., 2016. *Resource Exploitation in Native North America. A Plague upon the Peoples*. Santa Barbara, CA: ABC-CLIO.

Johnson v McIntosh, 1823. *Johnson and Graham's Lessee v. McIntosh*. United States Supreme Court. 21 U.S. (Wheat.) 543. February 28, 1823.

Johnson, Matthew, 2012. "Landscape Studies: The Future of the Field," in Sjoerd Kluiving and Erika Guttmann-Bond (eds.) *Landscape Archaeology between Art and Science. From a Multi- to an Interdisciplinary Approach*, pp.515-525. Landscape and Heritage Series. Amsterdam: Amsterdam University Press.

Jones, Christopher F., 2016. *Routes of Power. Energy and Modern America*. Cambridge, MA: Harvard University Press.

Jones, Nathan F., Liba Pejchar, and Joseph M. Kiesecker 2015 "The Energy Footprint: How Oil, Natural Gas, and Wind Energy Affect Land for Biodiversity and the Flow of Ecosystem Services" *BioScience*, 65 (3), 290-301.

Jorgensen, Joseph G. (ed.), 1984. *Native Americans and Energy Development II*. Boston: Anthropology Resource Center and Forestville, CA: Seventh Generation Fund.

Jumbunna, n.d. Hydraulic Fracturing and Free, Prior, and Informed Consent (FPIC) in the Northern Territory: A Literature Review. Jumbunna Institute for Indigenous Education and Research.

Karl, Terry L., 2007. *Oil-Led Development: Social, Political, and Economic Consequences*. CDDRL Working Papers Number 80. Stanford: Center on Democracy, Development, and The Rule of Law.

Keeler, Jacqueline, 2021. *Standoff. Standing Rock, the Bundy Movement, and the American Story of Sacred Lands*. Salt Lake City: Torrey House Press.

Kirsch, Stuart, 2014. *Mining Capitalism. The Relationship between Corporations and their Critics*. Oakland: University of California Press.

KLJ, 2014. *North Dakota Oil and Gas Impact Study, 2014-2019. Phase II Update, April 8, 2014. Appendix M*. Bismarck, ND: Kadrmas, Lee & Jackson.

Kluiving, Sjoerd, and Erika Guttmann-Bond (eds.), 2012. *Landscape Archaeology between Art and Science. From a Multi- to an Interdisciplinary Approach*. Landscape and Heritage Series. Amsterdam: Amsterdam University Press.

Knobloch, Frieda, 1996. *The Culture of Wilderness. Agriculture as Colonization in the American West*. Chapel Hill: The University of North Carolina Press.

Krech, Shepard, III, 2000. *The Ecological Indian: Myth and History*. New York: W.W. Norton.

Kreps, Bart Hawkins, 2020. "The Rising Costs of Fossil-Fual Extraction: An Energy Crisis that will Not Go Away." *American Journal of Economics and Sociology, 79*(3), pp.695-717.

Kroshus, Brian, 2011. "The Beat Goes On…" *Bakken Breakout, 2*(2), pp.5-7.

Krupnik, Igor, 1993. *Arctic Adaptations. Native Whalers and Reindeer Herders of Northern Eurasia*. Hanover, NH: University Press of New England.

Kube, Hanno, 1997. "Private Property in Natural Resources and the Public Weal in German Law - Latent Similarities to the Public Trust Doctrine?" *Natural Resources Journal, 37*(4), pp.857-880.

Kurkiala, Mikael, 1997. *"Building the Nation Back Up." The Politics of Identity on the Pine Ridge Indian Reservation*. Uppsala Studies in *Cultural Anthropology, 22*. Uppsala: Acta Universitatis Upsaliensis.

Ladd, Anthony E. (ed.), 2018. *Fractured Communities. Risk, Impacts, and Protest against Hydraulic Fracking in U.S. Shale Regions*. New Brunswick, NJ: Rutgers University Press.

LaDuke, Winona, 1984. "The Council of Energy Resource Tribes," in Joseph G. Jorgensen (ed.) *Native Americans and Energy Development II*, pp.58-70. Boston: Anthropology Resource Center / Forestville, CA: Seventh Generation Fund.

Laird, Wilson M., 1952. "The Geology of the Basin in North Dakota" in Petroleum Information *An Introduction to the Williston Basin*, pp.16-40. Petroleum Information: Casper, WY.

Laird, Wilson M., 1956. "The Williston Basin – A Backward Look with a Look to the Future" in *First International Williston Basin Symposium*, pp.14-22. North Dakota Geological Society and Saskatchewan Geological Society.

Lambert, Jessica G., Charles A.S. Hall, and Stephen Balogh, 2013. *EROI of Global Energy Resources. Status, Trends, and Implications.* Prepared for the United Kingdom Department for International Development by the SUNY Environmental Science and Forestry Next Generation Energy Initiative.

Lamm, Richard D., and Michael McCarthy, 1982. *The Angry West. A Vulnerable Land and Its Future*. Boston: Houghton Mifflin.

Larnaudie, Valeria, 2018. *Sustainable Production of Fuel Bioethanol from Switchgrass in Uruguay*. Universidad de la Republica Uruguay, Facultad de Ingenieria.

Larocque, Francois-Antoine, 1985. "Missouri Jounral Winter 1804-1805," in W. Raymond Wood and Thomas D. Thiessen (eds.) *Early Fur Trade on the Northern Plains. Canadian Traders Among the Mandan and Hidatsa Indians, 1738-1818*, pp.133-155. Norman: University of Oklahoma Press.

Lawson, Michael L., 1994. *Dammed Indians. The Pick-Sloan Plan and the Missouri River Sioux, 1944-1980*. Norman: University of Oklahoma Press.

LeFever, Julie A., Carol D. Martiniuk, Edward F. R. Dancsok, and Paul A. Mahnik, 1991. "Petroleum Potential of the Middle Member, Bakken Formation, Williston Basin," in *Sixth International Williston Basin Symposium*, pp.74-94. Regina: Saskatchewan Geological Society.

Lehr, Amy K. and Gare A. Smith, 2010. *Implementing a Corporate Free, Prior, and Informed Consent Policy: Benefits and Challenges*. Foley Hoag LLP.

Leonard, Lori, 2016. *Life in the Time of Oil. A Pipeline and Poverty in Chad*. Bloomington: Indiana University Press.

Leopold, Aldo, 1991. *The River of the Mother of God and Other Essays by Aldo Leopold*. Edited by Susan L. Flader and J. Baird Callicott. Madison: The University of Wisconsin Press.

Lévi-Strauss, Claude, 1969. *The Elementary Structures of Kinship*. Boston: Beacon Press.

Lévi-Strauss, Claude, 1992. *Tristes Tropiques*. New York: Penguin.

Li, Fabiana, 2015. *Unearthing Conflict. Corporate Mining, Activism, and Expertise in Peru*. Durham: Duke University Press.

Liboiron, Max, 2021. *Pollution is Colonialism*. Durham: Duke University Press.

Lin, Zhulu, Tong Lin, Siew Hoon Lim, Michael H. Hove, and William M. Schuh, 2018. "Impacts of Bakken Shale Oil Development on Regional Water Uses and Supply," *Journal of the American Water Resources Association, 54*(1), pp.225-239.

Little, Ronald L., 1978. "Energy Boom Towns: Views from Within," in *Native Americans and Energy Development*, pp.63-88. Cambridge, MA: Anthropology Resource Center.

Lone Wolf v Hitchcock, 1903. *Lone Wolf et al. v. Ethan A. Hitchcock et al.* Supreme Court of the United States. 187 U.S. 553. January 5, 1903.

Lustgarten, Abrahm, 2012. "Injection Wells: The Poison Beneath Us." *ProPublica*, June 21, 2012.

Lyons, Scott Richard, 2010. *X-marks. Native Signatures of Assent*. Minneapolis: University of Minnesota Press.

Ma, Guanyu, Mengistu Geza, and Pei Xu, 2014. "Review of Flowback and Produced Water Management, Treatment and Beneficial Use for Major Shale Gas Development Basins" in Christopher Meehan, Jeanne M. VanBriesen, Farshid Vahedifard, and Xiong Yu (eds.) *Shale Energy Engineering 2014. Technical Challenges, Environmental Issues, and Public Policy*, pp.53-62. Proceedings of the 2014 Shale Energy Engineering Conference. American Society of Civil Engineers.

MacPherson, James, 2010. "State, tribe garner millions from oil tax accord" *Associated Press*, 18 January 2010.

Maharidge, Dale, and Michael S. Williamson, 2011. *Someplace like America. Tales from the New Great Depression*. Updated Edition. Berkeley: University of California Press.

Malinowski, Bronislaw, 1966. *Argonauts of the Western Pacific. An Account of Native Enterprise and Adventure in the Archipelagoes of Melanesian New Guinea*. Sixth Edition. London: Routledge and Kegan Paul.

Mall, Amy, and Melissa Troutman, 2020. *North Dakota Frack Waste Report. The Failure to Safely Manage Oil and Gas Waste*. Earthworks.

Marrin, Albert, 2012. *Black Gold. The Story of Oil in Our Lives*. New York: Alfred A. Knopf.

Matlock, Staci, 2015. "Federal Judge Overturns Mora County's Drilling Ordinance," *The New Mexican*, January 20, 2015.

Maugh, Thomas H, II, 1978. "Tar Sands: A New Fuels Industry Takes Shape," in *Science, N.S. 199*(4330), pp.756-760.

May, Theresa, 2014. *Salmon is Everything. Community-Based Theatre in the Klamath Watershed.* With Suzanne Burcell, Kathleen McCovey, and Jean O'Hara. Corvallis: Oregan State University Press.

McDevitt, Bonnie, Molly C. McLaughlin, David S. Vinson, Thomas J. Geeza, Jens Blotevogel, Thomas Borch, and Nathanial R. Warner, 2020. "Isotopic and Element Ratios Fingerprint Salinization Impact from Beneficial Use of Oil and Gas Produced Water in the Western U.S." *Science of the Total Environment, 716*, p.137006.

McDevitt, Bonnie, Aaron M. Jubb, Matthew S. Varonka, Madalyn S. Blondes, Mark A. Engle, Tanya J. Gallegos, and Jenna L. Shelton, 2022. "Dissolved Organic Matter within Oil and Gas Associated Wastewaters from U.S. Unconventional Petroleum Plays: Comparisons and Consequences for Disposal and Reuse," *Science of the Total Environment, 838*, p.156331.

McDonald Robert I., Joseph Fargione, Joe Kiesecker, William M. Miller, and Jimmie Powell, 2009. "Energy Sprawl or Energy Efficiency: Climate Policy Impacts on Natural Habitat for the United States of America," *PLoS ONE, 4*(8): e6802, pp.1-11.

McGraw, Seamus, 2012. *The End of Country. Dispatches from the Frack Zone.* New York: Random House.

McKenzie County, 2012-16. Planning and Zoning Minutes, 2012-16. McKenzie County Planning and Zoning Commission.

MCMPR, 2005. *Principles for Engagement with Community and Stakeholders.* Canberra: Ministerial Council on Mineral and Petroleum Resources.

Meier, Thomas, 2012. "'Landscape,' 'Environment' and a Vision of Interdisciplinarity," in Sjoerd Kluiving and Erika Guttmann-Bond (eds.) *Landscape Archaeology between Art and Science. From a Multi- to an Interdisciplinary Approach*, pp.503-514. Landscape and Heritage Series. Amsterdam: Amsterdam University Press.

Merry, Stu, 2011. "Oil: Creating a Sustainable Roar," *Boom and Bloom*, 4,7.

MHA Nation, 2012. *Request to the United States Army Corps of Engineers to Refrain from Issuing Permits for the Use or Taking of Surplus Water from Lake Sakakawea for Commercial or Industrial Purposes within the Exterior Boundaries of the Fort Berthold Indian*

*Reservation.* Resolution No. 12-048-VJB. Resolution of the Governing Body of the Three Affiliated Tribes of the Fort Berthold Indian Reservation. May 14, 2012.

MHA Nation, 2015. *Grant of Right of Way.* Resolution No. 15-065-KH. Resolution of the Governing Body of the Three Affiliated Tribes of the Fort Berthold Indian Reservation. April 16, 2015.

MHA Nation, 2016a. *Correction to Resolution No. 15-065-KH.* Resolution No. 16-127-CSB. Resolution of the Governing Body of the Three Affiliated Tribes of the Fort Berthold Indian Reservation. June 9, 2016.

MHA Nation, 2016b. *Rescission of Resolution No. 16-127-CSB.* Resolution No. 16-183-FF. Resolution of the Governing Body of the Three Affiliated Tribes of the Fort Berthold Indian Reservation. August 11, 2016.

MHA TERO Ordinance, n.d. *TERO Ordinance of the Three Affiliated Tribes.* Retrieved from https://mhatero.com/ordinances-and-regulations/ on 6/29/2022.

MHA Tero Regulations, n.d. *MHA TERO Regulations.* Retrieved from https://mhatero.com/ordinances-and-regulations/ on 6/29/2022.

Miller, Patrick C., 2016. "Telling the Bakken's True Story," *The Bakken Magazine, 4*(6), pp.14-18.

Minot State University and Dickinson State University, 2012. *Energy Impact Solutions Conference. Tuesday, August 14, 2012.* DVD. In possession of author.

Müller, Birgit, 2008. "Still Feeding the World? The Political Ecology of Canadian Prairie Farmers," in *Anthropologica, 50*(2), pp.389-407.

Murphy, David J., 2014. "The Implications of the Declining Energy Return on Investment of Oil Production." *Philosophical Transactions of the Royal Society A*, 372:20130126.

Murphy, Robert P., 2020. *Managing the Risks of Hydraulic Fracturing, 2020.* Fraser Institute.

Myers, Tom, 2012. "Potential Contaminant Pathways from Hydraulically Fractured Shale to Aquifers," *Groundwater, 50*(6), pp.872-882.

Myler, Glade A., 1981-82. "Mitigating Boom Town Effects of Energy Development: A Survey," in *Journal of Energy Law and Policy, 2*, pp.211-235.

Nasen, Lawrence C., Bram F. Noble, and Jill F. Johnstone, 2011. "Environmental Effects of Oil and Gas Lease Sites in a Grassland Ecosystem," *Journal of Environmental Management, 92*, pp.195-204.

Nash, Gerald D., 1999. *The Federal Landscape. An Economic History of the Twentieth-Century West.* Tucson: University of Arizona Press.

Nash, Roderick Frazier, 2001. *Wilderness and the American Mind.* Fourth Edition. New Haven: Yale University Press.

NCPS, 1971a. North Central Power Study. *Report of Phase I, Volume I. Study of Mine-Mouth Thermal Powerplants with Extra-High-Voltage Transmission for Delivery of Power to Load Centers.*

NCPS, 1971b. North Central Power Study. *Report of Phase I, Volume II. Study of Mine-Mouth Thermal Powerplants with Extra-High-Voltage Transmission for Delivery of Power to Load Centers.*

NDPC, 2013. North Dakota Petroleum Council, North Dakota – Oil Can! Advertisement, *Bakken Magazine, 1*(1) April, 2.

NDPC, 2016. Notice to All Interested Parties that own oil and gas mineral interests under Lake Sakakawea. http://nwlandowners.com/wp-content/uploads/2016/09/Lake-Sakakawea-claim-FInal.pdf accessed 12/8/2016.

Ness, Ron, 2011. "The Bakken: What lies ahead?" *Bakken Breakout, 2*(2), 28, 31.

Newell, Richard G., and Daniel Raimi, 2015. "Shale Public Finance: Local Government Revenues and Costs Associated with Oil and Gas Development," *NBER Working Paper 21542.* Cambridge, MA: National Bureau of Economic Research.

Nicholls, 2007. *Mobile Workers in the Wood Buffalo Region. Final Report.* Nichols Applied Management.

Nikiforuk, Andrew, 2010. *Tar Sands. Dirty Oil and the Future of a Continent.* Vancouver: Greystone Books.

Nikiforuk, Andrew, 2012. *The Energy of Slaves. Oil and the New Servitude.* Vancouver: Greystone Books.

Norris, Timothy B., 2014. "Bridging the Great Divide: State, Civil Society, and 'Participatory' Conservation Mapping in a Resource Extraction Zone," *Applied Geography, 54*, pp.262-274.

North Dakota Legislative Council, 2010. *Fort Berthold Reservation Oil Development under 2007 Senate Bill No. 2419 and Subsequent State-Tribal Agreements.* March 2010.

Nowatzki, Mike, 2015. "Abandoned oil waste pit eroding into Little Missouri River in western N.D." *Grand Forks Herald*, October 16, 2015.

Nuttall, Mark, 2010. *Pipeline Dreams. People, Environment, and the Arctic Energy Frontier*. Copenhagen: IWGIA.

OCS, 1978. Alaska OCS Socioeconomic Studies Program, Technical Report Number 1. *Definition of Alaska Petroleum Development Regions*. Bureau of Land Management, Alaska Outer Continental Shelf Office.

Oklahoma v Castro-Huerta, 2022. *Oklahoma v. Victor Manuel Castro-Huerta*. Supreme Court of the United States. 597 U.S. June 29, 2022.

Olivas, John, 2018. "The Truth Behind Fracking and Mora County," *The New Mexican*, May 28, 2018.

Oliver-Smith, Anthony, 2005. "Communities after Catastrophe. Reconstructing the Material, Reconstituting the Social." in Stanley E. Hyland (ed.) *Community-Building in the Twenty-First Century*, pp.45-70. Santa Fe: School of American Research Press.

Orlowski, Aaron, 2011. "Workers come in search of one thing – a paycheck," *Boom Times*, supplement to *The Journal* and *The Tioga Tribune*, Wed., Dec. 7, 2011, pp.2-4.

ORVI, 2021. *Appalachia's Natural Gas Counties: Contributing More to the U.S. Economy and Getting Less in Return. The Natural Gas Fracking Boom and Appalachia's Lost Economic Decade*. Update February 12, 2021. Ohio River Valley Institute.

Owens, Nancy J., 1978. "Can Tribes Control Energy Development?" in *Native Americans and Energy Development*, pp.49-62. Cambridge, MA: Anthropology Resource Center.

Paradigm v Fox and Heart, 2016. *Paradigm Energy Partners v. Mark Fox and Nelson Heart*. Case No. 1:16-cv-304. Order Granting Plaintiff's Motion for Preliminary Injunction. United States District Court for the District of North Dakota. September 13, 2016.

Parker, Angela K., 2011. *Taken Lands. Territory and Sovereignty on the Fort Berthold Indian Reservation, 1934-1960*. Ph.D. Dissertation, University of Michigan.

Parker, Chad H., 2014. "Aramco's Frontier Story. The Arabian American Oil Company and Creative Mapping in Postwar Saudi Arabia," in Ross Barrett and Daniel Worden (eds.) *Oil Culture*, pp.171-188. Minneapolis: University of Minnesota Press.

Patel, Tara, 2011. "France Should Ban Shale Exploration on Risks, Minister Says," *Bloomberg*, May 10, 2011.

Pearson, Thomas W.,2017. *When the Hills are Gone. Frac Sand Mining and the Struggle for Community*. Minneapolis: University of Minnesota Press.

Pendley, William Perry, 1995. *War on the West. Government Tyranny on America's Great Frontier*. Washington, D.C.: Regnery.

Persson, Torsten, Gerard Roland, and Guido Tabellini, 2000. "Comparative Politics and Public Finance," *The Journal of Political Economy, 108*(6), pp.1121-1161.

Peters, Lisa Westberg, 2014. *Fractured Land. The Price of Inheriting Oil*. St. Paul, MN: Minnesota Historical Society Press.

Peterson, James A., 1988. *Geologic Summary and Hydrocarbon Plays, Williston Basin, Montana, North and South Dakota, and Sioux Arch, South Dakota and Nebraska, U.S.* Open-File Report 87-450-N, U.S. Geological Survey.

Pickering, Kathleen Ann, 2000. *Lakota Culture, World Economy*. Lincoln: University of Nebraska Press.

Pierre, Jon Paul, Michael H. Young, Brad D. Wolaver, John R. Andrews, and Caroline L. Breton, 2017. "Time Series Analysis of Energy Production and Associated Landscape Fragmentation in the Eagle Ford Shale Play," *Environmental Management, 60*, pp.852-866.

Popper, Deborah E. and Frank Popper, 2006. "The Buffalo Commons: Its Antecedents and Their Implications," *Online Journal of Rural Research and Policy, 1*(6).

Powell, John Wesley, 1879. *Report on the Lands of the Arid Region of the United States*. Second Edition. Washington, D.C.: Government Printing Office.

Preston, Todd M., Joanna N. Thamke, Bruce D. Smith, and Zell E. Peterman, 2014. "Brine Contamination of Prairie Pothole Environments at Three Study Sites in the Williston Basin, United States," in Robert A. Gleason and Brian A. Tangen (eds.) *Brine Contamination to Aquatic Resources from Oil and gas Development in the Williston Basin, United States*. Scientific Investigations Report 2014-5017. U.S. Geological Service.

Rajak, Dinah, 2011. *In Good Company. An Anatomy of Corporate Social Responsibility*. Stanford: Stanford University Press.

Ramirez, Pedro, Jr., 2009. *Reserve Pit Management. Risks to Migratory Birds*. U.S. Fish and Wildlife Service, Region 6. Environmental Contaminants Program.

Ramudo, Andrea, and Sean Murphy, 2010. *Hydraulic Fracturing – Effects on Water Quality*. CRP 5072. Cornell University, City and Regional Planning.

RAN, 2020. *Fracking Fiasco. The Banks that Fueled the U.S. Shale Bust*. Rainforest Action Network.

Rao, Maya, 2018. *Great American Outpost. Dreamers, Mavericks, and the Making of an Oil Frontier*. New York: Public Affairs.

Ray, Arthur J. 1998 *Indians in the Fur Trade*. Toronto: University of Toronto Press.

Resolute v Greenpeace, 2016. *Resolute Forest Products, et al. v. Greenpeace International, et al.* Case No. 3:17-cv-02824-JST. Plaintiff's Amended Complaint. United States District Court for the Northern District of California. November 8, 2016.

Rio Tinto, 2021. *Protecting Cultural Heritage*. https://www.riotinto.com/sustainability/communities/cultural-heritage. Accessed 7/8/2021.

Robbins, Lynn A., 1980. "Native American Experiences with Energy Development," in Joseph Davenport, III and Judith Ann Davenport (eds.) *The Boom Town: Problems and Promises of the Energy Vortex*. Laramie: University of Wyoming Department of Social Work.

Robinson, Elwyn B., 1966. *History of North Dakota*. Lincoln: University of Nebraska Press.

Rogers, Douglas, 2015. *The Depths of Russia. Oil, Power, and Culture after Socialism*. Ithaca: Cornell University Press.

Roosevelt, Franklin D., 1937. *The Future of the Great Plains*. Message from the President of the United States, Transmitting the Report of the Great Plains Committee under the Title "The Future of the Great Plains." 75th Congress 1st Session, Document No. 144. United States House of Representatives.

Ross, Wilbur L., 2020. *Remarks by Commerce Secretary Wilbur L. Ross at the Rio Tinto Resolution Copper Site Visit Roundtable in Phoenix, Arizona*. As Prepared for Delivery, Friday, October 9, 2020. https://www.commerce.gov/news/speeches/2020/10/remarks-commerce-secretary-wilbur-l-ross-rio-tinto-resolution-copper-site Accessed 12/31/2020.

Rumsey, Alan, and James Weiner (eds.), 2004. *Mining and Indigenous Lifeworlds in Australia and Papua New Guinea.* Oxon, UK: Sean Kingston Publishing.

Ruppel, Kristin T., 2008. *Unearthing Indian Land. Living with the Legacies of Allotment.* Tucson: The University of Arizona Press.

Russell, Paul L., 1980. *History of Western Oil Shale.* East Brunswick, NJ: Center for Professional Advancement.

Sacco, Joe, 2020. *Paying the Land.* New York: Metropolitan Books.

Sachs, Jeffrey D., and Andrew M. Warner, 2001. "The Curse of Natural Resources" *European Economic Review, 45*, pp.827-838.

Sahlins, M.D., 1965. "On the Sociology of Primitive Exchange," In M. Banton (editor) *The Relevance of Models for Social Anthropology.* (Ass. social Anthrop. Monogr. I). London: Tavistock.

Sahlins, Marshall, 1972. *Stone Age Economics.* New York: Routledge.

Samson, Fred B. and Fritz L. Knopf (eds.), 1996. *Prairie Conservation. Preserving North America's Most Endangered Ecosystem.* Washington, D.C.: Island Press.

Sandberg, Charles A., 1962. *Geology of the Williston basin, North Dakota, Montana, and South Dakota, with Reference to Subsurface Disposal of Radioactive Wastes.* Open-File Report 62-115, U.S. Geological Survey.

Sanders, Andreas R.D., Pal Thonstad Sandvik, and Espen Storli (eds.), 2019. *The Political Economy of Resource Regulation. An International and Comparative History, 1850-2015.* Vancouver: UBS Press.

Sardar, Ziauddin, and Merryl Wyn Davies, 2002. *Why Do People Hate America?* New York: Disinformation.

Scazzosi, Lionella, 2004. "Reading and Assessing the Landscape as Cultural and Historical Heritage," *Landscape Research, 29*(4), pp.335-355.

Schäfer, Sylvia, 1996. *Kulturraum Oberrhein. Grenzüberschreitende Kulturarbeit in der deutsch-französisch-schweizerischen EuroRegion.* Schriften der Regio 15. Frankfurt a.M.: Helbing und Lichtenhahn.

Schettler, Jill, 2011. "Welcome to the New Frontier! Frontier Energy Group Invests in Local Communities," *Bakken Oil Report 2011*, pp.36,38.

Schmer, M. R., K. P. Vogel, R. B. Mitchell, and R. K. Perrin, 2008. "Net Energy of Cellulosic Ethanol from Switchgrass," *Proceedings of the National Academy of Sciences, 105*(2), pp.464-469.

Schneider, David 1980 *American Kinship: A Cultural Account.* Second edition. Chicago: University of Chicago Press.

Schuh, W.M., 2010. *Water Appropriation Requirements, Current Water Use, and Water Availability for Energy Industries in North Dakota: A 2010 Summary*. Response to House Bill 1322, Section 2 of the 61st Legislative Assembly of North Dakota. Water Resources Investigation No. 49. Bismarck: North Dakota State Water Commission.

Shay, C. Thomas, 2022. *Under Prairie Skies. The Plants and Native Peoples of the Northern Plains*. Lincoln: University of Nebraska Press.

Shell, 1998. *Profits and Principles – Does there have to be a Choice?* London: Shell International.

Sherrill v Oneida, 2005. *City of Sherrill, New York v. Oneida Indian Nation of New York et al.* Supreme Court of the United States. 544 U.S. 197. March 29, 2005.

Shiva, Vandana, 2015. *Soil not Oil. Environmental Justice in an Age of Climate Crisis*. Berkeley: North Atlantic Books.Sirivedhin, T., J. McCue, and L. Dallbauman, 2004. "Reclaiming Produced Water for Beneficial Use: Salt Removal by Electrodialysis," *Journal of Membrane Science, 243*(1-2), pp.335-343.

Singer, Joseph William 2014 "Property as the Law of Democracy" *Duke Law Journal,* 63, 1287-1335.

Slonecker, E. Terrence, and Lesley E. Milheim, 2015. "Landscape Disturbance from Unconventional and Conventional Oil and Gas Development in the Marcellus Shale Region of Pennsylvania, USA," *Environments, 2*, pp.200-220.

Smith, James K., 1977. *The Mackenzie River: Yesterday's Fur Frontier, Tomorrow's Energy Battleground*. Agincourt: Gage Publishing.

Smith, Mick, and Jason Young, 2022. *Does the Earth Care? Indifference, Providence, and Provisional Ecology*. Minneapolis: University of Minnesota Press.

Smith, Sherry L. and Brian Frehner, 2010. "Introduction," in Sherry L. Smith and Brian Frehner (eds.) *Indians and Energy. Exploitation and Opportunity in the American Southwest*, pp.3-19. Santa Fe: School for Advanced Research Press.

Sontag, Deborah, and Brent McDonald, 2014. "In North Dakota, a Tale of Oil, Corruption and Death," *New York Times*, December 28, 2014.

SRF, 2008. *Record of Meeting. Williston Comprehensive & Transportation Plan Update*. Focus Group of Emergency Services Providers, September 23, 2008. SRF Consulting Group.

Standing Rock v Corps of Engineers, 2020. *Standing Rock Sioux Teribe et al. v. U.S. Army Corps of Engineers et al.* Civil Action No. 16-1534 (JEB). Memorandum Opinion. United States District Court for the District of Columbia. March 25, 2020.

Standing Rock v Corps of Engineers, 2021. *Standing Rock Sioux Tribe et al. v. United States Army Corps of Engineers.* No. 20-5197. Consolidated with 20-5201. Appeals from the United States District Court for the District of Columbia (no. 1:16-cv-01534). United States Court of Appeals for the District of Columbia Circuit. January 26, 2021.

Standing Rock and Cheyenne River v Corps of Engineers and Dakota Access, 2020. *Standing Rock Sioux Tribe et al. and Cheyenne River Sioux Tribe et al. v. U.S. Army Corps of Engineers and Dakota Access, LLC.* Civil Action No. 16-1534 (JEB). Memorandum Opinion. United States District Court for the District of Columbia. July 6, 2020.

Stantec, 2017. *Site-Specific Risk Assessment for Keystone XL Project's Missouri River Crossing. Prepared for TransCanada Keystone Pipeline LP.* Stantec Consulting Services, Inc.

State Water Conservation Commission and State Engineer, 1946. *Fifth Biennial Report of the State Water Conservation Commision and the Twenty-Second Biennial Report of the State Engineer of North Dakota.* From November 1, 1944 to October 1, 1946.

Steffen, Will, Jacques Grinevald, Paul Crutzen, and John McNeil, 2011. "The Anthropocene: Conceptual and Historical Perspectives," *Philosophical Transactions of the Royal Society A, 369*, pp.842-867.

Stief, Sheena B., Kristen L. Figgins, and Rebecca Day Babcock (eds.), 2021. *Boom or Bust. Narrative, Life, and Culture from the West Texas Oil Patch.* Norman: University of Oklahoma Press.

Stinger, Joseph William, 2014. "Property as the Law of Democracy," *Duke Law Journal, 63*, pp.1287-1335.

Stohler, Hans, 1939. "Über die Orientierung der Stadtpläne von Augusta Raurica und Basilia Romana," *Basler Zeitschrift für Geschichte und Altertumskunde, 38*, pp.295-325.

Stronen, Iselin Asedotter, 2017. *Grassroots Politics and Oil Culture in Venezuela. The Revolutionary Petro-State.* Cham, CH: Palgrave Macmillan.

SWC, 2016. *Biennial Report for the Period July1, 2013 to June 30, 2015.* State Water Commission and Office of the State Engineer.

SWC, 2019. *Biennial Report for the Period July1, 2017 to June 30, 2019*. State Water Commission and Offce of the State Engineer.

SWCA, 2016. *Environmental Assessment Addendum and Mitigated Finding of No Significant Impact*. Sacagawea Pipeline, McKenzie and Mountrail Counties, North Dakota. Prepared by SWCA Environmental Consultants. U.S. Army Corps of Engineers, Omaha District.

SWEPI v Mora County, 2015. *SWEPI, LP v Mora County*. United States District Court for the District of New Mexico, No. CIV 14-0035 JB/SCY. Memorandum Opinion and Order. Filed 01/19/2015.

Sydow, Johanna, 2016. "Global Concepts in Local Contexts. CSR as 'Anti-Politics Machine' in the Extractive Sector in Ghana and Peru," in Catherine Dolan and Dinah Rajak (eds.) *The Anthropology of Corporate Social Responsibility*, pp.217-242. New York: Berghahn.

T'Seleie, Frank, 1977. "Statement to the Mackenzie Valley Pipeline Inquiry," in Mel Watkins (ed.) *Dene Nation. The Colony Within*, pp.12-17. Toronto: University of Toronto Press.

Tauxe, Caroline S., 1993. *Farms, Mines, and Main Streets. Uneven Development in a Dakota County*. Philadelphia: Temple University Press.

Thamke, Joanna N., and Steven D. Craigg, 1997. *Saline-Water Contamination in Quaternary Deposits and the Poplar River, East Poplar Oil Field, Northeastern Montana*. Water-Resources Investigations Report 97-4000. Prepared in Cooperation with the Water Resources Office of the Fort Peck Tribes. Helena, MT: U.S. Geological Service.

Thamke, Joanna, 2008. *City of Poplar Well Threat Plume Capture and Remediation Team*. U.S. Geological Survey.

Thamke, Joanna N, and Bruce D. Smith, 2014. *Delineation of Brine Contamination in and near the East Poplar Oil Field, Fort Peck Indian Reservation, Northeastern Montana, 2004-09*. Scientific Investigations Report 2014-5024. Prepared in Cooperation with the Fort Peck tribes Office of Environmental Protection. Reston, VA: U.S. Geological Survey.

Theriot, Jason P., 2014. *American Energy, Imperiled Coast. Oil and Gas Development in Louisiana's Wetlands*. Baton Rouge: Louisiana State University Press.

Thompson, Niobe, 2008. *Settlers on the Edge. Identity and Modernization on Russia's Arctic Frontier*. Vancouver: UBC Press.

Thornton, Thomas F. 2008. *Being and Place among the Tlingit*. Seattle: University of Washington Press.

Todrys, Katherine Wiltenburg, 2021. *Black Snake. Standing Rock, the Dakota Access Pipeline, and Environmental Justice*. Lincoln: University of Nebraska Press.

Turner, Frederick Jackson, 1953. *The Frontier in American History*. New York: Henry Holt and Company.

Turner, Sam, 2006. "Historic Landscape Characterisation: A Landscape Archaeology for Research, Management and Planning," *Landscape Research, 31(*4), pp.385-398.

United Nations. 1987. *Our Common Future. Report of the World Commission on Environment and Development.*

USACE, 2011a. *Final Surplus Water Report, Garrison Dam/Lake Sakakawea Project, North Dakota, Volume 1*. US Army Corps of Engineers, Omaha District.

USACE, 2011b. *Final Surplus Water Report, Garrison Dam/Lake Sakakawea Project, North Dakota, Volume 2: Appendix B – Public and Agency Coordination Letters / Views from Federal, State, and Local Interests*. US Army Corps of Engineers, Omaha District.

USACE, 2012. *Addendum No.1 to Garrison Dam/Lake Sakakawea Project, North Dakota, Final Surplus Water Report and Environmental Assessment, March 2011*. US Army Corps of Engineers, July 10, 2012.

USFWS, n.d. *Threats to Birds*. https://www.fws.gov/library/collections/threats-birds. Accessed 7/28/2022.

Uwiera-Gartner, Michelle, 2013. "Groundwater Considerations of Shale Gas Developments Using Hydraulic Fracturing: Examples, Additional Study and Social Responsibility." SPE 167233. Paper prepared for the SPE Unconventional Resources Conference-Canada, November 2013. Society of Petroleum Engineers.

Veil, John, 2020. *U.S. Produced Water Volumes and Management Practices in 2017*. Prepared for the Ground Water Research and Education Foundation.

Vision West ND, 2015. *Summary of the Regional Plan for Sustainable Development.*

Voyles, Traci Brynne, 2015. *Wastelanding. Legacies of Uranium Mining in Navajo Country*. Minneapolis: University of Minnesota Press.

Wagoner, Paula L., 2002. *"They Treated Us Just Like Indians." The Worlds of Bennett County, South Dakota*. Lincoln: University of Nebraska Press.

Wainwright, Joel, 2019. "Human Geography, Indigenous Mapping, and the US Military: A Response to Kelly and Others' 'From Cognitive Maps to Transparent Static Web Maps'" *Cartographica*, 54 (4), 288-296.

Wallace, Alfred Russell, 1864. "The Origin of Human Races and the Antiquity of Man Deduced from the Theory of 'Natural Selection,'" *Journal of the Anthropological Society of London, 2*, pp.clviii-clxxxvii.

Warner, Nathaniel R., Robert B. Jackson, Thomas H. Darrah, Stephen G. Osborn, Adrian Down, Kaiguang Zhao, Alissa White, and Avner Vengosh, 2012. "Geochemical Evidence for Possible Natural Migration of Marcellus Formation Brine to Shallow Aquifers in Pennsylvania," *Proceedings of the National Academy of Sciences, 109*(30), pp.11961-11966.

Washburn, Kevin K., 2017. "What the Future Holds: The Changing Landscape of Federal Indian Policy," *Harvard Law Review Forum, 130,* pp.200-232.

Watkins, Mel, 1977. "From Underdevelopment to Development," in Mel Watkins (ed.) *Dene Nation. The Colony Within*, pp.84-99. Toronto: University of Toronto Press.

Webb, Walter Prescott, 1931. *The Great Plains*. Boston: Ginn.

Weingarten, Debbie, 2018. "Why are America's farmers killing themselves?" *The Guardian*, Dec 11, 2018.

Western Dakota Energy Association, 2021. *Oil and Gas Tax Revenue*. Oil Tax Distribution Study – 2021 Update.

Wethe, David, and Kevin Crowley, 2020. "Shale's Bust Shows Basis of Boom: Debt, Debt, and Debt," *Washington Post*, July 23, 2020.

Wharton, 2018. *Could Fracking Debt Set Off Big Financial Tremors?* Knowledge at Wharton, September 21, 2018. Wharton School at the University of Pennsylvania.

Whitmore, Andy (ed.), 2012. *Pitfalls and Pipelines. Indigenous Peoples and Extractive Industries*. Baguio City, PH: Tebtebba Foundation and Copenhagen: IWGIA.

Whyte, William and Allan Holmberg, 1956. "Human Problems of U.S. Enterprise in Latin America," *Human Organization, 15*(3), pp.1-40

Wieland, James S., F. Larry Leistritz, and Steven H. Murdock, 1977. *Characteristics and Settlement Patterns of Energy Related Operating Workers in the Northern Great Plains*. Agricultural Economics Report No. 123. Fargo, ND: North Dakota State University.

Wilber, Tom, 2012. *Under the Surface. Fracking Fortunes, and the Fate of the Marcellus Shale*. Ithaca, NY: Cornell University Press.

Wilder, Forrest, 2013. "Observer Analysis Finds Fracking Water Use Underestimated in Eagle Ford Shale," *Texas Observer*, June 24, 2013.

Will, George F. and George E. Hyde, 1964. *Corn Among the Indians of the Upper Missouri*. Lincoln: University of Nebraska Press.

Williams, Bradford B. and Mary E. Bluemle, 1978. *Status of Mineral Resource Information for the Fort Berthold Indian Reservation, North Dakota*. Bureau of Indian Affairs, Administrative Report BIA-40.

Willis, Adam, 2021. "Under Biden, North Dakota and Tribal Officials looked to strike an Oil Deal. Here's How It Went Sour," *Dickinson Press*, March 20, 2021.

Willox, Ashlee Cunsolo, and Karen Landman (eds.), 2017. *Mourning Nature: Hope at the Heart of Ecological Loss and Grief*. Montreal: McGill-Queens University Press.

Wilson, M.P., F. Worrall, R.J. Davies, and A. Hart, 2017. "Shallow Aquifer Vulnerability from Subsurface Fluid Injection at a Proposed Shale Gas Hydraulic Fracturing Site," *Water Resources Research, 53*, pp.9922-9940.

Wood, W. Raymond 1967 *An Interpretation of Mandan Cultural History. Smithsonian Institution, Bureau of American Ethnology, Bulletin 198. Inter-Agency Archaeological Salvage Program. River Basin Surveys Papers*. Washington, D.C.: U.S. Government Printing Service.

Wood, W. Raymond, 1980. *The Origins of the Hidatsa Indians: A Review of Ethnohistorical and Traditional Data*. Lincoln: Midwest Archaeological Center.

Wood, W. Raymond and Thomas D. Thiessen, 1985. "The Canadian-Missouri River Fur Trade," in W. Raymond Wood and Thomas D. Thiessen (eds.) *Early Fur Trade on the Northern Plains. Canadian Traders Among the Mandan and Hidatsa Indians, 1738-1818*, pp.3-17. Norman: University of Oklahoma Press.

WORC, 2013. *Gone for Good: Fracking and Water Loss in the West*. Billings, MT: Western Organization of Resource Councils.

WORC, 2021. *Reclaiming Oil and Gas Wells and Addressing Climate Impacts: State Policy Recommendations*. Western Organization of Resource Councils.

Worster, Donald, 1977. *Nature's Economy. A History of Ecological Ideas*. Cambridge: Cambridge University Press.

Wylie, Sara Ann, 2018. *Fractivism. Corporate Bodies and Chemical Bonds*. Durham, NC: Duke University Press.

Wynn, Graeme, 2015. "Foreword: The Paradoxical Politics of Participatory Praxis." in Carly A. Dokis, *Where the Rivers Meet. Pipelines, Participatory Resource Management, and Aboriginal-State Relations in the Northwest Territories*, pp.vii-xx. Vancouver: UBC Press.

Young, Elspeth 1995 *Third World in the First. Development and Indigenous Peoples*. London: Routledge.

Zibel, Alan, and Kelly Mitchell, 2021. *Fueling Failure. How Execs at Bankrupt U.S. Oil and Gas Companies Pocketed nearly $200M in Payouts while Leaving more than 10,000 Workers Jobless and at least $10B in Cleanup Costs*. August 2021. Public Citizen.

## About the Author

Sebastian Felix Braun took his lic.phil.I in ethnology and history from Universität Basel and his PhD in anthropology from Indiana University. He worked for the Department of American Indian Studies at the University of North Dakota for over ten years, the last three as chair. He has been Director of the American Indian Studies program at Iowa State University since, where he is also Professor of Political Science. Braun is the author of *Buffalo Inc. American Indians and Economic Development* (2008) and editor of *Transforming Ethnohistories. Narrative, Meaning, and Community* (2013). Since 2005, he has contributed the chapters on the United States to *The Indigenous World*, the yearbook of the International Work Group for Indigenous Affairs (IWGIA). His interests are located in the intersections of culture, the environment, politics, language, kinship, and economics.

www.ingramcontent.com/pod-product-compliance
Lightning Source LLC
LaVergne TN
LVHW020708110826
845149LV00012B/2166

* 9 7 8 1 9 6 6 3 6 0 8 9 6 *